Democratic Legitimacy

Routledge Studies in Social and Political Thought

For a full list of titles in this series, please visit www.routledge.com

Democratic Legitimacy

Fabienne Peter

Routledge
Taylor & Francis Group
New York   London

First published 2009
by Routledge
711 Third Avenue, New York, NY 10017

Simultaneously published in the UK
by Routledge
2 Park Square, Milton Park, Abingdon, Oxon OX14 4RN

Routledge is an imprint of the Taylor & Francis Group, an informa business

First issued in paperback 2011

Typeset in Sabon by IBT Global.

Library of Congress Cataloging in Publication Data
Peter, Fabienne.
Democratic legitimacy / by Fabienne Peter.
    p. cm. — (Routledge studies in social and political thought ; 62)
    Includes bibliographical references and index.
1. Democracy. 2. Legitimacy of governments. I. Title.
JC423.P383 2009
321.8—dc22
                                    2008033991

ISBN10: 0-415-33282-6 (hbk)
ISBN10: 0-415-89663-0 (pbk)
ISBN10: 0-203-40139-5 (ebk)

ISBN13: 978-0-415-33282-8 (hbk)
ISBN13: 978-0-415-89663-4 (pbk)
ISBN13: 978-0-203-40139-2 (ebk)

Contents

Acknowledgements

Inevitably, many people have, in many different ways, contributed to this book and it would not exist without them. I am deeply grateful for all the comments and criticisms that I have received over time, as well as for all the encouragement and even for the occasional skeptical look. Specifically, I would like to express my thanks to the following persons—for comments, advice, and/or for their friendship: Arun Abraham, Bina Agarwal, Elisabeth Allgoewer, Franck Amalric, Paul Anand, Sorin Baiasu, Luc Bovens, Geoff Brennan, Harry Brighouse, Boudewijn de Bruin, Matthew Clayton, David Estlund, Philippe Fontaine, Jerry Gaus, Asha George, Paul Gomberg, Bob Goodin, Nien-hê Hsieh, Susan Hurley, Eileen John, Eva Kittay, Roland Kley, Tony Laden, Christian List, Alain Marciano, Stephen Marglin, Katrin Meyer, John Rawls, Norbert Reetz, Sanjay Reddy, Andrew Reeve, Ingrid Robeyns, Herlinde Pauer-Studer, Ben Saunders, Hans Bernhard Schmid, Amartya Sen, Kai Spiekermann, Alex Voorhoeve, Jonathan Wolff, Mark Yakes, and Chris Zuern. I would also like to express special thanks to my parents and to my two sisters for their ongoing support.

Over the last couple of years, when I did most of the writing for this book, I very much benefitted from regular discussions with and comments from Arun Abraham, Matthew Clayton, and Herlinde Pauer-Studer. I am very grateful to them. And while I did not have many discussions about the content of this book with Mark Yakes, his contribution has, in many ways, been the most important one. I could not have finished the book without his companionship during this time, and without what he has taught me about life. I dedicate this book to him.

Many more persons have contributed than those just mentioned. I have presented different parts of what eventually became this book at conferences and workshops taking place at All Souls College Oxford, University of Reims, the APSA meetings in Chicago, University of Lisbon, University College London, Freie Universitaet Berlin, and the University of Manchester, and have received much helpful feedback. In addition, I have greatly benefitted from comments that I received on presentations I gave in seminars at Harvard University, Max Weber Kolleg, Erfurt, the London School of Economics, University of Bristol, University of Oxford, Erasmus University Rotterdam, and at the political philosophy seminar that Matthew Clayton has been hosting at the University of Warwick since 2004.

I am also very grateful to the Philosophy Department at the University of Warwick for providing a great work environment in general, but particularly for granting me an extra period of leave this year in order to finish this book. Naomi Eilan, in her capacity as Head of Department, made this extra leave possible and without it, I would probably have lost courage.

The project has its roots in my doctoral dissertation; it is in that context that I became interested in legitimacy as a normative concept. I completed the dissertation in 1996, under the title "The Possibility of Justice: Aggregation versus Deliberation in Social Choice." I did an important part of my research for the dissertation during a year spent at Harvard University in 1994/5. As will be evident from many pages of this book, I am deeply indebted to Amartya Sen. Amartya's writings in both economics and philosophy inspired me to embark on a dissertation in the first place and he supervised my work during that first year at Harvard. More importantly, the deep insight that his writings reveal— sometimes even between the lines—has shaped my thinking on many issues and it continues to enlighten and guide me. It will also be evident that I am very much indebted to the late John Rawls; I cherish memories of two challenging, inspiring, and encouraging discussions.

The shape and content of the argument I present in this book are based, not on the dissertation, but on articles on democratic legitimacy that I have published in various journals in the last few years. While the book goes much beyond previously published material, some sections are based on articles in print elsewhere.

Sections 4.1.c. and 7.1.of the book are based on my article "Pure Epistemic Proceduralism." *Episteme* 5(1) 2008: 33–55 (http://www.eup-journals.com/journal/epi). I thank Edinburgh University Press for permission to use this material.

Section 6.2. of the book consists of revised sections of my chapter "Democratic Legitimacy without Collective Rationality" in Boudewijn de Bruin and Christopher Zurn (eds) *New Waves in Political Philosophy.* Basingstoke: Macmillan Publishers, 2008. I thank Palgrave Macmillan for permission to reproduce this material.

Sections 4.2. and 7.2. of the book consist of revised sections of my article "Democratic Legitimacy and Proceduralist Social Epistemology." *Politics, Philosophy, and Economics* 6(3) 2007: 329–353. I thank SAGE for permission to use this material.

Chapter 5 ("Political Equality") consists of revised parts of my article "The Political Egalitarian's Dilemma." *Ethical Theory and Moral Practice*

10(4) 2007: 373–387. I thank Springer Netherlands for permission to use this material.

Section 6.1. consists of revised parts of my article "Rawls' Idea of Public Reason and Democratic Legitimacy." *Politics and Ethics Review* 3(1) 2007: 129–143. http://www.eupjournals.com/journal/jipt. I thank Edinburgh University Press for permission to use this material.

1 Introduction

1.1. DEMOCRATIC LEGITIMACY

What normative conditions should apply to democratic decision-making? The concept that covers this form of evaluative exercise is democratic legitimacy. Legitimacy entails an ideal for how the members of a democratic constituency ought to make decisions about how to organize their life together. Democracy can mean many things, of course. There are numerous recognizably democratic forms in which the members of a democratic constituency might collectively exercise their political authority. And it is not my goal here to prescribe a particular form. The question that this book seeks to answer is primarily a philosophical question, not one of institutional design. Taking democracy as the starting-point, and allowing that there are many different recognizably democratic institutional arrangements, I am interested in what kind of considerations should matter in the evaluation of the democratic exercise of political authority.

Democratic legitimacy is a distinct normative concept. In contemporary political philosophy, this concept has tended to be somewhat in the shadow of another normative concept: distributive justice. Distributive justice spells out what is owed to people. But no amount of insight into what might be owed to people will settle the question of how decisions about distributive policies ought to be made. The latter is a question about legitimacy and it is clearly a normative question in its own right.

This said, what democratic legitimacy might require is not a new question. But in contemporary debates, the issue has taken on a new twist. The situation in contemporary democratic theory is characterized by the opposition between two main paradigms—aggregative and deliberative democracy. Deliberative democracy was introduced as an alternative to aggregative democracy (e.g. Manin 1987), and as a solution to the problems encountered in that account. Deliberative democrats stress that while voting might be an important feature of democratic decision-making, it is not, as aggregative democrats have presumed, the only feature that matters. The aggregative account of democracy fails to consider how the ideal of democracy embeds voting in an environment of open discussions and sustained controversy. What characterizes both the deliberative and the aggregative accounts of democracy, however, is a preoccupation with the democratic decision-making process. This constellation has focused the debate on the conditions that democratic decision-making needs to satisfy. Social contract theory looms in the background, of course.[1] But the current debates address a more specific question. Over and above the broad concern with moral standards for evaluating the legitimacy of political authority and political obligations that is typical for social contract theory, the narrower focus of the current debate is on the standards that apply to democratic decision-making. This also constitutes a shift away from the Weberian focus on the legitimacy of the state (Weber 1964).[2]

In contemporary democratic theory, the question of what conditions democratic decision-making processes ought to satisfy has been posed by economists such as Kenneth Arrow (1963) and political philosophers such as Joshua Cohen (1997a, b) alike. Indeed, ever since the literature on deliberative democracy started to emerge in the late 1980s, democratic legitimacy, thus interpreted, has been attracting more and more the attention of scholars working in a range of disciplines. As a result, one can identify an increasing diversity of conceptions of democratic legitimacy in the literature.

My principal aim in this book is to offer a systematic treatment of the requirements of democratic legitimacy, interpreted as the set of conditions that applies to the evaluation of democratic decision-making. What should be the normative anchor in the evaluation of democratic decision-making processes? Is it sufficient for democratic legitimacy that the decisions are made through appropriate procedures, or do the decisions also have to satisfy some normative conditions that apply to them directly? To put the same point differently, is it necessary for democratic legitimacy that the decisions themselves can be justified or is it sufficient that the decision-making process can be justified? A lot of different, and often confusing, answers tend to be given to these questions. The study I present here rests on a conceptual framework that I have developed to clearly differentiate between alternative conceptions of democratic legitimacy.

The framework distinguishes between purely procedural conceptions of democratic legitimacy, which only include conditions that apply to the decision-making process, and conceptions that combine criteria that apply to the decision-making process with criteria that relate to the quality of the decisions made. Since the framework targets democratic legitimacy, it only includes conceptions of legitimacy that build on the value of democratic decision-making processes. I call such conceptions proceduralist—in contrast to conceptions of political legitimacy that only attribute instrumental value to democratic decision-making. I think there are two main problems with democratic instrumentalism. It shows insufficient respect for value pluralism by neglecting the constitutive role of democratic decision-making processes for groups of individual agents who try to determine how they should act together. And it ignores the "constructive function" (Sen 1999a) of democracy, i.e. how individual agents learn from each other in deliberative decision-making processes about what the problems are that affect them and what the best means are to solve them. Taking seriously this constructive function points to an epistemic account of democracy, i.e. an account that values democratic decision-making not just for its commitment to political equality but also for its knowledge-generating potential.

I use this framework to identify and defend a particular conception of democratic legitimacy. This conception, which I call Pure Epistemic Proceduralism, has tended to be overlooked so far. This conception of democratic legitimacy identifies a democratic decision as legitimate if it is the outcome of a decision-making process that satisfies certain conditions of political and epistemic fairness. It thus belongs to the category of purely procedural conceptions of democratic legitimacy. What is important for democratic legitimacy, in this view, is that the normative and empirical premises of policy proposals have been subjected to the scrutiny of an inclusive process of public deliberation prior to voting. What distinguishes the conception I shall defend from other conceptions that have been put forward in the literature is that it incorporates procedural epistemic values as part of the conditions that apply to the decision-making process. That is to say, it rejects the common interpretation that epistemic democracy values democratic processes for their ability to track a correct outcome. I shall also argue against the quite common assumption that legitimate democratic decisions need to satisfy some conditions of collective rationality. I will try to show that Pure Epistemic Proceduralism is best able to honor the learning potential that deliberative democratic decision processes contain—the constructive function of democracy—while providing an effective safeguard against the unwarranted appropriation of political authority based on contestable claims to expert knowledge.

1.2. PLAN OF THE BOOK

The topic of the first part of the book is the description of democratic decision-making. Theories of democracy differ in what they single out as the main features of the democratic process and the significance attached to them. For example, is voting the main feature of democratic decision-making, or is that only one feature among many, and perhaps not even the most important one? And is public deliberation, in which people's views about alternative proposals are formed and subject to scrutiny from others, an essential feature of democratic decision-making and if so, what is its role? In this part of the book, I shall focus on the two main theories of democracy currently on offer; I shall discuss aggregative democracy in Chapter 2, and deliberative democracy in Chapter 3. Aggregative democracy treats voting as the constitutive ingredient of democratic decision-making and does not attribute significance to the deliberative process. Deliberative democracy, by contrast, makes the process of public discussion and the exchange of reasons central to democratic decision-making. Since deliberation, even under ideal circumstances, cannot be expected to lead to a consensus, many deliberative democrats still treat voting as a necessary feature of democratic decision-making, but one to which they attribute less normative significance than aggregative democrats. My aim in this part of the book is twofold. I shall want to both introduce these two theories of democracy and defend deliberative democracy over aggregative democracy. In Chapter 2, after presenting aggregative democracy, I shall discuss a series of problems that aggregative democracy faces in its treatment of democratic social evaluation. I shall be focusing on the account given by Arrow in his book *Social Choice and Individual Values* as this is probably the most sophisticated version of aggregative democracy. In Chapter 3, after presenting an account of deliberative democracy, I shall compare the two theories and argue for deliberative democracy.

The topic of the second part of the book is democratic legitimacy. By democratic legitimacy I mean the normative concept that establishes under what conditions the members of a democratic constituency ought to respect a democratic decision. In Chapter 4, I shall first discuss the concept of legitimacy itself. I shall defend a broadly Rawlsian account, one that treats legitimacy as a fundamental normative concept that is related to, but weaker than, a conception of justice. In this view, a particular democratic decision may thus be legitimate without being just.

I then discuss different interpretations of what democratic legitimacy requires. To this end, I develop a taxonomy by means of which alternative interpretations of the requirements of legitimacy can be distinguished. The taxonomy is geared towards the recent literature on democratic theory. It provides a simple way of classifying alternative proceduralist conceptions of legitimacy and helps to clarify the issues that underlie current debates. A first version of the taxonomy distinguishes between aggregative and deliberative democracy on the one hand, and between different categories of requirements of legitimacy on the other. Some conceptions of democratic legitimacy only impose conditions of political equality, or fair process. These are the Pure Proceduralist conceptions. Other conceptions of democratic legitimacy also impose conditions that relate to the rationality of outcomes—to political quality (Estlund 2000)—in addition to those that refer to fair process. I call such conceptions Rational Proceduralist. In Chapter 4, I shall focus on aggregative and deliberative variants of Pure and Rational Proceduralism. In Chapter 7, I shall add an epistemic account of democracy and compare Rational and Pure Epistemic Proceduralist conceptions of democratic legitimacy.

Chapters 5 and 6 discuss specific requirements of democratic legitimacy in greater detail. The topic of Chapter 5 is political equality. I shall show that establishing what political equality requires creates a fundamental problem for deliberative democracy. The problem arises from a dilemma I call the "political egalitarian's dilemma." If the conditions of political equality are weak, many will be formally included in the deliberative decision-making process, but will not have a fair chance to actually participate. If many remain factually excluded from democratic decision-making, legitimacy is undermined. If, in an attempt to correct for this situation, the conditions of political equality are strong, then many potentially controversial decisions will be made in the attempt to create a fair process. These decisions will not be subject to democratic deliberation, and this will potentially undermine democratic legitimacy.

Some have argued that deliberative democracy, in contrast to aggregative democracy, can reconcile the tension between procedural and substantive considerations. I interpret the political egalitarian dilemma as showing that deliberative democracy, too, is affected by this tension. But if deliberative democracy cannot solve this problem, this suggests that a trade-off needs to be made between these two types of considerations. I shall argue that procedures should get more weight in a conception of democratic legitimacy than it is commonly thought. I shall reject both the idea that the outcomes of democratic decisions ought to satisfy some conditions of collective rationality (Chapter 6) and the idea that there are correct outcomes of democratic decision-making that the democratic process ought to track (Chapter 7).

In Chapter 6, I shall discuss the requirement of collective rationality. Most democratic theorists, whether in the aggregative or the deliberative tradition, defend a version of Rational Proceduralism. They take it that the rationality of the outcomes of decision-making is an essential part of their legitimacy. The premise seems to be that an irrational outcome cannot bind; a decision that we ought to respect must be one that satisfies some requirement of collective rationality. I shall argue against this premise and reject the view that democratic legitimacy demands rational outcomes. I shall defend the weaker claim that the deliberative decision-making process needs to be embedded in an institutional structure that can be publicly justified. I shall defend this claim on the basis of a procedural interpretation of John Rawls's idea of public reason and its role in a conception of democratic legitimacy.

In the last chapter, I shall add to the taxonomy presented in Chapter 4 by introducing epistemic democracy—a variant of both aggregative and deliberative democracy. Epistemic democracy emphasizes the knowledge-generating capacity of processes of collective decision-making. As such, it captures an important feature of democratic decision-making that the standard interpretations of aggregative and deliberative democracy neglect. Epistemic accounts of democracy focus on belief formation. Whereas the standard aggregative view characterizes democracy as an aggregation of preferences over alternative outcomes, the epistemic interpretation of aggregative democracy characterizes it as an aggregation of beliefs about outcomes. The epistemic interpretation of deliberative democracy, similarly, focuses on deliberation as a process of belief formation. Epistemic democracy is typically understood as making the value of democratic decision-making processes dependent on their ability to track a correct outcome that exists procedure-independently. I shall propose a different interpretation of the epistemology of democracy, one that focuses on procedural values and does not treat the outcomes of the process as a source of normativity. My main aim in this last chapter is to defend Pure Epistemic Proceduralism. As a version of Pure Proceduralism, this conception of democratic legitimacy does not make legitimacy dependent on criteria that refer to the quality of the outcomes the procedure generates. Instead, it defines legitimacy exclusively with respect to the fairness of democratic procedures, but interprets political fairness as including conditions of epistemic fairness. Comparing this conception with the Rational Proceduralist conception of legitimacy that is advocated in the standard account of epistemic democracy, I shall show that the normative commitments of Rational Epistemic Proceduralism are unnecessary and misleading and that Pure Epistemic Proceduralism is a more plausible conception of democratic legitimacy.

2   Aggregative Democracy

2.1. THE AGGREGATIVE ACCOUNT OF DEMOCRACY

In the intuitive understanding of many, democracy is foremost about voting. The aggregative account develops this intuition into a full-blown theory of democracy. It focuses on mechanisms for aggregating the preferences individuals express to a collective choice. The aggregative account gained importance in the contemporary literature in the form of an economic theory of democracy through the works of Duncan Black (1948, 1958) and Kenneth Arrow (1963). In this section, I shall give a brief description of this account, as well as discuss features of its theoretical background. I shall focus on Arrow's framework for social choice theory, as it is arguably the most sophisticated account of aggregative democracy.

2.1.a. Arrow's Framework

Arrow attempted to break away from the received approach in normative economics by seeking to ground the evaluation of alternative policy proposals in democratic decisions. Arrow's project in *Social Choice and Individual Values* (1963) was to identify a collective decision-making mechanism, or a class of such mechanisms, which would yield a consistent social preference ordering of alternative social states, and thus a social choice, for every constellation of individual preferences. There are obvious parallels between this project and the works of the Marquis de Condorcet (1785) and Jean-Charles de Borda (1784), but apparently Arrow did not know these authors (McLean 1995).

The relevant theoretical background for Arrow is welfare economics, a branch of normative economics dedicated to the identifcation of best policies. Before Arrow's contribution, it was standard practice in welfare economics to represent policy evaluation with the decisions of a "benevolent dictator." The so-called new welfare economics equipped the dictator with a (Bergson-Samuelson) social welfare function that would capture the social value judgments pertaining on policy decisions. The problem with this approach is that in a democratic society characterized by value pluralism, there is no single set of value judgments that the benevolent dictator could feed into a social welfare function. Arrow thus asked whether the benevolent dictator could be replaced by a system that would be able to respect the diversity of individual values. In answer, he interpreted a social welfare function as a collective decision-making mechanism that would aggregate individual preferences for alternative policies to a social preference ordering and thus enable rational social choice. In addition, he imposed a set of conditions that should ensure that the decision-making mechanism is recognizably democratic. Characterized at this most general level, Arrow's approach appears as a normative theory of democracy, just like deliberative democracy. Both are theories that aim at an account of how a democratic public ought to evaluate alternative courses of actions and make its decisions.

Let me discuss the framework, and its implications, in some more detail. Social choice theory builds on an analogy between the market mechanism and voting. Voting is, just like the market, a mechanism that aggregates individual preferences. Individual preferences thus form the basis of this theoretical framework. Arrow makes an important distinction, however, between individual preferences interpreted as "values" and as "tastes" (Arrow 1963: 18). The latter belong to the market sphere and describe the preferences over the individual's own consumption bundle. They are usually assumed to be self-regarding. But tastes are only a part of individual values. When individuals evaluate alternative policies and vote, they may value not just the goods they consume themselves, but also take into account equity standards or other normative considerations. Arrow assumes that the voting mechanism can aggregate such individual value judgments about alternative social policies. To capture this broader spectrum of considerations, Arrow assumes that individuals have preferences over alternative social states. A social state stands for a full description of all the economic, political, and social circumstances, and each policy option, as well as the status quo, is modeled as an alternative social state.

Individual preferences over such social states are assumed to be rational, where rationality means that individual preferences satisfy the axioms of completeness and transitivity.[1] Completeness requires that every pair of alternatives can be ranked. Transitivity demands that if an alternative x is ranked as at least as good as an alternative y, and y as at least as good as z, then x should also be ranked as at least as good as z. In addition, there is also a condition stating that the alternative chosen is ranked as at least as good as any other alternative available—a maximizing condition. Arrow calls a preference ranking that is fully rational in this sense an "ordering." Although he acknowledges that there might be some difficulties with the notion of rationality that he uses, Arrow defends it as being "at the heart of modern economic analysis" and having "great intuitive appeal" (Arrow 1963: 19).[2]

Arrow works with the revealed preference model (Samuelson 1938). That is to say, he assumes that the choices individuals make reveal their preferences. According to this model, individual preferences are nothing above and beyond what underlies and explains rational individual choices, and can be reconstructed on the basis of the choices individuals make. In the analysis of markets, standard economic theory looks at how individual choices of consumption goods reveal individual preferences over these goods. In the context of the social evaluation and choice of alternative public policies, Arrow assumes that how individuals vote reveals their values.

Such individual preference orderings form the input of this account of democratic decision-making. Arrow makes no further substantive assumptions about the origin and nature of these preferences. This implies that his interpretation of the aggregative account of democracy treats individual preferences as given and as independent of the specific environment—both of the social states and of the decision-making process itself. Arrow admits that the latter is a contestable assumption, but he defends it with the argument that his theoretical framework needs an anchor. He writes, "[i]f individual values can themselves be affected by the method of social choice, it becomes much more difficult to learn what is meant by one method's being preferable to another" (Arrow 1963: 8).[3]

The output is a social choice, a collective decision. Arrow models social choice in exactly the same way as standard economic theory models individual choice—as based on preferences. And just like individual preferences are interpreted as what is expressed by individual choices, Arrow assumes that social preferences are expressed by the democratic choices the collective makes. The voting mechanism thus reveals social preferences, or social "values," and they are what is underlying, and revealed by, the choices society makes by means of a collective decision-making mechanism.[4]

Consider the following simple example with three individuals and three alternatives x, y and z. Suppose the individual preference orderings are as represented in Table 2.1.

If pair wise majority voting was the decision-making mechanism, x would be chosen out of the pair $\{x, y\}$ because both individual 1 and 3 prefer x to y, and only individual 2 thinks y is better than x. Similarly, y would be chosen out of the pair $\{y, z\}$ and x out of the pair $\{x, z\}$. The choices of this mini-society in this situation could thus be interpreted as revealing social preferences that rank alternative x as better than y and alternative y better than z.

Table 2.1 Voting

	Individual 1	*Individual 2*	*Individual 3*
Most preferred	x	y	x
Middle ranked	y	z	z
Least preferred	z	x	y

Table 2.2   Paradox of Voting

	Individual 1	Individual 2	Individual 3
Most preferred	x	y	z
Middle ranked	y	z	x
Least preferred	z	x	y

Already Condorcet was aware, however, that such majoritarian collective choice may fail to yield a consistent ranking. Consider the example of what Arrow calls the "paradox of voting." Assume that the individual preference orderings are the following as represented in Table 2.2.

If this mini-society uses pairwise majority rule to make its social decisions, it would prefer x to y in the choice between x and y and choose y out of the pair $\{y, z\}$. If the social preference ranking was consistent, we would expect this society to prefer x to z. However, if the society is to make a choice between x and z, it will choose z. We therefore have a cycle. None of the choices can be taken as a meaningful reflection of individual preferences since they depend on the order in which the choices are made. The paradox of voting occurs whenever individual preferences form a so-called *Condorcet triple*, as is the case in the example above.

The paradox of voting is an essential motivation for Arrow's framework for social choice. Arrow asks whether there is a democratic collective decision-making mechanism that for any constellation of individual preferences yields a social preference ordering. If social preferences fulfill the same conditions of rationality as individual preferences, then such cycles cannot occur. To exclude problems of cyclicity, Arrow thus modeled a decision-making mechanism as a function that maps a profile of individual preference orderings to a social preference ordering. Arrow alternatively calls this mapping function a social welfare function or a constitution (1963: 105).

One can imagine many different such decision-making mechanisms. Dictatorship, where the preference ordering of one individual always determines the social preference ordering, is just one example. But dictatorship is clearly not a democratic decision-making mechanism. To ensure that the collective decision-making mechanism is recognizably democratic, it is thus necessary to restrict the class of admissible decision-making mechanisms. This can be achieved by demanding that admissible decision-making mechanisms satisfy a set of normative conditions that capture democratic values.

Arrow proposed the following four conditions. The first condition, Unrestricted Domain (condition U), requires that all possible profiles of individual preferences be admitted. The idea is that the collective decision-making mechanism should not discriminate against some preference profiles. Since individuals are described only via their preference profiles, this condition contains an ideal of political equality. The Independence of Irrelevant Alternatives (condition I) requires that social preferences between two alternative social states should depend only on the individual preferences over this pair of alternatives. Collective decision-making should not be affected by individual preferences over other alternatives, or indeed by any considerations other than people's preferences over pairs of alternatives in the subset. According to the weak Pareto principle (condition P), if all individuals judge an alternative x to be (strictly) better than an alternative y, the social preference ordering should also rank x as (strictly) better than y. If there is unanimity in the society about which of two alternatives is better than the other, then the social preference ranking should reflect this unanimity.[5] The fourth condition, finally, Non-Dictatorship (condition D), rules out dictatorial social choice by demanding that social choice should not be determined by the preferences of a single individual. This is another very weak condition of political equality.

Pairwise majority voting, the decision-making mechanism discussed above, satisfies all four conditions. Plurality rule, however, another common majoritarian decision-making mechanism, satisfies U, P, and D, but violates condition I. Plurality voting counts how many votes each alternative in the feasible set gets, assuming that each individual votes for his or her top-ranked alternative. With this rule, it is possible that there is a profile of individual preferences, say over three alternatives x, y, and z, which yields x as a winner, and another profile, created by changing the preferences of some individuals over the pair $\{y, z\}$, which yields a different winner.[6] Since plurality rule is a common democratic decision-making mechanism, it would seem that Arrow would have to provide an argument for why plurality voting is ruled-out. More generally, it would seem imperative to have a further justification for which conditions are necessary to render a decision-making mechanism recognizably democratic. Arrow does not, however, try to show that these conditions are necessary for democracy. His only justification for them is that they are reasonable.[7]

As it is well-known, the four conditions are sufficient to bring about a rather devastating result for aggregative democracy. Arrow's famous impossibility theorem establishes that there is no collective decision-making mechanism that simultaneously satisfies the four conditions.[8] The only collective decision-making mechanism that yields a complete, transitive social preference ordering and that satisfies conditions P, I, and U is dictatorial. Any decision-making mechanism that satisfies all four conditions may violate the conditions of collective rationality.[9]

The impossibility result implies that it cannot be guaranteed that democratic decision-making does not issue in cyclic social preferences. Only a dictatorial collective decision-making process yields rational social preferences. Any democratic, i.e. non-dictatorial, decision-making mechanism may yield intransitive social preferences. The impossibility theorem thus generalizes the problem we have encountered above with the voting para-dox: aggregative democracy is prone to generate cyclic social preferences. As discussed in this context, if there is a possibility of cycles, then there are difficulties with identifying the social choice that can be said to be a true reflection of individual preferences.

Some have drawn very pessimistic conclusions from Arrow's impossibil-ity theorem. William Riker (1982), for example, has argued that it demon-strates the impossibility of any meaningful democratic policy evaluation.[10] An objection that immediately suggests itself against such negative inter-pretations is that Arrow's framework is very restrictive and that the impos-sibility result is overcome once either the rationality postulates or one or several of the four conditions are weakened or dropped entirely. This has of course been explored extensively; it is what characterizes the literature on social choice theory.[11] But unfortunately the impossibility theorem proved to be very robust. Similar impossibility results occurred again and again.

One way of escaping the impossibility result that Arrow discusses in *Social Choice and Individual Values* is to restrict the domain of individual preferences. This amounts to modifying condition U. If individual prefer-ences over social states are similar—with unanimity as the extreme case—or if individual preferences show a common structure, then the impossibility result vanishes.[12] The latter is the case with so-called single-peaked pref-erences.[13] Arrow gives the example of single-peaked preferences in elec-tions. Preferences are single-peaked if the individuals have a most preferred candidate that best reflects their position in the political spectrum and if the other candidates are ranked according to their vicinity to the preferred political position. This obtains, for instance, if candidates differ only with respect to their position in the left–right political spectrum. More gener-ally, single-peakedness means that alternatives vary only with respect to one dimension. Arrow shows that if preferences are single-peaked and if the number of individuals is odd, pair wise majority rule would satisfy all conditions and yield rational social preferences. This can easily be checked in the case of three alternatives. If preferences are single-peaked, the pos-sibility of Condorcet triples is ruled out and majority rule thus yields a transitive social preference ranking. Take three candidates, where x may stand for the one on the political left, y for center, and z for a right-wing candidate. The individual preference orderings can be either (x, y, z), (z, y, x), (y, x, z) or (y, z, x). Since (x, z, y) and (z, x, y) are ruled out by single-peakedness, there will be no Condorcet triple.

This escape route does not lead very far however, as Arrow himself recognized. For one, democratic social evaluation becomes necessary, not when there is unanimity or something close to it, but when individual interests conflict and values about how to evaluate these conflicts are plu-ral. This solution thus seems to beg the question. In addition, the case of preferences differing only according to one dimension does not seem to be the standard one in pluralist democratic collectives. To continue with the election example, gender and ethnicity, ecological considerations, or issues of global reach may add additional dimensions that detract from the left-right spectrum of traditional national politics.

If revising condition U does not offer an attractive escape route, what about the other conditions? The Pareto and the Non-Dictatorship conditions are often seen as making only very weak demands. Social choice theorists have explored the consequences of further weakening conditions P and D, but these rather technical explorations have not yielded very promising results either, and I shall refrain from reviewing them here. The Pareto condition is far from being just a technical condition, of course, and I shall come back to this condition later in this chapter, when I discuss Amartya Sen's response to Arrow's impossibility theorem, which focuses on the combined effects of different conditions.

The Independence condition is the one that has perhaps caused most debate in the literature. Condition I rules out decision-making mechanisms that rely on more information than individual preferences over pairs of alternatives. This shows that this condition, although satisfied by pairwise majority rule, is a fairly strong one to impose on democratic processes. The Borda count, for example, which gives points to the rank-order of the alternatives in individual preferences, and then determines social choice by identifying the alternative that receives the most points, is ruled out by condition I.[14] Weakening, or dropping, condition I thus allows for a broader spectrum of aggregative mechanisms to be considered. In spite of this result, many have defended majority rule as the core decision-making mechanism of aggregative democracy, arguing that its intrinsic properties render it preferable to other forms of decision-making (e.g. Waldron 1999; Dasgupta and Maskin 2004). Indeed, this escape route is not one that I shall pursue. I shall argue below that there are objections to aggregative democracy that affect other decision-making rules as well. I shall defend the view that broadening the class of admissible aggregative decision rules is not sufficient, and that the account of aggregative democracy needs to be replaced by an alternative account of democracy that rests on different normative premises. This alternative account includes majoritarian decision-making but treats majority rule as not sufficient for legitimacy.

Another escape route that I want to briefly discuss here is to weaken the rationality conditions that Arrow imposes on social preferences. Transitivity has attracted most of the attention.[15] A weaker condition than transitivity is quasi-transitivity. It requires transitivity of strict preferences ("better than"), but not of the weak ("at least as good as") preference relation. It can be shown, however, that the only collective decision-making mechanisms that satisfy reflexivity, completeness, quasi-transitivity and conditions U, I, P, and D, are oligarchic (Sen 1970a). An oligarchy is defined as a group of individuals that is decisive over all pairs of alternatives—if social preferences always mirror the unanimous preferences of the oligarchy—and where each individual has a veto.[16] An example for a social decision function that yields a quasi-transitive social preference ranking is the so-called "Pareto-extension rule." It identifies an alternative x as socially preferred to y whenever all individuals unanimously strictly prefer x to y, and ranks all alternatives that are either Pareto-indifferent or Pareto-noncomparable as socially indifferent (Sen 1969).[17] As many have pointed out, one problem with the Pareto-extension rule is that it is not discriminating enough. It may rank as indifferent two alternatives that are clearly not of equal value, such as one in which everyone but one person almost starves and another in which everyone has enough. Opinions differ about whether or not the Pareto principle is a necessary condition that any social evaluation function ought to satisfy. But many will agree that because of its indifference towards considerations of justice, it is not a sufficient condition. I shall come back to this issue below (3.2.b.)

Thus while weakening the rationality requirements on social preferences leads to some social decision-mechanisms, the spectrum is still very narrow and the mechanisms themselves are not very appealing. Majority rule is still excluded. Instead of weakening the conditions imposed on social preference rankings, the alternative is to drop the idea of a social preference ranking completely. This was suggested by James Buchanan already in 1954, in reaction to the first publication of *Social Choice and Individual Values* in 1951. Buchanan criticized Arrow's attempt to deduce a value ordering for society from individual values. According to him, while individuals have preferences, society, viewed as an aggregate of individuals, can only make choices.[18] The appropriate focus of social choice theory should thus be the decision-making process, not its result. He objects that Arrow overlooks the difference between imposing normative conditions on the decision-making process, and imposing them on the function that maps profiles of individual preference orderings onto a social preference ordering. As he puts the point (Buchanan 1954: 116):

> [D]oes not the very attempt to examine [social] rationality in terms of individual values introduce logical inconsistency at the outset? Can the rationality of the social organism be evaluated with any value ordering other than its own?

For Buchanan's objection to work, it has to be shown that it is possible that a collective makes consistent choices, even if these choices cannot be interpreted as based on a rational social preference ranking that maps individual values. The idea would be to define social choice with reference to choice sets, not a social preference ordering (e.g. Fishburn 1973). This escape route proved to be illusory, however. If some requirements of internal consistency are imposed on the choice function, the problems that affect the relational framework sneak back in. The reason is that requiring internal consistency of choices from different sets can be interpreted as implying a pairwise comparison underlying the choices. This links the choice-centered framework with the relational formulation. Furthermore, Sen (1993b) shows that the impossibility result can be reestablished even if all requirements of internal consistency of choice are dropped and the conditions refer to choices from one set only.[19]

Even if Buchanan's objection to Arrow thus rests on some problematic assumptions of its own and ultimately fails, the distinction he makes between imposing normative conditions on the democratic decision-making process itself and on its outcomes is important, I think. I also agree with Buchanan that Arrow does not have a good defense of the idea of modeling democratic decision-making as a function that maps profiles of individual preference orderings onto a social preference ordering. I shall have more to say on this distinction in Chapters 4 to 7, where I shall defend the claim that it is not necessary to impose conditions that refer to the outcomes of democratic decision-making and that conditions that apply to the decision-making process are sufficient.

In the rest of this section, I want to discuss some aspects of the philosophical background on which Arrow's framework rests, as this background forms the target of my critique of aggregative democracy in section 2.2.

2.1.b. The Utilitarian Background of Social Choice Theory

If we accept the conclusion that Arrow's impossibility theorem is very robust, and that its negative implications cannot be avoided by tinkering with single elements of the framework he proposed, it seems necessary to probe deeper and to examine the philosophical underpinnings of the framework as a whole. What led Arrow to model democratic decision-making in this particular way?

Utilitarianism forms an important part of this background, as Arrow acknowledges (1963: 22–23):

> The utilitarian philosophy of Jeremy Bentham and his followers sought [. . .] to ground the social good on the good of individuals. The hedonist psychology associated with utilitarian philosophy was further used to imply that each individual's good was identical with his desires. [. . .] The hedonist psychology finds its expression here in the assumption that individual's behavior is expressed by individual ordering relations R_i. Utilitarian philosophy is expressed by saying that for each pair of social states the choice depends on the ordering relations of all individuals [. . .].

Generally speaking, utilitarianism models the problem of moral evaluation as a choice between different alternatives. If utilitarianism is understood as a system of individual morality, the moral choice is between alternative options—acts, rules, motives—the individual has. Arrow interprets utilitarianism as guiding the choice between alternative social states. I shall stick to this interpretation here, according to which utilitarianism advises us to compare alternative social states in terms of their consequences on individual utility and select the social state that maximizes individual utility.

Classical utilitarianism—as expounded in the writings of Jeremy Bentham, John Stuart Mill, and Henry Sidgwick, among others[20]—is helpfully factorized into the following three component principles (Sen and Williams 1982: introduction). The first component is consequentialism. According to John Rawls's definition, in consequentialist theories, "the good is defined independently from the right, and then the right is defined as that what maximizes the good" (Rawls 1971: 24). The second component specifies goodness. Classical utilitarianism rests on what Sen (1977b) has labeled "welfarism," and it identifies individual happiness as the ultimate good. In the passage just quoted, Arrow refers to welfarism as "hedonist psychology," but this term underplays the normative content of the idea and I shall thus not use it. Later forms of utilitarianism use different conceptions of individual utility.

The combination of consequentialism and welfarism characterizes the core of the utilitarian approach to social evaluation: what is assessed is the social welfare produced by different social states, where social welfare depends exclusively on individual utility. The last component of utilitarianism is a principle that determines how individual utility should be aggregated to determine the greatest good. In classical utilitarianism, this principle is sum-ranking. According to sum-ranking, the alternatives should be ranked according to the total happiness they produce, as calculated by adding up happiness across individuals and giving the interests of individuals equal weight.[21] Other versions of utilitarianism use different alternative aggregative principles.

The utilitarian influence on Arrow's framework for social choice theory is inherited from welfare economics. The so-called old welfare economics was a straightforward application of classical utilitarianism; it proposed an operationalization of the principle of maximizing the sum of individual utilities (Pigou 1929). The idea of sum-ranking as the default aggregative principle was dropped following Lionel Robbins's influential critique of interpersonal comparisons of utility (Robbins 1938). The new welfare economics, exemplified by the Bergson-Samuelson social welfare function, started from ordinally measurable, interpersonally non-comparable utility functions. The Bergson-Samuelson welfare function is a function of a particular profile of individual utilities. It is a formal approach that is compatible with different judgments about how individual utility should be aggregated in the evaluation of social states. It is supposed to be a tool for a social planner, a policy-maker, who needs to make a decision among alternative social states given a certain profile of individual utilities. Arrow, by contrast, was searching for a collective decision mechanism by way of which a democratic society could select social states on the basis of individual values about them. In his framework, what is aggregated is not the individual utilities generated by a particular social state, but individual values about how to rank social states.

In spite of this important difference, Arrow's framework still includes elements of welfarism and consequentialism. The utilitarian content of his analysis can be described as lying, firstly, in his restriction of the informational basis of social choice to individual preference orderings. This is a version of welfarism. Secondly, Arrow's formulation of the problem of social choice aims at identifying the "best" social state, taking expressed individual preferences as the measure. This is a version of consequentialism. While the ordinal approach Arrow adopts rules out the classical utilitarian principle of sum-ranking, the question he poses nevertheless parallels the maximization postulate of utilitarian moral philosophy. In fact, Arrow himself refers to this preference-based combination of consequentialism and welfarism as "ordinal utilitarianism."[22]

Sen's work has probably contributed most to our understanding of the utilitarian roots of Arrow's framework for social choice, and in particular his commitment to welfarism. Sen has shown that the conditions U, P, and I that Arrow imposes on a collective decision-making mechanism have the secondary effect of specifying a very narrow informational basis for social choice (e.g. 1979, 1986b). Each of these three conditions can be interpreted as ruling out certain types of information from affecting social choice, thereby tightening the spectrum of what counts as admissible information until only a very narrow version of welfarism remains.

The informational constraint implicit in the "Unrestricted Domain" condition is that social preferences should depend only on individual preferences—the informational domain over which the aggregative mechanism should work does not include information other than preferences. Condition I, as we saw, demands that social choice should depend only on individual preferences over the alternatives over which the choice is actually to be made and not on preferences over additional alternatives. Sen (1970a: 89–90) calls this the "irrelevance" aspect of condition I. The "ordering" aspect of condition I implies, in combination with condition U, that social choice should depend on individual preferences over pairs of alternatives only. This rules out decision-making mechanisms such as the Borda count, which depends on the ranking of all alternatives in the set, not just of pairs. This aspect also rules out any direct consideration of intensity of preferences. Considerations of preference intensities would require more than only ordinally measurable utility. But any such utility index would depend on all alternatives in the set and thus violate the informational restriction to preferences over pairs of alternatives. The two aspects are not independent of each other, however. The irrelevance aspect is, rather, only a part of the ordering aspect. If social choice is to depend only on individual preferences over the pairs in S, it is clear that alternatives not included in S will not affect the social choice. If the weak Pareto principle is added to the first two conditions, the implication is that when individual preferences are strict ("better than"), social preferences and social choice should depend exclusively on individual preferences over pairs of alternatives. This is a version of welfarism.[23]

Sen (1970a) has shown that Arrow's framework for social choice can be reformulated to take into account individual utility functions instead of individual preference rankings. This revised framework makes it possible to explore the consequences that broadening the informational basis of social choice has for the impossibility result. A famous theorem (Sen 1970a, theorem 8*2) proves that introducing cardinal measurability of utility alone does not change anything. But if Arrow's framework is modified in order to allow for interpersonal comparisons, whether at the ordinal or at the cardinal level, a variety of non-dictatorial social welfare functions become available. With ordinal level comparability, maximin is a possible aggregative mechanism. This social welfare function ranks social states according to how well-off the worst-off individual is. If individual utility functions are cardinally measurable and interpersonally comparable, then the sum of individual utilities becomes a possible aggregative mechanism. We have come full circle, back to utilitarianism.[24]

With interpersonal comparisons, it is thus possible to derive consistent social welfare judgments from information about individual welfare.[25] This important result moreover sheds light on the working of the impossibility theorem itself. Sen (1979: 539) concludes that "[t]he impossibility theorem can be seen as resulting from combining a version of welfarism ruling out the use of non-utility information with making the utility information remarkably poor." But how attractive is such an escape route? Arrow considered and rejected the idea of relying on interpersonal comparisons of utility in *Social Choice and Individual Values*.[26] He was aware that excluding interpersonal comparisons of utility played a crucial role in bringing about the impossibility result, as this characterization of his theorem confirms (1963: 59):

> If we exclude the possibility of interpersonal comparisons of utility, then the only method of passing from individual tastes to social preferences which will be satisfactory [i.e. leading to rational social preferences] and which will be defined for a wide range of sets of individual orderings are either imposed or dictatorial.

He later defended excluding the possibility of interpersonal comparisons of utility in the following way (1984: 160):

> In a way that I cannot articulate well and am none too sure about defending, the autonomy of the individuals, an element of mutual incommensurability among people, seems denied by the possibility of

interpersonal comparisons. No doubt it is some such feeling as this that has made me so reluctant to shift from pure ordinalism, despite my desire to seek a basis for a theory of justice.

Arrow thus wanted to exclude interpersonal comparisons of utility on grounds that they constitute an inadmissible value judgment. This view has been prominent among economists ever since Robbins's influential attack on welfare economics and its reliance on interpersonal comparisons (Robbins 1938).

While historically important, the standard objection against interpersonal utility comparisons—that they involve a value judgment—lacks a persuasive argument to back it up, however. The objection rests on the dubious assumption that value judgments enter only through individual comparisons of utility, and that no value judgments are involved, for example, in the idea of individual preferences, or the idea of interpreting social evaluation as a problem of aggregative democracy, etc.[27] I share Sen's view on this issue—that it is not interpersonal comparability that is the real problem, but utility itself. I shall discuss problems with the utility framework in section 2.2.

Sen is a powerful advocate of the escape route offered by introducing interpersonal comparisons—but not of interpersonal comparisons of utility. The alternative informational framework he proposes, the capability approach, has an objective component that renders interpersonal comparisons possible.[28] As is well-known, Sen has applied this approach to the evaluation of social states, and to comparisons between how different individuals fare in different social states in the context of studies of development, poverty and inequality (e.g. Sen 1985a, 1992a). The problem with this escape route, if pursued in isolation, is that it reverts to the evaluative approach of welfare economics. Sen (1977b, 1995) distinguishes between two separate dimensions of social choice theory: the social welfare judgment dimension and the collective decision-making dimension. The former is in continuation with the project of welfare economics. It focuses on the possibility of passing social welfare judgments, i.e. of selecting among alternative social states on the basis of a given set of values. The latter dimension is associated with the study of collective decision-making rules that can be traced back to Cusanus, Borda, and Condorcet. The original contribution Arrow made in *Social Choice and Individual Values* was to combine the utilitarian tradition in welfare economics with the formal theory of collective decision-making mechanisms in an axiomatic theory of aggregative democracy. Both the impossibility result and the exploration of avenues to escape it reveal the difficulties that affect an aggregative account of democratic evaluation. It is one of the great merits of Arrow's original framework that it sought to bring research on democratic decision-making to bear on the problem of evaluating alternative social states. Exploring escape routes from the impossibility result has again driven a wedge between these two research programs. The research program that focuses on interpersonal comparisons has shifted the focus back to the original preoccupation with social welfare judgments, while neglecting the possibility of grounding such value judgments in democratic processes.[29] The alternative research program on properties of collective decision-making mechanisms stopped paying much attention to the normative aspects of democratic social evaluation. Arrow's attempt to integrate the two dimensions thus seems to have failed, at least within an aggregative account of democratic decision-making. As I shall argue in Chapter 3, deliberative democracy is an account of democracy that is better able than aggregative democracy to integrate the social welfare judgment dimension with the collective decision-making dimension. According to the deliberative account, democracy is, and ought to be, essentially a process of collective deliberation over alternative institutional arrangements and policies. But before turning to deliberative democracy, there are some further objections to aggregative democracy that I want to raise.

2.2 PROBLEMS WITH AGGREGATIVE DEMOCRACY

The previous section focused on the presentation of Arrow's framework of social choice, and on the internal critique of aggregative democracy in relation to the impossibility theorem. This section takes up some lines of external criticism. I want to argue that there are important considerations that aggregative democracy neglects.

2.2.a. Justice

A first objection is that Arrow's framework makes it hard to address considerations of justice. The reason for this problem can be traced back to the utilitarian legacy in social choice theory. It is a well known objection against utilitarianism that it places insufficient value on distributive justice (e.g. Williams 1973). The standard version of the objection is directed against the sum-ranking principle. If only the sum of individual utilities matters in utilitarian moral evaluation, this neglects the distribution of individual utilities. This is not to deny that the distribution of utilities may matter instrumentally. It is perfectly plausible that redistribution increases the sum-total. But there may be tremendous variations in the distribution of individual utility across social states with the same sum-total, and the utilitarian calculus will not differentiate between such social states.

Another version of this objection applies also to variations of utilitarianism that are not committed to sum-ranking—i.e. versions of ordinal utilitarianism that stick to consequentialism and welfarism, but use a different principle for aggregation. This version of the objection was famously raised by Rawls. It says that utilitarianism "does not take seriously the distinction between persons" (Rawls 1971: 27). The main target of this objection is the combination of consequentialism and welfarism. This combination is sufficient to reduce individuals to carriers of utility. Because it rules out that any considerations other than those about individual utility are independently valued, it attaches insufficient value to considerations that arise when separate persons try to decide how to organize their life together. Such considerations might include their rights, whether human rights or legal rights, their freedom to live according to principles they endorse, and their opportunities to partake in the shaping of the institutions that structure their life together.

An example from Sen (1995) illustrates how the problems with accommodating considerations of justice reappear in the Arrowian version of welfarist consequentialism. Take a classic cake-division problem with three people. And suppose the aggregative mechanism is majority rule. Suppose there are two situations: (a) the case where two of the three people already have most of the cake and take away more cake from the third, who has practically nothing, and (b) the case where two of them have very little and get some more from the third person, who has the bigger part of the cake. Now, if all individuals prefer more to less cake and vote accordingly, there is a 2:1 majority for redistribution in each case. The problem is, of course, that while the information processed by aggregative democracy suggests that the two cases are alike, the distributive situation in the two cases clearly differs. The example shows that an assessment of distributive justice would require more information than what majority rule alone can process. The Arrowian account of democratic social evaluation thus suffers from the same problem as classical utilitarianism in that it also tends to gloss over considerations that affect the evaluation of distributive justice.

Both welfarism and consequentialism are sometimes defended as minimal moral commitments: what can be wrong with trying to bring about something good, and what is wrong with identifying the good with individual welfare? But, as Bernard Williams points out, the minimal commitment of utilitarianism is a result of its blindness for problems of justice and should not be seen as providing a defense for it:

> The appeal at the social level of utilitarianism's minimal commitment is therefore to some extent not peculiar to it, and to some extent illusory. It is also to some extent real, in the sense that utilitarianism really does make do with fewer ancillary principles and moral notions, but [. . .] the lightness of its burden in this respect to a great extent merely shows how little of the world's moral luggage it is prepared to pick up. A system of social decision which is indifferent to issues of justice or equity certainly has less to worry about than one that is not indifferent to those considerations.[30]

Because the combination of welfarism and consequentialism neglects the separateness of individuals—the conflicts and mutual exclusion of individual goals and the problems this poses for distributive issues—it ignores important aspects of moral evaluation. The allegedly innocuous commitment to only minimal value premises turns out to be loaded with contestable claims. It is thus necessary to discuss in some more detail how the commitments of utilitarian moral philosophy bear on aggregative democracy.

2.2.b. Welfarism

Welfarism forms one element of Arrow's framework, as uncovered by Sen's informational interpretation of the impossibility result. Arrow's conditions imply that aggregative mechanisms should only take into account information contained in individual preference orderings over social states. Other sources of values are ruled out. Arrow defends the welfarism commitment on grounds of its subjectivism about value; he rejects the idea "that there exists an objective social good defined independently of individual desires" (Arrow 1963: 22). There are two main objections against welfarism that I regard as significant for aggregative democracy. One concerns precisely the subjectivist idea of identifying goodness with the satisfaction of individual preferences. The other concerns the difficulties welfarism has with the formation of preferences.

Let me start with a version of the objection against welfarism that focuses on the identification of individual welfare with the satisfaction of individual preferences. This account of individual welfare is common in welfare economics, but also sometimes invoked by utilitarian moral philosophers. It is especially problematic if welfare judgments are based on actual preferences.[31] Actual preferences are revealed, according to the theory of revealed preferences, through the choices individuals make. As we have seen above, Arrow has endorsed this approach to preferences. But what an individual chooses is not necessarily linked to his or her well-being, for preferences may be based on false information or beliefs. Equally, an individual may decide according to values other than maximizing his or her well-being, such as responsibility, moral commitments, standards of politeness, etc. and make choices that reduce his or her well-being (Sen 1977a).

But let us assume that it can be ensured that individual utility actually reflects individual welfare. Does that solve the problem with welfarism? The answer is no. A further objection targets the idea that goodness is rooted in individual welfare. The objection is that welfarism may exclude important other sources of value from becoming relevant in the evaluation of alternative social states. Consider the following example (Sen 1979: 547–48). Take two individuals in two social states x and y. In x, individual 2 is very well-off, whereas 1 is almost starving. State y is reached by some redistribution that leaves 2 slightly less well-off, but greatly improves the standard of living of individual 1. Assume that the pattern of utilities in the two states is as represented in Table 2.3.

Table 2.3   A Problem with Welfarism

	x	y
Individual 1	4	7
Individual 2	10	8

Aggregate utility is higher in social state y than in x. Since 1 is now much better off and 2 suffers only a little, let us agree that the utilitarian calculus gets it right in this situation and that y is better than x. But now assume a third social state y', which has the same utility profile as y. According to welfarism, y and y' should thus be regarded as equally good. But if we know that y' is reached from x by letting sadist individual 1 torture individual 2, we would probably not want to agree with this verdict. Welfarism thus fails to register important differences between social states.

This version of the objection is not just a problem for welfare economics and applied utilitarian philosophy; it can be adapted to aggregative democracy. If the preference profile over two social states is the same in two scenarios, welfarism demands that they be treated equally. But we may want to discriminate between the two scenarios if we know that one involves torture. This is impossible in a welfarist framework that takes individual preferences as the ultimate basis of social evaluation. Or recall the cake-division problem, which compared a redistribution scenario with an exploitation scenario. In the informational space of preferences, the two cases look the same. In each, two individuals preferred the new social state and one individual was against it. As long as the preference profiles are the same, welfarism demands that two social states be valued the same—even if the two social states differ greatly in non-welfare informational spaces, and if there are good reasons to discriminate between, say, redistribution and exploitation.

The second objection is that welfarism cannot handle the formation of individual preferences. Welfarism brackets this issue, and there are several problems that might arise as a result. A first problem concerns adaptive preferences—when individuals unintentionally tend to adjust their preferences to their possibilities.[32] Adaptive preferences pose a serious obstacle for social evaluation based on individual preferences. For one, if preferences are formed adaptively, the satisfaction of these preferences would yield a distorted picture of individual well-being. This connects the second objection to the first. But the additional problem that arises from neglecting preference formation is that if preferences vary with social states, how should the social choice between the alternative states be made? If there is a different preference profile for every alternative in the choice set, a decision regarding the relevant profile in terms of which the social choice is to be made is needed first.[33] For example, before the introduction of women's right to vote in Switzerland in the 1970s, many Swiss women opposed the idea. Which preferences matter: the one before the introduction of the vote or the ones after the introduction? Arrow, as discussed in section 2.1.a., deals with this problem by assuming that preferences are independent of social states. The completeness condition, which requires that individuals have a complete preference ordering over all conceivable social states, rules out that individuals rank alternatives differently depending on what the status quo is. As a result, his framework is not equipped to deal with the possibility of adaptive preference formation and may neglect information about how different social states affect individuals.

A further problem is captured in the so-called "expensive tastes" objection.[34] This objection says that individuals may have voluntarily cultivated expensive tastes, and the resulting preferences should not receive equal weight in social evaluation as the preferences of those who have remained modest. Whereas the problem of adaptive preferences points to the inappropriateness of using given preferences as the basis of moral assessment due to their dependence on the individual situation to be evaluated, the expensive tastes argument focuses on the opposite issue. That is, it is concerned with the individual capacity to reflect upon preferences and to exert a certain control over them. To the extent to which individuals have this capacity, they can also be held responsible for them. And, so the argument goes, if some individual has voluntarily cultivated expensive tastes, these preferences cannot be taken as the given basis for claims on society's resources. It is necessary to discriminate among preferences with respect to their origins if they are still to be the informational framework for social evaluation. Thus, while the problem of expensive taste is just an example, the more fundamental issue is that preferences over which the individuals have control and for which they can be held responsible may not form an adequate informational framework for settling matters of distributive justice.

One answer to these problems with welfarism is to argue for some kind of correction of actual preferences in order to eliminate preferences with objectionable or ambiguous content (e.g. Griffin 1986). To a certain extent, Arrow takes this idea on board when he distinguishes between "values" and "tastes," and views the former as relevant for social choice. But as argued above, all that this distinction achieves is that it allows for the possibility that individual preferences include considerations other than self-interest. It does not rule out adaptive preferences, or demand that individuals take responsibility for their preferences. John Harsanyi's (1955) distinction between personal and moral preferences, by contrast, is a step in this direction. Moral preferences reflect preferences "in those possibly rare moments when [the individual] forces a special impartial and impersonal attitude upon himself" (Harsanyi 1955: 315).

This solutions gets some things right. It is certainly plausible that preferences can be laundered in the sense of being subject to critical examination—either privately, or in the context of an exchange with others. I shall have more to say on this issue in the next chapter. And there is no problem either, of course, with feeding a decision-making mechanism with laundered preferences, as opposed to unexamined preferences. But that is not to say that the laundering preferences idea provides a solution to the problems that welfarism poses for aggregative democracy. For it is not clear how aggregative democracy would be able to incorporate such processes of critical examination. Aggregative democracy does not have the tools for answering the question of who should "launder" actual preferences. If laundering preferences is left to the individuals themselves, then it is not clear when we are dealing with "polluted" preferences and when with preferences that have been corrected. If, by contrast, discriminating among preferences is not done by the individuals themselves, but delegated to some public official in charge with aggregation, this violates the fundamental principle of preferences-based welfarism—that the individual is the best judge of his or her well-being.[35] Since laundering preferences thus does not solve the problems with preference-based evaluation on which aggregative democracy relies, I conclude that democratic social evaluation cannot be based on individual preferences alone. Non-utility information, such as individual rights, has to be included.[36]

2.2.c. Agency

A further argument for the need to go beyond utility information is based on Sen's distinction between well-being and agency (1985b). Welfarism neglects that people value and pursue other things than their own well-being; to focus on individual well-being only is to neglect people's agency. Agency is the ability to set and pursue one's own goals and interests, of which the pursuit of one's own well-being may be only one. Other ends may include furthering the well-being of others, respecting social and moral norms, or acting upon personal commitments and the pursuit of a variety of values.

I regard the argument from agency as the most fundamental objection against the Arrowian framework for social choice theory, welfare economics, and welfarist moral philosophy. The claim is that it makes a fundamental difference to the evaluation of policy alternatives if persons are respected as agents and not just treated as "patients"—who do or do not have well-being (Sen 1999a: 190). Taking agency seriously brings to the fore a person's actions and the motivating principles behind them: how a person acts or refuses to act, and her reasons and motives for choosing one action over another. As Sen (1985b: 204) puts it:

> The importance of the agency aspect . . . relates to the view of persons as responsible agents. Persons must enter the moral accounting by others not only as people whose well-being demands concern, but also as people whose responsible agency must be recognized.[37]

In contrast to the outcome-based structure of the received view of individual rational choice and social choice, taking agency seriously highlights how individuals may attribute value not just to what they receive, but to the relation between their own acts and the resulting outcomes, as well as to the relation between what they receive and their interactions with other agents.

Because individual agents may value and pursue a wide range of goals, taking into account the agency aspect requires a broader informational basis than the evaluation of well-being, which may be just one of these goals, alone. But agency is not easily incorporated into aggregative democracy. The problems this poses are best discussed with reference to Sen's "liberal paradox."[38] Let me briefly explain the liberal paradox first, and then show how it can be used to illustrate the difficulties aggregative democracy has with taking seriously individual agency.

The liberal paradox uses a slightly modified version of Arrow's axiomatic framework to describe a possible conflict between liberty and rights on the one hand, and efficiency—or purely utility-based evaluation of outcomes—on the other. As such it presents a further argument against welfarism, one that stands in the tradition of the literature on utilitarianism and rights (cf. n. 36). To get off the ground, the liberal paradox requires highly differentiated social states: they have to keep track of the different actions of individuals. Preference-based evaluation is interpreted in the same way as in Arrow's original framework—Sen uses conditions U and P. Condition I, which is often regarded as the most problematic one in Arrow's framework, is not used. Instead, Sen uses a condition called "Minimal Liberty," which states that each individual should have the right to determine some social states irrespective of what others think or want. In the language of social choice theory, such rights make individuals decisive. Sen's theorem says that social evaluation based on respecting liberty rights may clash with the overall evaluation of social states in terms of individual preferences about these social states, i.e. that the condition specifying liberty may be inconsistent with the other two conditions.

Sen uses an example to illustrate the paradox. There are two people—Prude and Lewd—and the question is who gets to read *Lady Chatterley's Lover*. There are three alternatives: Prude reads it (x), Lewd reads it (y), or no one reads it (z). In Sen's example, Prude strongly dislikes the book and prefers to read it himself rather than knowing that Lewd reads it. His preference ordering is thus (z, x, y). Lewd likes the book, but gets even more pleasure from thinking that uptight Prude reads the book. He thus prefers that Prude read it, to reading it himself, to no one reading it (x, y, z). The paradox is the following: if the choice is between x and z, from a perspective of liberal rights, society should leave it up to Prude to decide whether he wants to read the book (Prude should be decisive). Since he prefers z to x, society should also prefer z to x. If the choice is between y and z, similarly, Lewd should be decisive and society should prefer y

to *z*. This leads to the social preference ranking (*y*, *z*, *x*). This preference ranking is, however, not Pareto optimal, as both Prude and Lewd prefer *x* to *y*—hence the paradox.

The paradox reveals a difficulty with trying to reconcile preference-based welfarism with respect for individual agency. Applied specifically to aggregative democracy, the paradox can be used to make the following point. If democratic social evaluation is cast in the welfarist informational framework, then considerations of rights that would protect individual agency will receive insufficient weight. If rights-based considerations are introduced, then these rights might trump preference-based evaluation even when no one thinks that this is warranted, thus violating a fundamental premise of preference-based, welfarist democratic evaluation. Either way, the paradox poses a problem for aggregative democracy and captures the difficulties aggregative democracy has with non-welfarist considerations.

The liberal paradox arises only if there are preferences regarding the choices of others. The paradox does not arise with completely separate individuals whose only concern is with their own benefits. In Sen's example, both Lewd and Prude have preferences about each other's actions. Many have taken issue with this assumption about interdependence, and argued that the best way to resolve the liberal paradox is by ruling out such interdependent preferences (e.g. Gibbard 1974; Blau 1975). But it is not clear how that would be possible, as social life does not seem to be constituted by solipsistic units, but by individual agents who interact with others in many and complex ways, and who cannot individually control these interactions. I thus believe that the assumption of interdependence is perfectly reasonable.[39]

What is more, such interdependence makes taking agency information into account all the more important. The clash between liberty rights and preference-based evaluation is only one consequence of trying to accommodate individual agency information. The general problem is that when a multitude of individual agents tries to organize their lives together, they may bring all sorts of values and principles to bear on this matter. When there is interdependence, reflecting on how this interdependence should be regulated forms an important part of social evaluation. Some libertarian views, for example, will insist on devising institutions so as to minimize interdependences (e.g. Nozick 1974). More liberal views will differentiate between positive and negative interdependences, and seek to foster the former and minimize the latter. Providing someone with the care he or she needs may be a case of positive interdependence, while any form of oppression is likely to be a case of harmful interdependence. Another example for how agency matters is the widely held view that the justice of a particular distribution depends on how that distribution came about. The roles individuals or institutions of collective agency have in shaping these interdependences are thus an important topic for social evaluation, and individuals will form views about how social institutions should regulate them.

Let me explain what is at stake on the basis of the following variation of Sen's original example. The example focuses on a problem of distributive justice. Take again two people and one possible action, for instance eating the last piece of chocolate cake. There are again three alternatives: Anthony eats it (x), Gina eats it (y), and no one eats it (z). Assume Anthony believes that chocolate is bad for Gina's health, as he has explained to her many times before. Since he knows how much she likes the cake, he would not want to eat it either, but would rather give it away. If Gina insists that he have it, he would eat it, however. His preference ordering is thus (z, x, y). Gina is unconvinced about chocolate's harm to her health. But although Gina likes chocolate very much, she would not want to eat the last piece of cake before making sure that Anthony does not want it. If they both want it, Gina prefers Anthony to have it. Her preference ordering is thus (x, y, z). Let us proceed as in Sen's original example. If the choice is between x and z, according to liberal values, Anthony should be decisive and, since he prefers z to x, society should also rank z above x. If the choice is between y and z, Gina should be decisive and, since she prefers y to z, society should also rank y above z. This leads to the social preference ordering (y, z, x). Again we have a conflict with the Pareto criterion, as both Anthony and Gina prefer x to y.

In the distributive justice context, the paradox is not the only problem, however. First, look at the rights-based social preference ranking. In Sen's original example, this ordering makes some sense, given the story. It makes sense that a rights framework should enable Lewd, who has a taste for it, to read the book and regard this case as better than the case where no one reads the book and better than the case where Prude, who hates the book, has to read it.[40] In the chocolate cake example, the ordering makes no sense whatsoever. Why, given that both equally like chocolate, should y be ranked first and x last? Should these two states not be regarded as indifferent from a liberal point of view? And why should a rights system identify y as the best social choice given that, as we know, Gina would prefer to forego the pleasure of eating the piece of cake for Anthony's sake? Should it not be Gina's right to give away the cake if she wanted to?

Abandoning rights-based evaluation and switching to preference-based evaluation would not be an adequate solution either, since the preference-based approach does not contain enough information to properly assess the situation. It neglects the value people assign to their actions above and beyond the outcomes that result from these actions. In our example, it is important to Anthony that Gina does not harm her health, and he will eat the piece of cake only if she insists that he does so. For Gina, it is important to express her care for Anthony by leaving the piece of cake to him. Assume that after a dinner together, they decide that Anthony should eat the cake. If, instead, a third party were to assign the cake to Anthony, we would have the same outcome in terms of who gets to eat it, but the crucial role of interdependent agency in this example would be neglected. Anthony would not enjoy the cake in the same way than if Gina had given it to him, and Gina may feel left out.

Of course, not too much should be inferred from a simple example. Nevertheless, in comparison with Sen's original example, it makes visible that different forms of interdependence bear differently on the evaluation of a situation. What is at stake can be further illustrated with the following variation of the Anthony and Gina example. Suppose that the rankings are now the result of a different story. Suppose that Anthony is Gina's older brother, and Gina has been brought up to leave the best things to him, while he is accustomed to enjoying them without concern for his sister's well-being. When Anthony does not feel like eating the chocolate cake, he either saves it for some other day, or he gives it to a friend of his. It does not occur to him to leave it for his sister. His preference ranking is thus still (z, x, y) and Gina's preferences also remain unchanged (x, y, z). In this case, there would be reasons to be skeptical about the result if Anthony were to get the piece of cake, even if Gina left it for him.

These variations of Sen's original example reinforce the point about the importance of agency in social evaluation. They illustrate that what matters is not only whether Anthony or Gina actually gets the piece of chocolate cake—though that matters too, of course—but also how they relate to each other and how their respective acts and motives affect each other. The following conclusions can be drawn from these examples. First, contrary to the welfarist principle, agency matters for the evaluation of what counts as a good outcome. Second, liberty rights alone cannot cover all aspects of how persons value their relationships and commitments to other people. There is thus need for a richer informational basis in social evaluation.

We can classify the three cases I have discussed in the following way. Sen's original example captures the main liberal case for limiting interference from others. The intuition is that Prude's agency should not extend to preventing Lewd from reading the book, just as Lewd's agency should not extend to compelling Prude to read it. The condition of Minimal Liberty is in line with the intuition that their agency should be thus restricted. The first Anthony and Gina example covers a case of procedural justice. The reasons behind their preferences about who should get the cake are such that intuition suggests that their agency should not be restricted. It should be left to them to decide how to distribute the cake. But neither the principle of Minimal Liberty nor that of preference-based respects these reasons. The decision that their agency should not be restricted would have to be made on other grounds. The second Anthony and Gina example focuses on oppression. This example draws attention to a situation where the intuitions about whether to restrict interdependence are conflicting. Preference-based evaluation would pick up on the fact that they both prefer that Anthony gets the cake rather than Gina. The problem is that in so far as it is based on overt choice, perhaps expressing adaptive preferences, preference-based evaluation may reinforce oppressive relations. Rights-based evaluation protects Gina in that it prevents Anthony from deciding whether Gina should get the piece of cake. It does so at the price of "feeding" Gina the cake, however, since it identifies the situation in which Gina eats the cake as socially "best." As such, it treats her as a "patient," which may even reinforce the restrictions on her agency. This suggests, again, that taking her seriously as an agent would require a decision-making process that can draw on more information than what is contained in these principles of preference-based or rights-based evaluation. Such a decision-making process should register the reasons that are underlying different preferences and have the tools to take into account not just preferences among given alternatives, but also preferences among counterfactual alternatives and the reasons that support them. In the oppression case, such a decision-making process may reveal that there is a previously neglected option of splitting the cake in two, and that this alternative is the one that finds most support.

In sum, the informational constraints of aggregative democracy are too restrictive to address the multiple considerations that interdependent agents may want to bring to bear on their decisions for how to shape their life together. We have thus reached another juncture at which a broader informational basis is called for. Social evaluation has to be responsive to agency information, including to information about the ways in which social institutions may unduly restrict individual agency. Deliberative democracy, I shall argue in the next chapter, is better able to take this kind of information into account.

3   Deliberative Democracy

3.1. THE DELIBERATIVE ACCOUNT OF DEMOCRACY

The deliberative account of democracy highlights the importance of public discussions prior to a vote. In an early and very influential article, Joshua Cohen gives the following characterization of deliberative democracy (1997a: 72):

> [t]he notion of deliberative democracy is rooted in the intuitive ideal of a democratic association in which the justification of the terms and conditions of association proceeds through public argument and reasoning among equal citizens. Citizens in such an order share a commitment to the resolution of problems of collective choice through public reasoning, and regard their basic institutions as legitimate in so far as they establish the framework for free public deliberation.

By now, deliberative democracy has established itself as a powerful democratic theory, the main real rival of aggregative democracy (Bohman 1998). It is not surprising, therefore, that many different accounts of deliberative democracy can be identified in the literature.[1] Nevertheless, there is some sort of an agreement about the two main features that make up Cohen's characterization: in deliberative democracy, decision-making is based on public reasoning among the members of the democratic collective (i) under conditions of political equality or fairness (ii). To characterize the deliberative account, I thus need to say a bit more about each of these two features.

3.1.a. Public Reasoning

The first essential feature of deliberative democracy is public reasoning. This feature has two dimensions that need to be commented on. The first dimension is reason.[2] In the deliberative account, reasons replace preferences as the main input into the democratic decision-making process. Such reasons may be directed at what is to be done, but also at the empirical claims and the causal hypotheses on which specific policy proposals rest. In most cases, the participants in the deliberative process will not agree on which proposal to support. Indeed, disagreement about the reasons for and against different courses of actions forms the starting-point for the deliberative process, and the evaluation of conflicting reasons its *raison d'être*.

It is this evaluation of conflicting reasons about what to do that sets deliberative democracy apart from aggregative democracy. The latter allows for individual reasoning about preferences, of course. It may even demand some form of individual deliberation, as part of the requirement that individual preferences be rational (complete and transitive). But the aggregative account does not entail the requirement that this individual deliberation issues in reasons for and against a particular ranking of social states. It suffices that individual preferences are consistent. The consistency in question may be a purely subjective one, one that is not accessible intersubjectively.

This point does not change if we take into account Arrow's important distinction between tastes and values (cf. section 2.1.a.). It is true that Arrow insists that aggregative democracy does not have to be seen as an aggregation of self-interested preferences, but may take into account a broad range of considerations that pertain to individuals' evaluation of social states. The distinction between tastes and values rests on their objects, however, not on the type of deliberation that they are based on. Tastes are defined over the individuals' own consumption bundles whereas values are defined over social states. Beyond that, there is no difference. It need not be the case that values, as defined by Arrow, are any more explicable than tastes; what kind of considerations underlie an individual's values, i.e. what determines his or her ordering of social states, may be purely subjective and cannot be explained to others.

In the aggregative account, it thus does not matter why people prefer one alternative to another. The aggregative process is attuned to sufficiently widely shared agreements on how to rank two alternatives, but not to the reasons for which they should perhaps be ranked in this way. In the deliberative account, it is precisely this exchange of reasons that lies at the heart of the democratic decision-making process. The deliberative account is thus more thoroughly procedural than aggregative democracy in this regard, as it considers the process of reasoning itself as an essential element of democratic decision-making. Aggregative democracy, by contrast, takes into account only the products of individual reflection. This amounts to an overly amorphous view of social evaluation that disregards how the structuring influence of the deliberative process may facilitate democratic decision-making.

The second dimension, publicity, is related to the emphasis on reason-giving in deliberative democracy. The deliberative view centers on the public discussion of reasons for and against alternative social states. In public discussion, individuals are expected to voice and justify the reasons for which they prefer particular social states and both the content of the preferences and their justifications are scrutinized by the participant discussants.

The requirement of publicity constitutes a first step toward specifying the kind of reasons that the members of the democratic collective owe to each other.[3] Publicity is not just about giving one's reason in public, as opposed to deliberating privately, but affects the type of reasons given. The possibility of a public exchange of reasons entails that the reasons are of a form that makes them potentially acceptable to others. In other words, what renders reasoning public is not simply the forum in which it takes place, but the accessibility of the reasons given for a particular view to people who might not share that view.

In the aggregative account, individual preferences, and deliberation about them, are primarily treated as a private matter. Hence, insofar as public deliberation is taken into account at all, it is through the lens of the benefits it may impart on individuals. Such individual benefits may be direct, as when participating in discussion with others is treated as an element of well-being (e.g. Hirschman 1989). They may also be indirect—for example insofar as public deliberation provides access to information that improves individual decisions (e.g. Bohnet and Frey). I am not trying to deny that such individual benefits may occur as side-effects of the deliberative process, but views of this kind fail to appreciate the public character of deliberation and its search for reasons that can be shared. For deliberative democrats, what stands at the center is the role of the public evaluation of justifications for alternative proposals through an exchange of reasons.[4]

Very importantly, for deliberative democrats, the mutual exchange and public scrutiny of reasons are likely to have a transformative effect on individual preferences—that is why reasons, not preferences, are regarded as the main input to democratic decision-making. As a result of deliberation, some initially expressed preferences will seem unsustainable and be transformed, and new preferences will emerge during the process of public deliberation. Deliberation may, for example, strengthen the reasons people have for not endorsing a policy that discriminates against women. Or it may lead some to abandon their strong initial preference to elect a woman to a high political office, if the deliberative process generates strong reasons in support of a previously lesser known male candidate.[5]

If public reasoning forms the input of democratic decision-making, what is, in the deliberative account, its output? Quite a few deliberative democrats hold the view that it is a decision that furthers the common good. According to this view, it is the focus on the common good that gives public reasoning its direction and that determines the content of decisions. This focus on the common good is taken to be another difference with aggregative democracy, in which decisions are based on individual preferences, whatever they happen to be, and may thus reflect the pursuit of narrow self-interest. The thought is that in public deliberation, reasons that refer to strictly individual benefits of certain policies will not be acceptable to others. Only reasons that refer to the common good will be potentially acceptable to everybody. Cohen expresses this thought in the following way. First, he highlights the pressure deliberation exercises on the content of individual preferences (1997a: 76):

> [T]he mere fact of having a preference, conviction or ideal does not by itself provide a reason in support of a proposal. While I may take my preferences as a sufficient reason for advancing a proposal, deliberation under conditions of pluralism requires that I can find reasons that make the proposal acceptable to others.

This pressure, he goes on to argue, "focuses debate on the common good" (1997a: 77).[6] This view need not entail that there is such a thing as the common good, the social state that all have reasons to endorse, even though some deliberative democrats do take this view (e.g. Habermas 1996). The view is quite compatible with allowing for the possibility that there is a range of possible decisions that is in accord with the pursuit of the common good.[7] Still, I regard the idea that the common good has to form the aim of public deliberation as more problematic than most deliberative democrats. I shall discuss my reservations in a moment.

Let me first note that some deliberative democrats have also argued that, ideally, beyond focusing on the common good, public reasoning also aims for consensus (e.g. Habermas 1990, 1996; Benhabib 1994; Postema 1995; Cohen, 1997a).[8] But others, though granting the focus on the common good, have argued that individuals will always differ in their interpretations of the common good and the transformative power of deliberation should thus not be theorized as leading to a consensus (e.g. Elster 1986; Manin 1987; Bohman 1996; Gaus 1997). I agree with this second set of deliberative democrats that consensus should not be taken to be the aim of deliberation. In a society characterized by value pluralism, differences over what constitutes the best social choice in a certain issue will always remain. If there are strong reasons in favor of a particular outcome that convince the majority to vote in its favor, this is not to deny that members of the minority may not also hold good reasons in favor of their views. This has been recognized by Isaiah Berlin, who argued that given scarcity, it is conceivable that some valuable alternative can be realized only at the expense of some other alternative, which may also be, with good reasons, regarded as valuable. As he puts the point (Berlin 1969: 168):

> The world that we encounter in ordinary experience is one in which we are faced with choices between ends equally ultimate, and claims equally absolute, the realization of some of which must inevitably involve the sacrifice of others.

I agree that public deliberation cannot transcend this pluralism. For this reason, it should not be seen as its purpose either.

If consensus is rejected as the aim, this implies, of course, that even a deliberative account of democratic decision-making relies on some aggregative mechanism to reach a decision. The contrast between the aggregative and the deliberative account is thus not that one relies on voting while the other does not. The difference is, rather, that the deliberative account has a broader view of the decision-making process, one that does not study voting mechanisms in isolation. John Dewey (1927: 207–08) captures the difference nicely when he writes that "[m]ajority rule, just as majority rule, is as foolish as its critics charge it with being." But this, he adds, ignores how the "antecedent debates, modification of views to meet the opinions of minorities, the relative satisfaction given the latter by the fact that it has had a chance and that next time it may be successful in becoming a majority" may affect the evaluation of the decision-making process as a whole. How exactly this works, how taking the deliberative process that precedes a vote into account changes our evaluation of the aggregative mechanism too, is something I cannot discuss here. I shall have more to say on this issue in Chapters 4–7.

Having rejected the idea that deliberative democracy needs to focus on consensus, I now also want to argue against the view that a focus on the common good is necessary. I am on the side of Iris Marion Young (2000) on this. Young argues that the view that takes public reasoning to be necessarily oriented towards the common good puts up a false dichotomy between aggregative democracy as based on subjective self-interest and deliberative democracy as based on the objective common good. A first problem with this dichotomy is, of course, that the aggregative account of democracy need not be limited to aggregating self-interested preferences, but can take into account of rational preferences of any content. This is not, however, Young's point. Her point is, rather, that the dichotomy is false because it both masks the deep value pluralism and diversity of experiences that may characterize a democratic society, and because it neglects how this multiplicity of perspectives feeds the deliberative process:

> Social movements mobilizing around experiences and analyses of the oppressive and unequal consequences of social differentiations of gender, race, sexuality, national origin, or religion, along with class, have expressed skepticism about appeals to a common good. . . . Issues of justice vary for structurally different groups, this politics of difference argues; oppressions and wrongful inequalities take many forms, and appeals to a common good do not adequately respond to and notice such differences. (Young 2000: 81)[9]

Taking the common good as the organizing principle of democratic deliberation, rather than "the politics of difference," obscures the multitude of perspectives about what the problems are and how they should be solved. In the alternative view that Young presents, difference is not seen as an obstacle to, but as a resource for democratic deliberation. I shall come back to this idea in Chapter 7.

The contrast between the "politics of difference" conception and the "common good" conception of public reasoning should not be overplayed, however, as both recognize that the need for deliberation occurs because of the diverging aims, interests, and perspectives of the individual partici-pants.[10] Still, the difference-centered conception of public reasoning, more so than the one that makes the common good its explicit focus, warns of invoking a false unity of perspectives that would unduly stall the delibera-tive process and fail to challenge mainstream—but flawed—opinions about shared interests. At the same time, this view does not imply that social pluralism is so deep and sacrosanct that no meaningful public discussion is possible. It thus does not endorse the aggregative account of democra-cy.[11] Instead, this conception of public reasoning stresses the possibility of deliberation being fuelled by ongoing disagreements about how to move forward without being undercut either by the refusal to share reasons (e.g. because of the authority of cultural identity) or the unwarranted invoking of the common good.

3.1.b. Political Equality

The second main feature of deliberative decision-making, besides public reasoning, is that the members of the democratic constituency acknowledge each other as equals. Political equality is, of course, a fundamental value of democracy; according to many, it is its most fundamental value. Among theories about who ought to have political authority, democracy is the most inclusive. It gives expression to the idea that people ought to be treated as equally free by granting them an equal share in the right to rule. This equal share in the right to rule can mean many things, of course. I follow Thomas Christiano's account and take it that democratic political equality means that the interests of each member of this constituency should receive equal consideration in collective decision-making (Christiano 1996: 53). In aggre-gative democracy, this requirement boils down to some principle of equal consideration of expressed votes and translates into the principle of "one person one vote." In deliberative democracy, a person's share in the right to rule must include opportunities to participate in public deliberation. Note that political equality must refer to opportunities to participate, not to par-ticipation itself, as the extent to which individuals participate will depend on investment decisions they make and personal tastes.[12] Roughly speak-ing, political equality in deliberative democracy means that individuals have equal opportunities to express their interests in the deliberative decision-making process and this process combines public deliberation and voting.

Political equality in deliberative democracy is a much more complex ideal than in aggregative democracy, as opportunities to participate in pub-lic deliberation depend on a great range of factors. Public deliberation does not take place in an isolated political forum, but has multiple centers and even more satellites. Deliberation takes place in and around parliaments, government councils and committees, media, lobbying networks, private meeting and associations, families and circles of friends, and increasingly, of course, the internet. As a result, the opportunity to participate in deliberation is influenced by a wide range of social and economic factors. This implies that in deliberative democracy, the ideal of political equality clearly must include within itself some requirements of social and economic equality. What renders the ideal even more complex is that it cannot be, to use a Rawlsian distinction, a merely formal requirement but must refer to fair equality of opportunities to participate in the deliberative process. A purely formal requirement, one that gives individual equal (political) rights to participate in the democratic process, but does not consider whether individuals can effectively use these rights, quite simply ends up neglecting those social and economic influences. Political equality in deliberative democracy thus must mean fair equality of opportunities to participate in the democratic process. As Cohen puts it (1997a: 74):

> In ideal deliberation, parties are both formally and substantively equal. Everyone . . . has equal standing at each stage of the deliberative process. Each can put issues on the agenda, propose solutions, and offer reasons in support of or in criticism of proposals. And each has an equal voice in the decision. The participants are substantively equal in that the existing distribution of power and resources does not shape their chances to contribute to deliberation, nor does that distribution play an authoritative role in their deliberation.

How best to give shape to the requirement of fair equality of opportunities and to spell out the demands of substantive equality is not an easy issue. I shall address it in Chapter 5, with reference to the "equality of what?" question, well-known from the literature on distributive justice. In particular, I shall discuss whether the best informational framework for interpreting the content of political equality in deliberative democracy is a resources-based framework, such as Rawls's primary goods, or Sen's capability approach.

The idea of political equality qualifies the idea of public reasoning discussed in the previous section by adding a demand of reciprocity. It specifies that it is not sufficient that the reasons that support a particular proposal are made public. Instead, it requires that there be equal opportunities for all to participate in the exchange of reasons—to demand justifications for a proposal and to present reasons for an alternative proposal. Public reasoning under conditions of political equality thus accentuates the "horizontal" dimension of the deliberative process: it is not sufficient that reasons are handed down—vertically—from public officials to the members of the democratic constituency. Instead, there have to be opportunities for all members to participate in the exchange of reasons as equals.[13] Public deliberation is not unidirectional, dedicated to the justification of a particular state of affairs, but multidirectional, capturing the exchange of reasons among participants viewed as equals.

The idea of political equality serves a multiple role in the deliberative account of democracy. On the one hand, as just sketched, it stands for the most important intrinsic value of democracy. But a multidirectional, de-centered process of public deliberation also serves other values. Very importantly, it facilitates learning about the reasons for which people prefer certain social states over alternatives. With Sen, I call this democracy's constructive function (Sen 1999a, b). I shall have more to say on the role of political equality in a normative theory of democracy in Chapters 4 and 7.[14]

3.1.c. Background

The deliberative account of democracy highlights public deliberation under conditions of reciprocity. It builds on individuals' recognition of each other's capacities to reason and acceptance that all have an equal right to use these capacities. As such, deliberative democracy has a background in the Kantian tradition in moral and political philosophy. The most important contemporary Kantians—John Rawls and Juergen Habermas—have both written on deliberative democracy, the latter more than the former. This contrasts with the utilitarian background of aggregative democracy, at least in Arrow's formulation. The difference between aggregative and deliberative democracy can thus be further elucidated by shedding some light on the place of deliberative democracy in the theories of Rawls and Habermas.

Rawls, unlike Habermas, did not develop an account of deliberative democracy. Nevertheless many elements of Rawls's theory of justice as fairness, and especially of the political conception of justice, fit in with and support deliberative democracy. Because I shall invoke the Rawlsian background again later, I want to explain here in some detail how the main features of deliberative democracy—public reasoning and political equality—can be given a Rawlsian foundation. I shall not attempt to give a full account of his theory of justice here, as this would detract from my topic, but I want to focus on the compatibility between core ideas of *A Theory of Justice* and *Political Liberalism* and deliberative democracy.

Rawls builds his theory of justice on fundamental ideas that he regards as implicit in the political culture of democratic societies. Among these ideas, two are especially important: the idea of citizens as free and equal persons and the idea of society as a fair system of cooperation.[15] Let me start with the latter. It expresses a political, not a psychological or metaphysical, conception of the person (Rawls 1993: 29–35; 2001: 18–24). Its function is both to capture the fact that people have diverse interests and to explain how they can reach an agreement in matters of justice. According to this conception, persons have two fundamental moral powers. These are the "capacity for a conception of the good," on the one hand, and the "capacity for a sense of justice," on the other (Rawls 1993: 34). Rawls (1993: 302) defines them as follows:

> [T]he capacity for a sense of justice is the capacity to understand, to apply and normally to be moved by an effective desire to act from (and not merely in accordance with) the principles of justice as the fair terms of social cooperation. The capacity for a conception of the good is the capacity to form, to revise, and rationally to pursue such a conception, that is, a conception of what we regard for us as a worthwhile human life.

By virtue of the capacity for a conception of the good, persons know what is to their advantage and are able to act rationally. Rawls works with a broader understanding of rationality than economic theory as it is not limited to how to best satisfy a consistent set of preferences. He adopts the Kantian conception of practical reason, which includes the capacity to deliberate about ends, to evaluate, prioritize, and—if necessary—to revise them, in addition to the capacity to choose the best means to reach a given end (Rawls 1993: 50). Moreover, persons are seen not only as potentially rational, but also as potentially reasonable. Being reasonable is defined in terms of the capacity for a sense of justice and this capacity refers to the second fundamental idea, that of society as a fair system of cooperation, which I shall discuss next. To complete this brief account of the first fundamental idea, let me point out that the theory of justice as fairness defines the freedom and equality of persons with regard to these two capacities. All citizens are assumed to hold these two principal moral powers and it is in this respect that they are equal and ought to be treated as such. They are free insofar as they can develop and pursue their own (reasonable) conception of the good.

The second fundamental idea of justice as fairness—that of society as a fair system of cooperation—is closely linked to the idea of citizens as free and equal persons. To understand Rawls's idea of cooperation, compare it with utilitarianism first. In the utilitarian view, the conception of the person is not a political but a psychological one—it uses individual utility both to represent what individuals value and to explain their (rational) actions. Moreover, the goodness of individual states is assessed exclusively in terms of the utility individuals derive from it—however utility is defined. Society is seen as a conglomeration of utility-maximizing individuals and cooperative arrangements should aim at maximal aggregate utility.

In contrast to utilitarianism, Rawls's theory of justice relies on a distinction between what is rational for individuals and what is reasonable. Persons are reasonable insofar as they recognize that, though they have good reasons to hold their own conception of the good, there are good reasons for other citizens to hold different views. Reasonable citizens accept that their society will always contain a plurality of conceptions of the good. They also accept what Rawls calls the "burdens of judgment"—a list of considerations for why reasonable disagreement over conceptions of the good is likely to persist (Rawls 1993: 54–58). In addition, by virtue of their sense of justice, persons are assumed to be willing to propose fair terms of cooperation, which guarantee fair prospects for all to pursue their respective rational advantage. Conceptions of the good that support this willingness are called reasonable, not just rational. The persons recognize, thanks to their capacity for a sense of justice, that the rational pursuit of their own advantage needs to be made compatible with the possibility for others to pursue their conception of the good, provided those conceptions are reasonable too. They are willing to refrain from imposing their own conception of the good upon others and will want principles of justice that are compatible with the fact of reasonable pluralism—an irreducible pluralism of reasonable comprehensive conceptions of the good.

Utilitarianism reduces the reasonable—reasons that refer to the regulation of the individual pursuit of a good life through cooperative arrangements—to the rational—reasons that refer to the individual pursuit of a good life. In the theory of justice as fairness, by contrast, the reasonable is an independent idea. Reasonable persons in Rawls's sense "are not moved by the general good as such but desire for its own sake a world in which they, as free and equal, can cooperate with others on terms all can accept" (Rawls 1993: 50). His idea of cooperation thus entails an idea of fair cooperation; it is based on reciprocity. Reciprocity refers to generally recognized rules that secure everybody an adequate share of the benefits produced through cooperation. As such, Rawls's idea of fair cooperation has to be distinguished from an idea of mutual advantage, which demands that everyone gains from cooperation. A conception of justice that specifies fair terms of cooperation entails that everybody is viewed as part of this cooperation and has a right to the benefits produced. It respects and ensures equal liberties for the citizens to develop and pursue their reasonable conceptions of the good.[16]

The idea of the reasonable is crucial for deliberative democracy. First, respect for the burdens of judgment entails that reasonable disagreement is the inevitable result of the confrontation between different conceptions of the good.[17] Secondly, the idea of the reasonable supports a person's willingness to engage in the process of public reasoning. Reasonable persons refrain from wanting to use state power to impose their own conception of the good upon others and propose fair terms of cooperation. They respect the plurality of conceptions of the good and this respect guides public deliberation. They are both willing to put their arguments in a way that makes them potentially acceptable to others and to listen to the arguments others advance.

Political equality occupies, not surprisingly, a central place in justice as fairness, and thus also in my account of how Rawls's theory of justice supports the description of democratic decision-making as embedded in a fair process of public reasoning. Rawls emphasizes that everybody must have a fair chance to participate in the political process. This requirement is discussed in *A Theory of Justice* (1971, 221–234) under the heading of the principle of participation. In his later writings, he includes it in the first principle of justice as fairness, the principle of basic rights and liberties, in the form of a guarantee of the fair value of the political liberties (Rawls 2001: 42ff.). The fair value of the political liberties requires that "citizens similarly gifted and motivated have roughly an equal chance of influencing the government's policy and of attaining positions of authority irrespective of their economic and social class" (Rawls 1993: 358).[18] Political equality, in this view, thus contains a substantive component. Social factors should not prevent people from being able to participate in the deliberative decision-making process as equals.

A further fundamental idea specifies the domain of justice. Reasonable pluralism makes it likely that the citizens will rarely—if ever—agree on the moral value of alternative social states. Taking this into account, Rawls limits the domain of justice as fairness. The fair terms of cooperation apply to what Rawls calls the "basic structure" of society, and only to that. The basic structure comprises "society's main political, social, and economic institutions, and how they fit together into one unified system of social cooperation from one generation to the next" (Rawls 1993: 11).[19] Rawls singles out the basic structure because inequalities that have their origin there have the most profound impact on the prospects of the individuals in society. Imposing rules of fairness on the basic structure is an attempt to correct these fundamental inequalities as far as possible, and to establish fair conditions of social cooperation. The intuition is that if the basic structure is just, so is the outcome generated by the social and economic processes it specifies and embeds. Thus being confined to a limited domain distinguishes justice as fairness both from utilitarianism and from those contractualist moral theories that are intended to apply to all questions of social evaluation (e.g. Scanlon 1998). Justice as fairness proposes principles for how to assess society's main institutions, and only them. Because it builds on fundamental political values instead, it circumvents the problem of value pluralism. That such a theory of justice is restricted in scope—that it does not apply not to all moral questions, but only to the problem of the justice of the basic structure of society—is for Rawls a small price to pay.

A conception of justice that builds on these fundamental ideas will be part of the family of what Rawls calls "political conceptions of justice." He defines such conceptions with the help of three criteria (2001: 26): (i) "it is worked out . . . for the basic structure of a democratic society"; (ii) it "does not presuppose accepting any particular comprehensive doctrine"; and (iii) it "is formulated so far as possible solely in terms of fundamental ideas familiar from, or implicit in, the public political culture of a democratic society."

As I have tried to show, a political conception of justice recognizes the deliberative capacities of persons and endorses a fair chance for everybody to participate in the process of deliberative decision-making, and thus supports the main features of deliberative democracy that I have highlighted in this chapter. Since the conception of democratic legitimacy that I shall develop in later chapters owes a lot to Rawls's work, I will come back to these Rawlsian themes there (especially in sections 4.1.b. and 6.2.).

Let me conclude this chapter with a few comments on Habermas's theory of deliberative democracy, and on why I shall opt for a Rawlsian framework. Habermas (1990, 1996, 1998) has a fully worked-out account of deliberative democracy, and deliberative democracy receives even greater moral weight than in Rawls's theory. This account draws on discourse ethics and its concern with the intersubjective rational justification of moral norms. The starting-point of discourse ethics is a hypothetical situation—an ideal discourse. In this hypothetical ideal discourse, participants deliberate about the moral principles that should guide their social arrangements. The goal is to reach an agreement on what "all can will in agreement to be a universal [moral] norm" (Habermas 1990: 67). The ideal discourse is inclusive in that it seeks to take the perspective of all participants into account and to allow for free deliberation undeterred by the influence of power. Only the force of the better argument is allowed to be decisive, and it is what all regard as the best argument that should bring the deliberative process to a close. As Habermas puts it, "practical reason . . . resides in . . . the rules of discourse and forms of argumentation that borrow their normative content from the validity basis of action oriented to reaching understanding" (1996: 296). Applied to democracy, this view makes deliberation constitutive of the rational justification of decisions that affect all. Conversely, it regards rational justification as characteristic of deliberative democracy and as the distinctive and superior feature that sets it apart from alternative accounts of democracy and forms of political authority in general. According to Habermas, "the procedures and communicative presuppositions of democratic opinion- and will-formation function as the most important sluices for the discursive rationalization of the decisions of an administration bound by law and statute" (1996: 300).

While, true to their Kantian backgrounds, both Rawls and Habermas rely on some idea of rational justification, they apply it to different domains. Both treat deliberative democracy as a moral requirement, but it has a different role in Habermas's account than in Rawls's. Even though Habermas recognizes some differences in content between the moral discourse and the political discourse, discourse theory assigns to them the same normative role. According to Habermas, the moral value of participating in public deliberation stems from its role in the substantive justification of particular outcomes. The only way in which a political community can determine its moral norms and find rational answers to moral problems is via the process of public deliberation under suitable conditions. For Rawls, as we saw, pluralism of reasonable conceptions of the good makes disagreement a fact of social life. In the Rawlsian view, it is thus the question of how societies can be just while respecting this diversity that is the main issue, not solving moral problems. Because of the focus on rational justification in discourse ethics, Habermas is also the leading advocate of the idea that, ideally, public deliberation leads to a consensus. Rawls does not endorse this idea.[20] As Rawls stresses in his "Reply to Habermas" (Rawls 1995), the normative focus of a political conception of justice is on the framework in which deliberation takes place. A political conception of justice has a limited domain: it applies to the basic structure. It does not aim at providing substantive solutions to moral problems beyond the regulation of the basic structure, and thus does not aim for a consensus about the substantive content of democratic decisions as they might be made in an appropriately constrained deliberative process.[21] For Habermas, by contrast, the aim of public deliberation is just that.

Some deliberative democrats follow Habermas here—e.g. the account Cohen gives in "Deliberation and Democratic Legitimacy," or Seyla Benhabib's in "Deliberative Rationality and Models of Democratic Legitimacy." Others, as discussed above, are more skeptical about the potential of public deliberation to reach a consensual, substantive justification of democratic decisions. A second strand in the literature on deliberative democracy thus does not link deliberative democracy to consensual decision-making, and this is the view I take as well, as explained earlier.

3.2. DELIBERATIVE DEMOCRACY DEFENDED

3.2.a. Examining Preferences

As argued in Chapter 2, unexamined preferences constitute a problematic informational basis for democratic decision-making. They may poorly reflect welfare-goals because of adaptive preferences or expensive tastes, or they may fail to distinguish between welfare and other goals. Deliberative democracy, unlike aggregative democracy, treats individuals not simply as passive carriers of preferences, but as political agents who can reason together about what to do. In the course of the process of public deliberation, individuals may reflect upon their preferences and, if necessary, revise them. In contrast to aggregative democracy, this more comprehensive account of democratic social evaluation and decision-making takes into account the process of preference formation. This process can be described as a dynamic link between individual and public deliberation. On the one hand, individual deliberation about preferences leads to arguments for and against certain preferences, which can then be expressed in the public sphere.[22] This makes public deliberation in principle possible. Public deliberation, on the other, influences the individuals' perceptions of their own preferences and may thus lead them to revise their initial preferences.

The objection that aggregative democracy neglects the formation of preferences is an often-stated one. According to this objection, because aggregative democracy fails to take into account the process of public deliberation that precedes the moment of voting, it also neglects the effects public reasoning may have on individual preferences. [23] A prominent version of this objection states that aggregative democracy only considers "prepolitical" preferences. Cass Sunstein (1991: 16) articulates it particularly clearly:

> [P]olitical choices will reflect a kind of deliberation and reasoning, transforming values and perceptions of interests, that is often inadequately captured in the marketplace. [This] amounts to a rejection or at least a renovation of subjective welfarism as a political conception. It is here that democracy becomes something other than an aggregative mechanism, that politics is seen to be irreducible to bargaining, and the prepolitical 'preferences' are not taken as the bedrock of political justification. [24]

Echoing the distinction between welfare and agency that I have discussed in the last section, Sunstein identifies two types of reasons that might justify interfering with preferences. According to him, "prepolitical preferences" ought to be overridden if a policy intervention is either autonomy- or welfare-enhancing. They ought to be overridden, for example, Sunstein argues, if an intervention acts on the causes of adaptive preferences, as this would be both welfare-enhancing and autonomy-enhancing.

There are, of course, potential threats for democratic legitimacy in any proposal that supports state intervention in the formation of preferences. [25] I shall discuss such problems later on, especially in Chapter 5. Here I want to focus on a more basic point, for this version of the objection to aggregative democracy is misleading. As discussed above, the Arrowian framework of aggregative democracy leaves it open what the content of individual preferences is that form the input of the aggregative mechanism, and how they have been formed. The condition of Unrestricted Domain specifies that the aggregative mechanism should function for all profiles of individual preferences—"pre"- or "post"- political.

The main problem with aggregative democracy is thus not that it necessarily refers to certain preferences and not to others. The main problem is, rather, that it treats the question of what counts as the relevant informational basis in the evaluation of policy alternatives as separate from the process of democratic evaluation itself. In deliberative democracy, this question is an element of the process of public deliberation. Conversely, the solution to problems that might arise from using certain "prepolitical" preferences as the input for democratic decision-making should not be to replace these preferences by some other, process-independent set of inputs, i.e. some preconceived conceptions of welfare. Instead, deliberative democrats suggest a procedural solution, one in which the decision about the appropriate informational basis for the evaluation of a particular set of policy alternatives is endogenized.

The real objection against aggregative democracy is thus not that it uses "prepolitical" preferences, but that by relying on expressed preferences, whatever they are, as the input of democratic decision-making, aggregative democracy uses the wrong model of practical reason. It fails to take into account the role of the kind of reasoning that deliberation enables.[26] Aggregative democracy is based on the standard model of rational choice. This model, as described in Chapter 2, focuses on a set of consistent preferences. As argued above, this model fails to cover the kind of deliberation on which deliberative democracy relies. As Sen puts it (2002: 39), it narrows the scope of (individual and collective) deliberation to "an instrumental requirement for the pursuit of some given—and unscrutinized—set of objectives and values." The best defense for the standard model of rational choice is that whatever an individual's ends, they can be translated into a single consistent ranking of the alternatives.[27] While this may or may not be so, the problem is that this model renders deliberation implicit. It has too little structure to differentiate among the different reasons individuals have for particular preferences.[28] As such, it is not of much use in accounting for the individual and social deliberation about ends as it takes place in deliberative decision-making.

Developing an alternative model of practical reason would be beyond the scope of this book. I shall thus just make a few comments on how the model of practical reason on which deliberative democracy relies differs from the standard model of rational choice. As discussed above, deliberative democracy does not take consistent preferences, whatever they are, as the main input of democratic decision-making. The deliberative account drives a wedge between the decisiveness of all individuals and the decisiveness of all preferences. Political equality, in deliberative democracy, demands that all individuals have an equal opportunity to participate in the political process—not that equal weight is given to all preferences.[29] Rather than preferences, the deliberative account takes reasons to be the main input of democratic decision-making. To accommodate the transformative force the reason-giving process has on individual preferences, deliberative democracy needs a different model of practical reason—one that rejects Humean skepticism about practical reason and includes the evaluation of alternative rankings of social states based on the values and principles that underlie those rankings. As discussed in relation to Rawls's idea of the rational, as well as Sen's distinction between well-being and agency, deliberative democracy needs the support of a model of practical reason that is broad enough to allow for the possibility of other ends besides individual welfare and that takes individual ends as accessible to deliberation—both individual and collective. Individual rationality, in this alternative model of reasoning, is not just about how to pursue given ends, but also about what to pursue and for what reasons. Accordingly, in deliberative democracy, participants in public deliberation are seen as able to express not just their preferences for certain alternatives, but also the welfare and non-welfare related reasons that underlie these preferences, and to revise their original preferences in light of reasons others confront them with. The alternative model of practical reason on which deliberative democracy relies has to allow for the possibility that individual ends can be scrutinized in the deliberative process and that there are reasons that support individual preferences—welfare-reasons, or reasons that relate to other values—that can be shared. As a result, the deliberative decision-making process can draw on more, and more richly structured, information than what rational choice theory makes available for the aggregative account.

3.2.b. Towards Justice and Inclusion

The next main advantage that deliberative democracy has compared to aggregative democracy is that it avoids the problems of the latter with incorporating considerations of justice (cf. section 2.2.a.). The utilitarian legacy of (Arrow's interpretation of) aggregative democracy makes it vulnerable to Rawls's objection against utilitarianism, that it fails to take seriously the difference between persons. A next argument in defense of deliberative democracy thus has to show that it is better able to deal with justice. Different theories of deliberative democracy have different versions of this argument, and I shall discuss some of them in later chapters. In this section I want to focus on an element that most theories of deliberative democracy have in common: how the emphasis on people's possibilities to participate in public deliberation makes deliberative democracy better suited than aggregative democracy to respect the difference between persons and to address considerations of justice.

Recall the cake-division example that I have used to illustrate the charge that aggregative democracy fails to deal adequately with considerations of justice. The objection, borrowed from Sen, states that majoritarian preference aggregation cannot distinguish between the case where the less well-off majority gets some more of the (symbolic) cake from the better-off minority and the case where the better-off majority gets some more of the cake from the worse-off minority, and that failing to distinguish between the two reveals an indifference towards considerations of justice. The failure to distinguish between the two cases has its origin in the informational implications of Arrow's Independence condition, which I have interpreted above as stating that the social preference between any pair of alternatives should only depend on individual preferences over this pair. The relevant pair here, in each of the two cases, is "redistribute" and "do not redistribute." Since in each case, two individuals prefer "redistribute" over "do not redistribute," the two cases look exactly alike, and should thus be treated alike by the aggregative mechanism. From the perspective of deliberative democracy, it is possible to differentiate between the two cases. In the first case, where the worse-off majority defends redistribution, the primary argument supporting their preference could be one from distributive justice. In the second case, where the better-off majority defends redistribution, the most likely argument is one from narrow self-interest. Clearly, the two cases will not be treated as identical in the deliberative process, nor is there any reason that they should.

The deliberative account of democratic decision-making is thus better equipped to deal with considerations of justice than aggregative democracy. And in contrast to utilitarian social evaluation, it is also better equipped to take seriously the distinction between persons. In the cake-division problem, the better-off and the worse-off individuals who constitute the minorities in the two cases are treated alike in aggregative democracy—they are both overruled for the sake of what the majority regards as the best outcome. In deliberative democracy, the veto of the poor person, who can plausibly argue that he or she is exploited by the better-off, is likely to receive more weight than the veto of the rich individual who wants to protect his or her assets from a minor loss which would benefit the poor. Insofar as deliberative democracy can respond, better than aggregative democracy, to minority arguments about interests that deserve protection, it is less likely to blindly trade off harms to a minority for the benefit of the majority and better able to take into account the difference between persons.

The emphasis on reason-giving offers further resources that aggregative democracy lacks in dealing with issues of justice as reasons that relate to the formulation of alternative policy proposals are part of the deliberative process. This stage is not theorized in aggregative democracy, at least not in Arrow's version of it. As we saw, the problem of social choice, for Arrow, consists in choosing from a given set of alternatives. His approach to the problem parallels how economists theorize individual choice in the market: there, the problem is to determine the best alternative given the goods the economy produces, prices, and the budget of the individual. Individual evaluation, in this perspective, is limited to the evaluation of a set of given alternatives, and does not extend to the evaluation of the conditions that brought about that particular set. Such an approach to evaluation is incomplete, and runs the risk of attributing too much to weight to the evaluation contained in the act of choice. In the case of individual choice, a choice between given alternatives need not imply a positive evaluation of the constraints that shape the set of alternatives, and is certainly not equivalent to an expression of one's evaluation of these constraints. There is nothing unusual about a situation in which one makes a choice, and at the same time objects to the conditions that brought about the set of alternatives from which one makes the choice. An example from the labor market is when a woman objects to the discriminating circumstances of a job offer, but still accepts the job. To take her choice to imply some form of assent to gender discrimination would be to fallaciously subsume the evaluation of the constraints that shape the set from which a choice is to be made under the evaluation of the alternatives from which one can choose (Peter 2004). In the case of collective choice, similarly, it is important to recognize the limitations that affect an account of democratic decision-making that starts from a given set of alternatives. For from the perspective of justice, it may well be the case that none of the alternatives on offer are satisfactory. Individuals may have certain preferences among the alternatives, but if they regard all options as deficient from the point of view of justice, their preferences should not be taken as an absolute judgment about what they think ought to be done in the name of justice. As a result, even if the aggregative mechanism were able to determine a "best" outcome, this outcome may have little in common with what justice might require.[30]

Deliberative democracy performs better in this regard, as public deliberation about the question of what the alternatives should be is very much part of this account. It encourages the participants to voice their dissent to what they perceive to be an unjust status quo and the policy alternatives it generates. Collective action organized around such dissent constitutes an engine for the exploration of alternatives that are more just and the transformation of the status quo. As such, deliberative democracy may help to make audible preferences for greater justice that the status quo tends to muffle.

Of course, people are likely to disagree about matters of justice. The fact that the deliberative process provides a forum in which considerations of justice can be raised more easily than in aggregative democracy does not mean that there will be agreement about what ought to be done. Yet, I contend, the fact that deliberative democracy gives weight to the possibilities people have to articulate their reasons for certain alternatives, and to question the political agenda, constitutes an important stepping-stone towards greater justice.

3.2.c. Enhancing Legitimacy

The most often made, and I think most important, arguments for deliberative democracy focus on its legitimacy-enhancing aspects.[31] These arguments aim at showing that deliberative democracy solves the legitimacy problems that arise in aggregative democracy. Some of the arguments relate to a positive concept of legitimacy, i.e. to whether people actually accept a democratic decision. The main argument of this kind is that participation in deliberation makes people more inclined to accept a decision, even if they have lost (e.g. Gutmann and Thompson 1996). I want to focus here on the arguments that relate to the normative concept, i.e. to the reasons people have to accept a democratic decision.[32] There are two main strategies that arguments of this kind tend to follow. A first argumentative strategy is to accept the problems as they arise from Arrow's impossibility theorem, and to argue that deliberative democracy can help create the conditions in which cycles do not occur and thus enable meaningful social choice. Many of the points made by those who argue in this way are illuminating. But this strategy fails to consider whether the conception of democratic legitimacy that underlies Arrow's framework for social choice theory is an appropriate conception in the first place. The second main strategy, therefore, does not take Arrow's framework as given, and seeks to defend deliberative democracy on grounds of the conception of legitimacy on which it builds. This strategy rests on the claim that the problem of legitimacy takes on a different form in the deliberative and the aggregative accounts of democracy, and that deliberative democracy offers a more satisfactory solution. The upshot of arguments of this kind is thus to show that the problems that arise within the Arrowian framework need not undermine democratic legitimacy—under the appropriate conception of democratic legitimacy.

Let me start with a discussion of the first strategy. The premise for arguments that try to show how public deliberation may solve problems that arise within Arrow's framework is that deliberation will not lead to a consensus and that some voting mechanism is thus necessary, even in a deliberative democracy. This is why Arrow-type problems may return through the backdoor. The goal of those who pursue the first strategy is to show that this need not be the case. Instead, they argue that treating the aggregative mechanism as embedded in a deliberative process justifies a modification of Arrow's framework and offers a way out of the impossibility result. As Jack Knight and James Johnson, in an early argument in support of the first strategy, put it (1994: 278): "The question is whether aggregative mechanisms are susceptible to systematic *endogenous* difficulties and, if so, whether enhanced, refined deliberative arrangements can either avoid or remedy those difficulties."

Those who pursue this strategy tend to focus on the link between deliberation and two conditions in Arrow's framework: Unrestricted Domain and Independence of Irrelevant Alternatives. We saw above (2.1.b.) that relaxing Unrestricted Domain and assuming instead that individual preferences have a certain structure offers a way out of Arrow's impossibility result—with single-peaked preferences, majority rule generates consistent decisions. John Dryzek and Christian List (2003) argue that public deliberation can introduce the kind of preference structuration that is necessary to avoid cycles. Preference structuration refers to an agreement at the meta-level. They thus need to show that public deliberation can bring about such agreements. How can it be argued that public deliberation can induce single-peaked preferences on one common issue? Public deliberation, as explained in the previous section, gives incentives to participants to present reasons that are potentially acceptable to others. As Dryzek and List (2003) put it, deliberation forces people to invoke generalizable interests, or "public goods." Insofar as these reasons, this orientation towards public goods, can influence the formation of preferences, deliberation will focus preferences on a single dimension and can thus mold single-peaked preferences. Deliberation may, for example, make it apparent to the participants that the main point of contention in a climate bill is how to trade off benefits to the current generation against benefits to later generations. Of course, this argument is vulnerable to the objection that although deliberation may bundle preferences in the public forum, people may privately vote differently. In response, Dryzek and List point to empirical studies that indicate that participating in public deliberation can have social conditioning effects that induce a cooperative disposition. The more established a deliberative democracy, the more extensive and inclusive public deliberation, the narrower the gap should be between what is expressed in the public forum and how people actually vote.[33]

What if the issues at stake are complex such that deliberation will fail to reduce preferences to a single dimension? For example, what if decision-making on a climate bill is not just contested along the dimension of intergenerational trade-offs? There may also be disagreements about which implementation method to use to reach particular results, as well as disagreements about what the problem is that the climate bill is meant to solve. Public deliberation may still be helpful, Dryzek and List argue. Insofar as deliberation contributes to the clarification of the issues at stake, it may influence not just the formation of preferences, but also the formulation of proposals. It may lead to the rejection or revision of existing proposals, or bring about entirely new proposals that are better suited to tackle multi-dimensional issues. Dryzek and List (2003) suggest the following procedures. A first possibility is that if public deliberation has identified different dimensions, then an aggregation procedure can be applied that yields a social ranking for each of the separate dimensions. Easiest is thus—if feasible—to carve up decisions according to the different dimensions. If this is not feasible, deliberation may produce an agreement on a lexicographical hierarchy of the dimensions and thus still lead to a social ranking. A third possibility is to use logrolling, which can provide information on preference intensity.[34] Finally, if none of these procedures work, the very recognition that there are disabling multiple-dimensions may bring about new proposals that lend themselves more easily to the formation of single-peaked preferences. In the climate bill example, this recognition may generate proposals that rely on less controversial implementation methods, and/or that target experimentation with alternative methods of energy usage.

Another set of important arguments in support of the first strategy relates to the Independence condition. If this condition is relaxed, a range of decision-making mechanisms becomes possible. Dryzek and List argue that relaxing Independence poses a problem for aggregative democracy, but not for deliberative democracy, as deliberative democracy has means to control agenda-setting that aggregative democracy does not have. They point out that (2003: 22):

> If the individuals agree on what the set of relevant alternatives X [the agenda] is, then there is little scope for an agenda-setter strategically to introduce or delete alternatives from X so as to affect the relative chances of other alternatives in X, and the logical possibility of agenda manipulation (implied by violations of (I)) no longer poses a problem.

Aggregative democracy focuses on social choice from a given agenda—I have discussed this problem earlier. How the particular set of alternatives got selected is thus not part of the account. In deliberative democracy, agenda-setting, and the formulation of alternative proposals, is just as much part of public deliberation as the evaluation of particular alternatives themselves. By making agenda-setting public, and demanding that it is embedded in a fair deliberative process in which people can participate as equals, deliberative democracy can help reduce the risk of agenda-manipulation and avoid one of the major threats to legitimacy that Arrow's account of aggregative democracy faces. If a deliberative democracy can ensure political equality, no social group should have the power to rig the outcome of the political process in its favor.

A final argument of those pursuing the first strategy is based on the link between public deliberation and Sen's informational interpretation of Arrow's impossibility result. As discussed above (section 2.1.b.), Sen has shown that Arrow's theorem can be explained as resulting from the combination of welfarism with minimal information about individual utility. This informational poverty rules out most decision rules. Deliberative democracy, by contrast, introduces a broader informational basis for democratic decision-making. Consequently, it allows for a much wider spectrum of principles and rules of allocation and distribution to be considered.[35]

This set of arguments for why deliberative democracy may enhance legitimacy has an empirical and a normative component. I will not discuss issues relating to empirical plausibility here, as I am primarily interested in what bearing the normative component of these arguments has, and indeed this is the one that does most of the work. This normative component consists of justifying a particular set of conditions (axioms) for democratic decision-making and showing that deliberative democracy is compatible with conditions necessary to bring about meaningful social choice. The empirical component then cites evidence for deliberative processes actually bringing about these conditions.

The strategy that gives shape to the arguments made by Dryzek and List is consistent. It takes the problems that arise within an Arrowian framework for social choice as a starting-point, and then focuses on showing how deliberative democracy can solve them. But is it, normatively speaking, the right strategy? Is this the right way to defend deliberative democracy? I do not think it is. The reason is that the argument rests on an overly shallow distinction between aggregative and deliberative democracy. Arguments of the kind that Dryzek and List present contrast the aggregative and the deliberative account at the descriptive level: one does while the other does not factor in public discussion. While such arguments reject Arrow's description of democratic decision-making, they fail to question the assumptions about the requirements of democratic legitimacy that are implicit in aggregative democracy.

Many have, however, drawn the distinction between aggregative and deliberative democracy precisely on grounds of their different conceptions of democratic legitimacy. Bernard Manin, for example, in a very early contribution to this debate, suggested that it is the deliberative process itself, or rather the conditions under which public deliberation takes place, that is the source of the legitimacy of collective decisions. He wrote (1987: 352; emphasis in the original):

> [A] legitimate decision does not represent the *will* of all, but is one that results from the *deliberation of all*. It is the process by which everyone's will is formed that confers its legitimacy on the outcome, rather than the sum of already formed wills.

On this basis, Manin went on to argue that since mapping individual preferences, whatever they happen to be, into a collective choice, is not the relevant frame for legitimacy in deliberative democracy, the problems that arise with this exercise are not legitimacy-undermining.

To be sure, to assert that deliberative democracy relies on a different conception of legitimacy does not amount to denying the need for a voting mechanism. If, as I have argued above, deliberation is not expected to result in a social consensus, there is still a need for some aggregative mechanism, for example majority rule, to make a social choice at the end of the deliberative process. Insofar as they consider this interplay between public deliberation and aggregation, the arguments that Dryzek and List (2003) present are valid and have a role in any full-fledged theory of deliberative democracy. I agree with them, for example, that it is an important feature of deliberative democracy that it can broaden the informational basis of democratic decision-making, help to structure preferences by creating greater clarity about what the points of contention are, and influence the formulation of proposals and hence the agenda. My objection to the argumentative strategy they pursue thus does not target the individual hypotheses they defend. It is more fundamental. My objection is that they fail to consider that the conditions that are necessary for democratic legitimacy differ in aggregative and deliberative democracy.

Referring to the alternative conception of legitimacy that underlies deliberative democracy will not, of course, resolve the impossibility theorem. The point is, rather, that the impossibility result looks less threatening if it can be shown that its implications do not affect the source of legitimacy. What this second argumentative strategy aims at is not—contrary to Dryzek and List—to solve the problem of social choice, but rather to show that deliberative democracy imposes different requirements of legitimacy. It is misleading to associate the problems that arise within a framework of aggregative democracy with the problems of democracy in general. If it can be shown that the problems that social choice theory highlights are specific to aggregative democracy, then these problems are pseudo-problems from the perspective of deliberative democracy. The challenge for deliberative democrats is thus to come up with arguments that prove that it can be ensured that a society's decisions, even if sometimes affected by cyclic patterns, have a continuing legitimate basis. If deliberative democrats can meet this challenge, then it becomes clear that the problems identified in social choice theory are not disabling for deliberative democracy and do not undermine the possibility of legitimate democratic decisions.[36]

Cohen (1997b) develops a prominent version of the second argumentative strategy.[37] He argues that deliberative democracy offers a solution to a well-known dilemma in democratic theory. The problem is the following. On the one hand, democrats will maintain that substantive judgments are legitimate only if they have been made through the appropriate democratic procedures. On the other, however, sometimes the results of such procedures are in conflict with certain widely held values such that their legitimacy is undermined. The well-known problem of the tyranny of the majority illustrates the dilemma. The tyranny exerted by the majority is compatible with respect of democratic procedures, but it can generate oppression like any other form of government. John Stuart Mill characterizes this problem well (1859: 8–9):

> Society can and does execute its own mandates; and if it issues wrong mandates instead of right, or any mandates at all in things with which it ought not to meddle, it practices a social tyranny more formidable than many kinds of political oppression . . . Protection, therefore, against the tyranny of the magistrate is not enough; there needs protection also against the tyranny of the prevailing opinion and feeling . . . There is a limit to the legitimate interference of collective opinion with individual independence; and to find that limit, and maintain it against encroachment, is as indispensable to a good condition of human affairs as protection against political despotism.

Mill's tyranny of the majority addresses the tension between "prevailing opinion" and "individual independence." The dilemma also manifests itself when a democratic collective, through regular procedure, sanctions a policy that infringes on the rights of some social groups, e.g. a policy that is sexist or racist. While the substantive judgment has been made through democratic procedure, and as such should qualify as legitimate, the judgment may nevertheless appear illegitimate because of its content. To give a last example for the kind of problem that Cohen has in mind, the possible cyclicity of the outcomes of majority rule that I have discussed in the context of aggregative democracy may also be taken as a case in point where a procedure that has certain democratic credentials fails to generate outcomes that appear legitimate. The resulting dilemma is thus the following. If a democratic collective relies exclusively on procedures, the resulting outcomes may fail to be legitimate because they conflict with certain values that are seen as necessary for legitimacy. If, however, substantive value judgments are made through avenues other than democratic procedures, these judgments do not have a legitimate basis.

Cohen argues that deliberative democracy offers a solution to this dilemma because, compared to aggregative democracy, it imposes more substantive constraints on the democratic process. The aggregative account, as discussed, only demands that the procedures give equal consideration to individual preferences. These preferences can be of any content. Deliberative democracy requires that the procedures ensure that reasons are given that are acceptable to everyone; not all substantive judgments will pass this test. Preferences that are an attempt at manipulation, or preferences for proposals that discriminate on the basis of race or gender, for example, will prove not to be justifiable in this way. Cohen argues, drawing on Habermas, that because it brings considerations of procedures and substance into harmony, deliberative democracy suggests a way for how the dilemma can be solved. According to the view that he defends, substantive judgments are legitimate if and only if they are compatible with the constraints deliberative democracy imposes on the democratic process. Deliberative democracy, in this view, can reconcile considerations of procedure and substance. The substantive constraints imposed on the democratic process limit the range of possible outcomes and guarantee the legitimacy of the decisions made. The problem of the tyranny of the majority, for example, does not occur because outcomes have to be justifiable to everyone. In other words, the line of argument concludes that the legitimacy requirements specific to deliberative democracy are more robust than those underlying aggregative democracy.

I believe that this line of argument—which I have only summarized here—characterizes not just Cohen's view but is quite widely held by deliberative democrats. Moreover, precisely the way in which it solves the tension between procedure and substance is often taken to be one of the main appeals of deliberative democracy as compared to aggregative democracy. It is this feature that is taken to tackle the problems that affect aggregative democracy. By bringing considerations of substance and of procedure into harmony, deliberative democracy avoids taking unexamined preferences as the basis of democratic justification, and it takes seriously at least some minimal conditions of justice and aligns them with the need to respect individual agency.

Even though it is a widely held view among deliberative democrats, I shall argue against it. While I shall also adopt the second argumentative strategy, I shall show in Chapter 5 that there is a problem with Cohen's argument. In that chapter, I will first give a more detailed account of his argument than I have done here and then show that it hides a further dilemma for democratic legitimacy. This dilemma relates to the interpretation of political equality. Deliberative democracy, as interpreted by Cohen and others, provides no solution to what I call the "political egalitarian's dilemma." In fact, because of the greater demands that deliberative democracy imposes on the democratic process, the dilemma affects deliberative democracy to a greater degree than it affects aggregative democracy. But before I can address these issues, I first need to accomplish some housekeeping tasks and provide a clearer idea of what democratic legitimacy might entail and what distinguishes alternative conceptions of legitimacy that have been proposed.

4 Conceptions of Democratic Legitimacy

My first aim in this chapter is to introduce the concept of legitimacy. I shall then describe and defend the Rawlsian approach to legitimacy and on that basis go on to argue for the importance of democratic procedures for political legitimacy. In section 2, I shall present a taxonomy that clarifies the differences between alternative conceptions of democratic legitimacy. The overall goal of this chapter is to clear the ground, so that in the rest of the book I can build my argument for the particular conception of democratic legitimacy that I want to advocate.

4.1. THE CONCEPT OF LEGITIMACY

4.1.a. Legitimacy, Authority, and Obligation

While much recent political philosophy has tended to focus on justice, this seems to be changing. The concept of legitimacy is attracting increasing attention in recent political theory and political philosophy. As I shall explain it in more detail, the concept of legitimacy qualifies political authority, the right to rule. In a democracy, political authority belongs to the members of the democratic constituency. Democratic legitimacy thus qualifies the right of the democratic constituency to impose laws and regulations on itself. In a common usage of the term legitimacy, the concept is interpreted descriptively—as referring to people's beliefs about how the right to rule is exercised. In the case of democratic legitimacy, it refers to people's beliefs about the acceptability of particular democratic decisions. In the descriptive sense, legitimacy prevails as long as people support—or at least do not challenge—democratic institutions and decisions. Another usage of the term is normative. In this interpretation, democratic legitimacy gives people a binding reason to support or not to challenge democratic institutions and the resulting decisions. If a democratic decision is legitimate, one ought to accept the decision and act accordingly—when action is required. If a decision is illegitimate, it does not have this binding force.

The normative concept of democratic legitimacy, on which I shall focus, is constituted by a set of conditions that the democratic decision-making must satisfy. These conditions specify how democratic decisions should be made, just like the concept of distributive justice specifies how goods should be distributed.

A main reason for the recent interest in legitimacy is how the debate on aggregative versus deliberative democracy has brought back the question of what democracy is about, and what the value of democratic decision-making is. The new twist that this debate has introduced into the theory of democratic legitimacy is the focus on the process of democratic decision-making itself, as opposed to the earlier focus, inherited from Max Weber's writings, on the legitimacy of democratic states, or democratically elected governments (Weber 1964; Connolly 1984). Another reason is how John Rawls's writings have paved the way for addressing the importance of procedural values in political philosophy. While *A Theory of Justice*—published in the early 1970s—has lead to a proliferation of writings on justice, his *Political Liberalism*—published in the early 1990s—coincides with the beginning of an increased interest in democracy and political legitimacy. One of the main concerns of the earlier book, as Rawls made it clear in its preface, is to overcome the utilitarian emphasis on outcomes and to think about procedural aspects of justice. In *Political Liberalism*, procedural considerations receive even greater weight. They are linked to the distinction Rawls draws between moral and political conceptions of justice. In that later book, Rawls defends justice as fairness as a political conception of justice. That is to say, he takes as a starting-point the problem of how the main political, social, and economic institutions in a democratic and pluralist society can be justified. The idea of a political conception of justice assigns a fundamental role to the concept of legitimacy in moral and political philosophy.

To get a better understanding of the concept of legitimacy, it is helpful to consider its relation to two further concepts—political authority and political obligation. Political authority refers to the right to rule. Political obligations are correlative to authority, as they specify duties to accept the right to rule and to act accordingly. There are different views in political and legal philosophy about the relationship between these three concepts, in particular about which one is fundamental.

According to a first view, taken by Ronald Dworkin (1986), for example, the concept of obligation is fundamental. What counts as legitimate authority depends on the political obligations people have. These obligations arise from membership in a political body and may be accrued non-voluntaristically.[1] Those who challenge the view that obligations are fundamental can do so on two grounds. First, they can defend the view that authority is the fundamental concept. A. John Simmons pursues this strategy. He argues in his essay "Associative Political Obligations" that even if it is granted that obligations arise from membership in a political body, or that obligations are owed to a government, it still needs to be clarified who counts as a member, and what kind of political organizations fall into the category of governments with authority (Simmons 2001: 72). According to the alternative (Lockean) view that Simmons defends, the concept of political authority is thus more fundamental than the concept of political obligations. The moral justification of political authority defines obligations and is separate from and prior to concerns with legitimacy.

But the authority-based view can be challenged too. If we focus, not just on political legitimacy in general, but specifically on democratic legitimacy, it is hard to see how the democratic assembly's right to rule can be characterized independently of the conditions under which this right is appropriately exercised. An analogous objection to the one Simmons raises against the obligation-based view can thus be raised against the authority-based view. The objection is that even if it is granted that the right to rule determines obligations, there is still the question of how a democratic collective ought to exercise this right. And that question concerns legitimacy.

In addition, there is a further objection to the obligation-based view, which also points to the primacy of legitimacy. The objection is that one cannot have an obligation unless certain background conditions are met. As Rawls (1971: 343) states it:

> obligations arise only if certain background conditions are satisfied. Acquiescence in, or even consent to, clearly unjust institutions does not give rise to obligations. It is generally agreed that extorted promises are void ab initio. But similarly, unjust social arrangements are themselves a kind of extortion, even violence, and consent to them does not bind.

Before one can determine whether individuals have certain political obligations, it is thus necessary to establish under what conditions they can incur such obligations, and this cannot be done without invoking voluntariness. This view implies that legitimacy determines which obligations are binding.

Taking these objections against the obligation-based and the authority-based views into account thus leads to the view that legitimacy is the fundamental concept that grounds both authority and obligations. In this view, expressed by Rawls (1971, 1993), for example, legitimacy explicates the conditions for the appropriate exercise of the right to rule and the conditions under which one has obligations to accept the bindingness of these rules and act accordingly.[2]

4.1.b. The Rawlsian Approach to Legitimacy

I now want to explain the idea that legitimacy is a fundamental normative concept in social evaluation. I shall draw on Rawls's *Political Liberalism*, which conceives of legitimacy as related to but weaker than justice. In this section, I shall focus on the broader concept of political legitimacy. In the next section, I shall address democratic legitimacy and provide two arguments for why democratic decision-making procedures are necessary for political legitimacy.[3]

What Rawls calls the problem of legitimacy arises from the tension between two facts. A first fact of liberal, democratic societies is that political power "is regarded as the power of free and equal citizens" (Rawls 2001: 40). A second fact is what he calls reasonable pluralism—an irreducible pluralism of reasonable comprehensive conceptions of the good (Rawls 1993: 63–64). Reasonable pluralism makes it likely that the citizens will rarely—if ever—agree on the moral value of alternative social states. The problem of legitimacy, then, is the following. If democratic legitimacy demands that political power is exercised by free and equal citizens and if these citizens hold a plurality of conceptions of the good, "in the light of what reasons and values . . . can citizens legitimately exercise . . . coercive power over one another" (Rawls 2001: 41)?

There are several features of Rawls's approach to legitimacy that I want to discuss here. The first concerns the link between justice and legitimacy. Rawls states (1993: 225):

> In justice as fairness, and I think in many other liberal views, the guidelines of inquiry of public reason, as well as its principle of legitimacy, have the same basis as the substantive principles of justice.[4]

The common basis between justice and legitimacy is formed, first of all, by the fundamental ideas that underlie Rawls's theory of justice as fairness and that he sees as implicit in the political culture of democratic societies. I have already discussed some of these ideas (section 3.1.c.): the idea of society as a fair system of cooperation, the idea of citizens as free and equal persons, and the idea of the basic structure. Rawls's conception of justice as fairness rests on these ideas, and they form the common basis between justice and legitimacy. But to say that justice and legitimacy have a common basis in fundamental political values does not imply that they impose the same demands, or that one reduces to the other. Rawls defines legitimacy in the following way: "political power is legitimate only when it is exercised in accordance with a constitution (written or unwritten) the essentials of which all citizens, as reasonable and rational, can endorse in the light of their common human reason" (Rawls 2001: 41). This definition demands clarification, as "constitutional essentials" is a Rawlsian technical term. There are two aspects to these essentials (Rawls 1993: 227):

(a) fundamental principles that specify the general structure of government and the political process: the powers of the legislature, executive and the judiciary; the scope of majority rule; and

(b) equal basic rights and liberties of citizenship that legislative majorities are to respect: such as the right to vote and to participate in politics, liberty of conscience, freedom of thought and of association, as well as the protections of the rule of law.

The constitutional essentials relate to the institutional structure of government and the resources to which citizens need to have access to be able to participate in this structure as equals. The holding and exercise of political authority is thus legitimate only if it is compatible with the constraints that the constitutional essentials impose.

The difference between justice and legitimacy lies in the contrast between what justice demands and the conditions that Rawls wants to impose on the constitutional essentials. Recall that according to Rawls's theory of justice as fairness, the basic structure of a society is just if it satisfies the two principles of justice.

(a) Each person has the same indefeasible claim to a fully adequate scheme of equal basic liberties, which scheme is compatible with the same scheme of liberties for all; and

(b) Social and economic inequalities are to satisfy two conditions: first, they are to be attached to offices and positions open to all under conditions of fair equality of opportunity; and second, they are to be to the greatest benefit of the least-advantaged members of society (the difference principle) (Rawls 2001: 42–43).

The first principle guarantees the citizens' equality with respect to a list of basic liberties and rights. These basic liberties and rights are the following: political liberties (i.e. the right to vote and to be eligible for public office) and freedom of speech and assembly, liberty of conscience and freedom of thought, freedom of the person and the right to hold personal property, and the freedom from arbitrary arrest and seizure (Rawls 1971: 61).[5] The first item on the list, political liberties, is of particular importance for the appropriate exercise of democratic political authority. In fact, Rawls's interpretation of the role of political liberties in the first principle of justice links his theory of justice to a conception of democratic legitimacy. As I have explained it earlier (3.1.c.), Rawls emphasizes that the first principle must include a guarantee that everybody has a fair chance to participate in the political process. The first principle thus seeks to ensure that members of all social groups are able to participate in the political process on an equal basis. This first principle of justice as fairness is also part of legitimacy, as Rawls demands that the constitutional essentials respect the first principle of justice. Rawls does not demand, however, that they satisfy the second principle. It follows that in the Rawlsian view, legitimacy is related to but weaker than justice.[6] Just situations are also legitimate, but democratic decisions can be legitimate without being just.[7]

In this Rawlsian view, the problem of legitimacy relates to how the basic institutions and public policies of a particular state can be justified to its free and equal citizens. Simmons (2001) objects to this statement of the problem of legitimacy that it mistakenly blurs the distinction between the (moral) justification of the state and the legitimacy of particular, historically realized, states. But this objection misunderstands Rawls's project. In the Rawlsian view, the moral justification of political authority and of political obligations depends on legitimacy—there is no independent source for moral justification. In addition, the Rawlsian view has the advantage that it does not narrow the focus on the state, but allows us to address questions about the conditions the democratic decision-making process ought to satisfy. This approach is thus more in line with the current debate on democratic legitimacy.

Another prominent objection against the Rawlsian approach is that because the idea of a political conception of justice refers to the possibility of a consensus based on fundamental political values, it is unsuitable for an understanding of democratic politics (e.g. Manin 1987; Wolin 1996; Mouffe 2006). Those who argue in this way thus reject the idea that the Rawlsian framework may serve as a foundation for deliberative democracy. I shall address this objection in Chapter 6, when I discuss the role of Rawls's idea of public reason in relation to legitimacy. The idea of public reason matters for a conception of democratic legitimacy, as it contains an account of how deliberative decision-making generates legitimacy. Unfortunately, there is some lack of clarity about how Rawls's idea of public reason should be interpreted. Does public reason apply to the justification of the constraints the democratic decision-process has to satisfy or the justification of democratic decisions themselves? I shall advocate the former—procedural—interpretation, and, in this context, argue that the objection against Rawls rests on a superficial reading of his approach, as well as on a confusion about the requirements of democratic legitimacy (see 6.1.b.). But an elaboration of this issue will have to wait.

The purpose of this section was to introduce Rawls's approach to the problem of legitimacy, as I shall use this Rawlsian approach as the foundation for my explorations into what democratic legitimacy might entail. The main idea is that individuals' comprehensive doctrines of justice are too different to serve as the basis for establishing and justifying the constitutional essentials which define the right to rule. The only justification that is available for the conditions that define the legitimate exercise of this rule is in fundamental democratic values. In a democratic society, the right to rule belongs to the democratic constituency. Insofar as it is conceivable that the legitimate exercise of the right to rule falls short of producing unified views on justice, there is a gap between justice and legitimacy, captured by the idea that legitimacy is weaker than justice.

It is important to note that this relationship between the two concepts should not be seen as depreciating the value of legitimacy. It follows from the Rawlsian view as I have presented it here that legitimacy is, in some sense, more fundamental than justice. It specifies a normative minimum: which social states ought to be respected even if they fall short of justice. In the Rawlsian view, moral justification thus incorporates the concept of legitimacy; the two are not independent ideas. Thus prioritizing legitimacy also has the practical implication that the only way to achieve justice is through a democratic process that satisfies the conditions of legitimacy. For Rawls, as Samuel Freeman (2000: 379) puts it, "deliberative democracy is a moral requirement of political legitimacy." This follows from how the fundamental ideas on which Rawlsian justice rests link in with the idea of deliberative democracy, as explained in section 3.1.c. It implies that in the Rawlsian view, a democratic decision-making procedure that gives individuals equal opportunities to participate forms an irreducible component of legitimacy and justice. In this light, we see that the constitutional essentials set the framework for the democratic exercise of political authority. Rawls's insistence that the constitutional essentials guarantee the fair value of the political liberties underlines the primacy of legitimacy over justice, and the idea that legitimacy and justice can only be achieved through a fair democratic process.[8] In the next section, I want to defend this view that democratic decision-making procedures are necessary for legitimacy.

4.1.c. Against Democratic Instrumentalism

The importance Rawls attributes to the principle of equal liberties and rights and its included guarantee of a fair value of the political liberties make Rawls a proceduralist about democratic legitimacy. Not just Rawls's conception, but all proceduralist conceptions of democratic legitimacy include some conditions of political equality, or "political fairness" (Beitz 1989). At the very least, these conditions capture what is minimally required for a procedure to still count as "recognizably democratic" (Estlund 2008). In many deliberative democratic conceptions of legitimacy, these conditions are interpreted more extensively, to capture requirements of substantive equality of opportunities to participate in the democratic decision-making process.[9]

Proceduralism about legitimacy can be contrasted with democratic instrumentalism (e.g. Wall 2007). According to instrumentalists, political equality only has instrumental value—the value of political equality depends on its contribution to good outcomes overall, but does not, as in proceduralism, form an irreducible component of legitimacy. In this view, some ideal of good outcomes, however defined, forms the standard that determines legitimacy. If political equality does not contribute to better outcomes, it is not necessary for political legitimacy. Those who defend instrumentalism take it as a premise that there is an ideal outcome that can be identified independently of the democratic process, and in terms of which the value of the democratic process, its legitimacy, can be gauged.

The instrumentalist accounts of Richard Arneson (2003) and Steven Wall (2007), for example, refer to some ideal egalitarian distribution. In their view, then, the greater the equality achieved, as measured with reference to the ideal egalitarian distribution, the greater the legitimacy of the democratic process. If sacrificing political equality allows for a better approximation of equality overall, so their argument goes, then this does not undermine legitimacy.

Proceduralists reject the idea that democratic procedures only have instrumental value. Different arguments have been made against instrumentalism and for why it matters that people can participate in democratic decision-making under some conditions of political fairness, and I shall not summarize them here. Instead, I want to focus on two arguments against instrumentalism, which I regard as the most important ones. The first argument focuses on the constitutive role of democratic procedures for legitimacy in pluralist societies. This argument takes "the fact of reasonable pluralism" (Rawls 1993: 63–64) as a premise; the interests and perspectives of the members of the democratic constituency inevitably diverge and they have different views—with good reasons—about which social state is best.

Instrumentalists probably do not want to deny this fact. Instead, they will try to brush it aside, hoping that reasonable pluralism will not be very deep on important matters and that there is sufficient congruence in people's conceptions of the good to identify some ideal outcome. But aside from the question of how deep this pluralism is, there is the issue of what it means to respect it. I want to claim that respect of reasonable value pluralism implies that people's possibility to participate in the evaluation of alternative social states is constitutive of democratic legitimacy. Here instrumentalists will not follow. It is, however, as explained above, the position that Rawls endorses. The claim can be defended by resorting once again to Sen's distinction between well-being and agency (cf. section 2.2.c.). This distinction highlights that even if the purpose is to evaluate the goodness of outcomes, it is not sufficient to take into account individuals' well-being—however interpreted. People should not simply be seen as patients, who do or do not have well-being, but as agents interested in the autonomous formulation and pursuit of their goals and values (Sen 1985b: 203ff.). Their well-being may be one of these goals, but how they conceive of well-being is again a result of their agency, and they may pursue goals other than their well-being (and perhaps even at the expense of their well-being). To respect value pluralism is thus to respect individual agency. But to respect individual agency is not just to respect some sphere of private autonomy or freedom, but, as I have argued on the basis of the liberal paradox (2.2.c.), also to ensure that individuals have the opportunity to participate in the determination of collective action. Consequently, if individuals are not just seen as passive carriers of well-being, but as causal forces in the forming of individual and collective goals and values, there is need for inclusive procedures that allow individuals with differing conceptions of the good to participate in the collective evaluation and choice of their social arrangements. We thus have an argument for why respect of reasonable value pluralism entails a demand for inclusive, fair procedures that enable individual agents to act together—for why respect of value pluralism entails that democratic procedures form an irreducible component of legitimacy.

It follows from this first argument for a proceduralist conception of legitimacy that the democratic decision-making process itself is at least one of the sources that confers normativity on its outcomes. [10] The instrumentalist view, which defines political legitimacy in relation to an ideal outcome that is assumed to be independent of a requirement of political equality, is deficient in this regard. It fails to acknowledge how respect of reasonable value pluralism implies that the collective evaluation and choice of social arrangements in pluralist constituencies necessarily involves democratic procedures. As a result, it wrongly denies how democratic procedures are constitutive of legitimacy.

There is a further argument for why democratic procedures are necessary for legitimacy that instrumentalists about political equality tend to neglect. This argument invokes what Sen calls democracy's constructive function and it applies specifically to deliberative democracy. As he puts it (1999b: 3):

> the practice of democracy gives the citizens an opportunity to learn from each other .... Even the idea of 'needs' (including the understanding of 'economic needs') requires public discussion and exchange of information, views and analyses. In this sense, democracy has constructive importance, in addition to the intrinsic value it has in the lives of the citizens and its instrumental role in political decisions.

The constructive function of deliberative democracy captures its knowledge-producing potential, and thus points to an epistemic interpretation of (deliberative) democracy. Epistemic democracy emphasizes the knowledge-generating capacity of processes of collective decision-making. Recognition of this constructive function is a common feature of all accounts of epistemic democracy, and indeed distinguishes them from non-epistemic accounts. But different accounts of epistemic democracy interpret the constructive function differently. I shall have more to say on that later (in Chapter 7). For the time being, let me just state that the constructive function captures learning processes that deliberative decision-making enables. To recognize the constructive function is thus to recognize that addressing differences in how people value alternative options is not the only function of deliberative processes. Deliberative democracy extends to the evaluation of different perspectives on and insights into what the problems are that need dealing with and the merits of alternative solutions. The constructive function of deliberative democratic decision-making lies in how it brings this multitude of perspectives to bear on the identification of alternative options for policy-making. The second argument against democratic instrumentalism thus shows how democratic procedures are epistemically necessary for legitimacy.

Naïve instrumentalists deny this aspect of the democratic decision-making process when they assume that there is a way of identifying the ideal outcome that does not require democratic participation. But sophisticated instrumentalists give some room to this constructive function. They allow for the possibility that democratic decision-making is instrumentally valuable for the identification of the ideal outcome. Indeed some arguments for epistemic democracy have precisely this structure: they defend democratic decision-making processes as necessary for the choice of the correct outcome, by arguing that the greater the number of sufficiently competent participants the greater the likelihood that the correct outcome will be chosen. I shall evaluate these arguments in Chapter 7.

4.2. A TAXONOMY

4.2.a. Rational and Pure Proceduralism

Having rejected democratic instrumentalism, I now want to turn my attention to proceduralist conceptions of democratic legitimacy. A great many such conceptions have been proposed in the literature, and the distinctions between them tend to get blurred. In this part of the chapter, as my final housekeeping task, I put forward a taxonomy for distinguishing among alternative proceduralist conceptions of democratic legitimacy. The taxonomy provides a simple way of classifying alternative conceptions of legitimacy and should thus help to clarify current debates.

The taxonomy is based on the following two dimensions. The first dimension captures alternative descriptions of the essential features of democratic decision-making. In a first step, I shall focus on the accounts of aggregative and deliberative democracy, as introduced in Chapters 2 and 3. In Chapter 7 I shall add to that the epistemic account of democracy, but for the time being I want to keep things simple.

The second dimension of the taxonomy captures different categories of requirements that are imposed on the democratic process in order to secure its legitimacy-generating force. Democratic theories differ in how much normative weight they place on procedures relative to substantive considerations about the quality of the outcomes of these processes. Thomas Christiano (2004) helpfully distinguishes between monistic conceptions of democratic legitimacy and non-monistic ones. Democratic instrumentalism, as discussed in the previous section, is a monistic view. It reduces the normativity of legitimacy to a single dimension: only the quality of the outcomes of the process is relevant for political legitimacy. Some proceduralist conceptions of legitimacy are, like the instrumentalist conceptions, also monistic. What is commonly called Pure Proceduralism is the view that only the dimension of political equality, or political fairness, is relevant for democratic legitimacy. According to conceptions of this kind, outcomes are legitimate as long as they are the result of an appropriately constrained process of democratic decision-making. This places all the normative weight on procedural values.

Most proceduralist conceptions of democratic legitimacy that have been put forward in the literature are not monistic, but add conditions that refer to the quality of outcomes to those that apply to procedural features. I call such conceptions of legitimacy Rational Proceduralist. This category of conceptions of democratic legitimacy is best explained by drawing a parallel to Rawls's distinctions between different categories of procedural justice. Rawls (1971: 85) distinguishes between (i) "pure" procedural justice and (ii) "perfect" and "imperfect" procedural justice, on grounds that the former does not, while the latter do, make reference to a desirable outcome that is defined procedure-independently. According to Rawls, perfect procedural justice describes the case where there is a procedure-independent criterion for ideal or correct outcomes, and it is possible to design a procedure that guarantees that such an outcome is reached. In imperfect procedural justice there is also a procedure-independent criterion for ideal or correct outcomes, but there is no procedure that can guarantee that such an outcome can be reached. Rawls gives the trial procedure as an example for imperfect proceduralist justice—it is desirable that only the guilty get charged, and the procedure is designed to achieve that, but it cannot be guaranteed. The same distinctions among versions of proceduralism can be applied to legitimacy. I call the category of conceptions of democratic legitimacy that have the same structure as either perfect or imperfect procedural justice Rational Proceduralism, in contrast to Pure Proceduralism, which has the same structure as pure procedural justice.

Rational Proceduralist conceptions place less value on procedural fairness than Pure Proceduralist ones as they incorporate a second type of conditions that need to be satisfied for democratic legitimacy to obtain. These conditions have their source in properties of the quality of outcomes. The general thought underlying Rational Proceduralist conceptions is that the fairness of the democratic decision-making process is not sufficient to establish legitimacy. A fair process, defenders argue, may lead to irrational outcomes—outcomes of unnecessarily and unacceptably low quality. Rational Proceduralist conceptions thus aim at fair decision-making procedures that can generate outcomes that satisfy certain conditions that define their quality.

Along the first dimension, the taxonomy thus distinguishes between aggregative and deliberative democracy and along the second dimension between Pure Proceduralist conceptions of democratic legitimacy and Rational Proceduralist conceptions. Combining the two dimensions of the taxonomy then yields a 2x2 matrix, into which alternative interpretations of the requirements of democratic legitimacy slot. The resulting four alternative categories of conceptions of democratic legitimacy are: (1) Pure Aggregative Proceduralism, (2) Rational Aggregative Proceduralism, (3) Pure Deliberative Proceduralism, (4) Rational Deliberative Proceduralism.[11]

Table 4.1 Categories of Conceptions of Democratic Legitimacy I

	Aggregative Democracy	Deliberative Democracy
Pure Proceduralism: Political Fairness	Pure Aggregative Proceduralism	Pure Deliberative Proceduralism
Rational Proceduralism: Political Fairness and Political Quality	Rational Aggregative Proceduralism	Rational Deliberative Proceduralism

Pure and Rational Proceduralism, while analogous in structure, mean different things, of course, in aggregative and deliberative democracy. As already discussed in Chapters 2 and 3, the demands of political equality differ greatly in aggregative and deliberative democracy. Whereas the aggregative model requires giving equal consideration to all expressed preferences, the deliberative model is primarily concerned with people's opportunities to participate in the process of public deliberation. Similarly, as I shall explain below, there is a wide range of conditions about the quality of outcomes that may be imposed, and aggregative and deliberative democrats tend to advocate different conditions.

In the rest of this chapter, I want to explain what these alternative categories of proceduralist conceptions of democratic legitimacy entail. Ultimately, my aim will be to defend a particular conception of legitimacy against rival candidates. Since I have already defended deliberative over aggregative democracy, it is clear that I will not endorse a version of Aggregative Proceduralism. But I shall argue later that there are problems with Pure and Rational Deliberative Proceduralism too, and I shall defend a conception that is based on an epistemic account of democratic decision-making in Chapter 7.

4.2.b. Aggregative Proceduralism

Aggregative democracy, as discussed in Chapter 2, focuses on the aggregation of individual preferences about alternative social states through some decision-making mechanism. What I call Pure Aggregative Proceduralism is the view that a collective decision-making mechanism—say majority rule—is fair because it gives equal consideration to all expressed preferences and that its outcome, whatever it might be, is politically legitimate for this reason. Such conceptions of legitimacy combine the emphasis of Pure Proceduralism on fair procedures with the aggregative account of democratic decision-making. Views of this sort can be identified in Robert Dahl's work, for example.[12] The defense of majority rule that follows from Kenneth O. May's theorem also falls into this category. May (1952) shows that majority rule is the only social decision rule that satisfies four minimal axioms.[13] The work that these axioms do is to specify a fair democratic procedure. One of them in particular, the axiom of Anonymity, is a straightforward axiom of political equality, and May himself had called it the "equality" condition (May 1952). It demands that the social decision rule does not discriminate among persons: a permutation of individual preferences—exchanging the name of the individuals while leaving the rankings as they are—should not change the decision. The other axioms are there to ensure that the equal consideration of individual preferences is indeed part and parcel of the decision process—not just a decorative sideshow. Together, these axioms provide a normative justification of majority rule and contain a conception of the democratic legitimacy of the outcomes it produces.[14]

Many aggregative democrats reject such a Pure Proceduralist conception of legitimacy and argue that procedural conditions are not sufficient to establish legitimacy. They worry about the quality of the resulting decisions. We have encountered the type of problem that these aggregative democrats worry about in section 2.1. above, in the discussion of the voting paradox. If there is a cycle in the social preference ordering, decisions made by pairwise majority rule will depend on the order in which the alternatives are presented. To avoid this kind of problem, variants of the second interpretation of democratic legitimacy in aggregative democracy include conditions for the quality of the outcomes chosen in addition to those specifying political equality. I call such conceptions of democratic legitimacy Rational Aggregative Proceduralism.

Arrow's formulation of the problem of social choice is an illustration of this second interpretation of legitimacy in aggregative democracy. On the one hand, there are conditions that capture the demands of a fair process—Unrestricted Domain and Non-Dictatorship—and those that secure a relation between the decision-making process and the outcome—the Pareto condition and Independence. On the other hand, however, he also imposes conditions that demand that the outcomes of the aggregative process be rational. He asks (Arrow 1963: 3): "Can we find . . . methods of aggregating individual tastes which imply rational behavior on the part of the community and which will be satisfactory in other ways?" The problem he poses is: are there methods of collective decision-making that are both based on equal consideration of individual interests and conducive to rational social choice?

Arrow imposes conditions of rationality to ensure that there are no cycles in the social preference ranking on which social choice is based. He reasons that "in the voting paradox . . . , if the method of majority choice is regarded as itself a value judgment, then we are forced to the conclusion that the value judgment . . . is self-contradictory" (Arrow 1963: 5). The thought is, I presume, that in the presence of cycles, there is a clash between different possible majority verdicts and that not one of them can thus count as "justified" by the process as such. In Arrow's view, the possible irrationality of majority rule undermines its defense on the basis of political fairness. Adding conditions of rationality that the outcomes of democratic decision-making ought to satisfy is meant to correct for that, and this renders the conception of legitimacy that underlies his account one of Rational Aggregative Proceduralism.

As discussed previously (2.1.a.), this attempt to avoid the problems that may affect a Pure Aggregative Proceduralism did not yield the desired result. Arrow's impossibility theorem shows that there is no collective decision-making mechanism that satisfies all four axioms and consistently maps individual preferences into a social preference ranking. The theorem thus reveals that the difficulty exemplified by the voting paradox is a feature that affects a large class of aggregative mechanisms.

Many have argued that these problems show that aggregative democracy fails to provide a satisfactory account of democratic legitimacy. On the one hand, there is the worry that if the demands of legitimacy are limited to the fairness of the aggregative mechanism, this may lead to insufficiently justified decisions. On the other hand, however, Arrow's theorem casts doubt on the possibility of coming up with more robust justifications. Thus interpreted, the impossibility theorem reveals the precariousness of aggregative conceptions of democratic legitimacy. I shall have more to say on the problems with Aggregative Rational Proceduralism in Chapter 6, problems that are quite independent of the impossibility theorem itself. First, I want to discuss Deliberative Proceduralist alternatives to Aggregative Proceduralism. As already mentioned in Chapter 3, deliberative democrats have often argued that their account of democratic decision-making can escape the difficulties that arise in aggregative conceptions of democratic legitimacy.

4.2.c. Deliberative Proceduralism

A first category of conceptions of democratic legitimacy that fits the deliberative account is Pure Deliberative Proceduralism. According to conceptions of this kind, legitimacy is ensured as long as the deliberative decision-making process meets some demands of procedural fairness. This implies that the content of the decisions does not receive independent weight in determining democratic legitimacy. All that matters for democratic legitimacy according to such conceptions is that collective decision-making proceeds through public deliberation among all those affected under some conditions of political fairness or equality. The view defended by Thomas Christiano in his book *The Rule of the Many* is an example for a conception of democratic legitimacy that falls in this category. According to him (Christiano 1996:35),

> democratic discussion, deliberation, and decisionmaking under certain conditions are what make the outcomes legitimate for each person. . . .
> [W]hatever the results of discussions, deliberation, and decisionmaking

. . ., they are legitimate. The results are made legitimate by being the results of the procedure.

Gerald Gaus also defends a variant of Pure Deliberative Proceduralism. He argues that the deliberative process inevitably produces disagreements that cannot be reconciled. Since agreement on a best solution is not to be had, there is no other justification for a particular decision than that it is the result of a fair process. As Gaus puts it (1997: 234): "In his or her deliberations, each citizen presents what he or she believes is the best public justification; the voting mechanism constitutes a fair way to adjudicate deep disagreements about what is publicly justified."

In parallel to the situation among defenders of aggregative democracy, adherents of Rational Deliberative Proceduralism are not satisfied with the justificatory power of Pure Proceduralism and hope to get more out of the democratic process. Rational Deliberative Proceduralists consider some form of justification of the collective decisions themselves as essential for democratic legitimacy and view public deliberation as the right means for achieving this. The requirement that the outcomes of collective decision-making satisfy some sort of rational justification is thus added to that of political equality. Democratic legitimacy, according to conceptions that fall into this category, is not only "backwards-looking"—towards the conditions under which a decision was reached—but also includes consideration of the rational quality of the outcomes chosen.

Rational Deliberative Proceduralism is the sister conception of Rational Aggregative Proceduralism. The notions of rationality invoked differ, of course. In Aggregative Proceduralism, rationality demands some sort of consistency among social preferences or social choices. In Rational Deliberative Proceduralism, rationality refers to the reasons given during deliberation in favor of or against certain alternatives. Whereas the difference between aggregative and deliberative versions of Pure Proceduralism hinges on their respective interpretation of political equality, the difference between the two Rational Proceduralist categories of conceptions of legitimacy also depends on their respective interpretations of what rational justification means. The distinction between the two versions of Rational Proceduralism sheds some light on the debate on aggregative versus deliberative democracy that I have addressed in section 3.2.c. There, I argued against the argumentative strategy that takes Arrow's framework for social choice as a starting-point and then shows how deliberative democracy solves the legitimacy problems that arise within that framework. My point was that this strategy rests on a confusion about the demands of legitimacy. In light of the distinction I have just drawn among versions of Rational Proceduralism, this objection can be restated. Those who argue in this way overlook how rational justification means different things in the contexts of aggregative and deliberative democracy, and the irrationality that affects legitimacy in the Arrowian framework need not play a role in the context of deliberative democracy. Similarly, the argument that Pure Proceduralism is insufficient in the aggregative context does not imply that Pure Proceduralism in general is deficient. I will have more to say on these issues later. First, I want to go into some more details about alternative interpretations of Rational Deliberative Proceduralism.

In a strong version of Rational Deliberative Proceduralism, deliberation is characterized by the aim to generate a consensus, and legitimacy depends on the availability of shared reasons to support an outcome. A famous example is the conception of democratic legitimacy propagated by Juergen Habermas (1990, 1996). In this conception, as discussed above, deliberation is constitutive of rational justification and, conversely, regards deliberative democracy as the only form of political authority that ensures rational justification. In Habermas's version of Rational Deliberative Proceduralism, considerations of political equality and of political quality intertwine and jointly determine democratic legitimacy. As he puts it: "Deliberative politics acquires its legitimating force from the discursive structure of an opinion- and will-formation that can fulfill its socially integrative function only because citizens expect its results to have a reasonable *quality*" (Habermas 1996: 304). The structure of Habermas's argument is to suggest that an ideal procedure will generate a desirable outcome: an ideally fair deliberative process is necessary and sufficient to generate a rationally justified collective decision. This structure is akin to what Rawls (1971: 85) has labeled "perfect proceduralism." The desirable outcome is a rationally justified decision—a decision everyone has reasons to endorse. And a fair deliberative process is the procedure that is able to generate this outcome.[15] For the sake of precision (and at the cost of terminological heaviness), Habermas's proposal for what constitutes democratic legitimacy can thus be labeled Rational Deliberative Perfect Proceduralism.[16]

As discussed in section 3.1.a., many have questioned the idea that public deliberation will generate a consensus, even under ideal circumstances.[17] Recent work on the so-called discursive dilemma reinforces this skepticism. Philip Pettit and Christian List have shown how occurrences of the discursive dilemma may undermine the rationality of the outcome of public deliberation.[18] This problem arises when the evaluation of alternative outcomes is logically connected to a set of independent premises. Take the following example from local politics. Suppose a town has to decide whether to build a new communal center. And suppose the decision depends on the perceived need for this in the community and as well as on an evaluation of the appropriateness of the site. The dilemma turns on the possibility that a collective decision on whether to build may clash with the separate evaluation of the individual premises—i.e. on the possibility that there is both a majority agreeing that there is such a need and a majority agreeing that the site is appropriate, but, if asked directly, the majority view is that the center should not be built. The problem is best represented for the simple case of three individuals:

Table 4.2 The Discursive Dilemma

	Need?	*Site ok?*	*Build?*
Individual 1	Yes	No	No
Individual 2	No	Yes	No
Individual 3	Yes	Yes	Yes
Collective	Yes	Yes	Yes / No?

The dilemma results from two alternative decision-making procedures yielding different decisions. There is a clash between the conclusion-based procedure, which consists of a direct collective evaluation of the outcomes, and the premise-based procedure, which chooses the outcome implied by the collective evaluation of the premises.[19] If the former is used, the outcome cannot be backed up by the premises that would justify the choice. If the latter is used, this problem is avoided, but at the cost of imposing a decision that the collective would not have chosen, if asked directly.

The discursive dilemma affects the demand endorsed by Rational Deliberative Proceduralists that, to be legitimate, the rational justification of outcomes plays a role. According to Pettit, the dilemma raises the question whether the "discipline of reason is meant to apply to each individual, taken singly, or to the group taken as a whole" (Pettit 2001b: 277). The conditions of rationality that apply here relate to the consistency between the evaluation of premises and the evaluation of the resulting conclusions. If the conclusion-based procedure is adopted, then the choices the collective makes cannot be backed up by the premises to which the decision is logically connected, and as such this strategy does not apply the "discipline of reason" to the group as a whole. This procedure may yield a collective choice that cannot be supported by the collective evaluation of the premises. Adopting the premise-based procedure reverses the situation. This strategy prioritizes public deliberation over individual deliberation by making the collective evaluation of the premises the input of decision-making, and letting collective choice be determined by the collective evaluation of the premises, even if the collective would have made a different choice had it been asked directly.

As an aside, note that the dichotomy that Pettit sets up is somewhat misleading. Rejecting the idea of applying "the discipline of reason" to the collective need not imply a purely individualistic or private view of deliberation.[20] Advocating the conclusion-based procedure is compatible with an account of deliberative democracy that values the public exchange of reasons. In fact, this possibility is what distinguishes Pure Deliberative Proceduralist conceptions of democratic legitimacy from their aggregative counterparts. The point is that the value of the public exchange of reason need not lie in its contribution to the rational justification of outcomes.

This can be illustrated with reference to the constructive function of public deliberation that I have introduced in section 4.1.c. Because of this constructive function, public deliberation may lead to the discovery of problems that affect existing policy proposals or to the formulation of new policy proposals. The value that this has for legitimacy may be quite unrelated to the value of deliberation for the justification of particular proposals.[21]

In any case, to return to the discussion of Rational Deliberative Proceduralism, the discursive dilemma renders doubtful the harmony between fair procedures and rational outcomes on which Rational Deliberative Perfect Proceduralism is based. It thus calls for an alternative conception of legitimacy. As I shall explain it in more detail below (6.2.), Pettit insists on the importance of rationality for democratic legitimacy and thus does not resort to a version of Pure Proceduralism. Instead, I would interpret his conception as falling into the subcategory of Rational Deliberative Imperfect Proceduralism. It is based on the recognition that although an ideal outcome exists—a collective decision endorsed by consistent collective evaluations of the premises and their conclusions—this outcome may not be obtainable, and adjustments have to be made in order to balance considerations of fairness with considerations of the quality of outcomes. The conception of democratic legitimacy that Pettit seems to endorse is thus one that seeks to balance considerations of political fairness with rational justification. He argues for the importance of imposing the "discipline of reason" on the collective. In his view, only the premise-based procedure can achieve this. It gives individuals an equal say (in the evaluation of premises) yet also ensures that the decisions made are supported by the evaluation of the premises.

Another influential view that falls into this category is the one expressed by Amy Gutmann and Dennis Thompson in *Democracy and Disagreement* (1996). Their account of the normative requirements of deliberative democracy is based on an irresolvable tension between procedural and substantive considerations. They view deliberative democracy as a mechanism to resolve moral dilemmas, but recognize that sometimes the demands of procedural fairness will lead to outcomes that are deficient in rational substantive justification. At the same time, they are not willing to exclude substantive considerations from the demands of democratic legitimacy, or even to rank the procedural considerations lexicographically above substantive considerations. Instead, they envision a dynamic deliberative process in which there is a continuous revision of both procedural and substantive considerations with the aim to avoid clashes between the two. There is thus an ideal outcome—harmony of procedural and substantive considerations—and, while this outcome cannot be guaranteed, a deliberative decision-making process is the best approximation.

Rational Deliberative Proceduralism—in either of its two subcategories—is probably the conception of democratic legitimacy that a majority of deliberative democrats today endorse. For adherents to this conception,

Pure Deliberative Proceduralism betrays what they see as the very essence of deliberative democracy—the rational justification of democratic decisions through public deliberation—and the ability of the deliberative account to address the problems that affect the aggregative conceptions of legitimacy. There are forceful critics of Rational Deliberative Proceduralism, however, such as Lynn Sanders (1997) and Iris Marion Young (1996, 2000). They argue against the attempt to integrate procedural fairness with substantive rationality because of the potentially exclusionary tendencies of attempts to provide a rational justification. Even after deliberation, they point out, people will differ in their assessment of what is the most justified way to proceed. If this is the case, to demand more than that the decision is the outcome of a fair process is to give undue weight to those who happen to be in agreement with a particular justification, at the expense of those who do not. This undermines the fairness of the deliberative process and hence its legitimacy. Over the next three chapters I shall evaluate Deliberative Proceduralist conceptions of legitimacy, and conclude that Rational Deliberative Proceduralists have indeed failed to show why a conception of legitimacy of this category is the most plausible one. But, I shall not endorse Pure Deliberative Proceduralism either. In Chapter 7, I shall reject Deliberative Proceduralism in favor of conceptions of democratic legitimacy that take seriously the epistemic dimension of deliberative decision-making. The mainstream interpretation of epistemic democracy, however, rests on a veritistic social epistemology and links democratic legitimacy to the truth-tracking potential of democratic decision-making. That is not the way in which I think we should incorporate the epistemic dimension. Consequently, I shall argue against forms of Rational Epistemic Proceduralism and defend instead a purely procedural conception of democratic legitimacy, one that includes epistemic values as part of the ideal of procedural fairness. In line with the terminology developed in this chapter, I call this conception Pure Epistemic Proceduralism.

5 Political Equality

Charles Beitz, in what is probably still the most important book on political equality, distinguishes between "the role or function of the egalitarian ideal in democratic theory and its content" (Beitz 1989: 17). I have given an explanation for what the role of political equality might be in the previous chapter, in relation to my defense of proceduralist conceptions of legitimacy. Here, I want to focus on the content of this ideal. Specifying the content of political equality is to spell out what conditions should be imposed on the process of democratic decision-making. Because there are many possible interpretations of political equality, and many different understandings of what political fairness entails, Beitz (ibid.) suggests that "the main philosophical task of a theory of political equality is to identify the best interpretation of the content of this idea." This is just the task that this chapter will focus on.

5.1. TWO DILEMMAS

Unfortunately, there is a dilemma that affects the attempt to answer the question of what political equality requires. I call it the "political egalitarian's dilemma." This dilemma is an instantiation of the "procedure vs. substance" dilemma that Joshua Cohen has argued deliberative democracy can solve (cf. section 3.2.c.). In deliberative democracy, as discussed above, political equality means that people have the opportunity to participate in the deliberative decision-making process as equals. Whereas political equality in aggregative democracy can be summarized with the "one person one vote" formula, in deliberative democracy it also demands access to the institutions of public deliberation. It is thus clearly a substantive ideal, not just a procedural one. Since I have already argued against aggregative democracy in Chapter 3, I shall focus here on how to interpret the content of political equality in the context of a Deliberative Proceduralist conception of democratic legitimacy.

5.1.a. Cohen's Procedure vs. Substance Dilemma

As summarized in Chapter 3, Cohen (1997b) has influentially argued that the procedure vs. substance dilemma does not arise in deliberative democracy—it only affects aggregative democracy. The reason is that deliberative democracy, unlike aggregative democracy, entails a certain set of substantive commitments. As such, it is able to create harmony between considerations of procedure and of substance. I want to argue here that there is a problem with this argument.[1] The political egalitarian's dilemma reveals that the tension between procedure and substance continues *within* deliberative democracy.

Here is a restatement of the procedure vs. substance dilemma and of Cohen's argument of how it can be solved. The dilemma can be characterized as a clash between the following two claims:

(i) Democratic procedures are necessary and sufficient for legitimacy.
(ii) Democratic procedures are not sufficient for legitimacy.

The dilemma is the following. Claim (ii) refers to the worry that the outcomes of democratic decision-making procedures may fail to be legitimate because they lack substantive justification. Claim (i), however, states that substantive value judgments that are made through avenues other than democratic procedures do not have a legitimate basis.

How does deliberative democracy solve this dilemma? Cohen argues that, compared to aggregative democracy, deliberative democracy imposes more substantive constraints on the democratic process. The aggregative conception only demands that the procedures give equal consideration to individual preferences. These preferences can be of any content. Deliberative democracy requires that the procedures ensure that reasons are given that are acceptable to everyone; not all substantive judgments will pass this test. Policies that discriminate on the basis of race or gender, for example, will prove not to be justifiable. Cohen argues that because it brings considerations of procedures and substance into harmony, deliberative democracy suggests a way for how the dilemma can be solved. According to this view, substantive judgments are legitimate if and only if they are compatible with the constraints deliberative democracy imposes on the democratic process.

Cohen's solution involves the following steps. On the basis of the difference between aggregative and deliberative democracy he argues, first, that claim (i) needs to be modified. Democratic procedures are necessary for legitimacy but, without further qualification, they are not sufficient.

(i') Democratic procedures are necessary for legitimacy.

This removes the tension and (trivially) yields

(iii) Democratic procedures are necessary, but not sufficient for legitimacy.

The next step consists in answering the question of how legitimacy can be guaranteed. To argue that deliberative democracy has an answer to this question, Cohen defends two further claims. The first concerns the constraints deliberative democracy imposes on the democratic process.

(iv) Deliberative democratic procedures are a subset of democratic procedures that fulfill a certain set of substantive criteria.

Cohen lists three principles that summarize the requirements of deliberative democracy: the principles of (1) deliberative inclusion; (2) orientation towards the common good; and (3) participation. The first principle requires that one need to justify one's views to others. The second specifies that justification should refer to a common good, not to private interests. These two principles refer to what I have characterized as the public reasoning component of the ideal of deliberative democracy (section 3.1.a.). I shall come back to this issue in the next chapter. The principle of participation, finally, refers specifically to political equality. Cohen spells out its demands in the following way. The deliberative process

> must ensure equal rights of participation, including rights of voting, association, and political expression, with a strong presumption against restrictions on the content or viewpoint of expression; rights to hold office; a strong presumption in favor of equally weighted votes; and a more general requirement of equal opportunities for effective influence. (Cohen 1997b: 422)

Cohen argues that the role of the three principles taken together is to render the outcomes of democratic procedures acceptable to everyone. As such, they are necessary for democratic legitimacy.

(v) The substantive criteria are necessary to ensure that the outcomes of democratic procedures are acceptable to everyone.

Finally, the last step in Cohen's argument is to defend the claim that because a deliberative process, properly constrained, yields outcomes that everyone finds acceptable, deliberative democracy is not only necessary, but also sufficient for democratic legitimacy.

(ii') Deliberative democratic procedures are sufficient for legitimacy.

From (i') and (ii') he concludes:

(vi) Deliberative democratic procedures are necessary and sufficient for legitimacy.

Deliberative democracy, according to this argument, reconciles considerations of procedure and substance and thus solves a dilemma that affects other accounts of democracy, notably aggregative democracy. Because the substantive constraints that deliberative democracy imposes on the democratic process limit the range of possible outcomes, they ensure the legitimacy of the decisions made. The problem of the tyranny of the majority, for example, does not occur because outcomes have to be justifiable to everyone. In an aggregative account of democracy, by contrast, there is no scope for the kind of rational justification that deliberative democracy enables. Aggregative democracy has an inbuilt legitimacy deficit due to its reliance on unexamined preferences.

While a view of this sort is quite widely held by deliberative democrats, there are several problems with this argument. One is that it does not consider how rational justification may be affected by the discursive dilemma, as discussed in section 4.2.c. I shall come back to this problem in the next chapter. Here I want to focus on a further dilemma for democratic legitimacy. This dilemma relates to the interpretation of political equality. Deliberative democracy, as interpreted by Cohen and others, provides no solution to the political egalitarian's dilemma. In fact, because of the greater demands that deliberative democracy imposes on the democratic process, the dilemma affects deliberative democracy to a greater degree than it affects aggregative democracy.

5.1.b. The Political Egalitarian's Dilemma

If deliberative democracy is to resolve the tension between considerations of procedure and of substance in the way that the previous argument suggests, it should be possible to specify the set of constraints imposed on the democratic process without theoretical ambivalence. This is to say, the ideal of deliberative democracy should determine, at least in principle, how the substantive criteria mentioned in claim (iv) should be interpreted. The point is perhaps best made by analogy to John Rawls's idea of a four-stage sequence, which describes how the ideas expressed in the principles of justice are rendered practicable (Rawls 1971: 195ff.). In Rawls's sequence, the first stage is the one in which the principles of justice get selected. The next three stages are the constitutional, the legislative, and, finally, the judicial and administrative stage, in that order. The point of this sequence is that what is decided at one stage restrains the range of possibilities in the next stage; there is thus no need for the principles of justice identified in the first stage to take account of all institutional details and special cases.

A similar construction should be applicable to the ideal of deliberative democracy. A first stage would identify the ideal of deliberative democracy. This ideal should offer sufficient guidance for how to spell out the set of substantive criteria in subsequent stages. For Cohen's argument to work, it has to be ruled out that the specification of the substantive criteria for deliberative democratic processes conflicts with other premises of his argument. I will argue that this is not the case. Focusing on political equality (what he calls the principle of participation), I will show that there is an ambivalence in the ideal of deliberative democracy about how it should be specified and that alternative specifications lead into clashes with other premises of Cohen's argument. This situation creates the political egalitarian's dilemma.

The dilemma arises from the tension between the following two desiderata. On the one hand, one might want to argue that political equality must mean that people have effectively equal opportunities to participate in the deliberative process. The idea is to avoid a situation where differences in people's effective ability to participate in the deliberative process undermine the legitimacy of democratic decisions. From this perspective, it seems important that the process of deliberative decision-making satisfies a strong criterion of political equality. I call a criterion of political equality strong if it is formulated with regard to people's effective abilities to participate in the deliberative decision-making process. As I shall explain it below, interpretations based on the capability approach lend themselves to the specification of such a strong criterion of political equality since they focus on the effective political freedoms of persons. On the other hand, however, one might want to argue that the purpose of deliberation is to reach a decision on contested issues under conditions of pervasive pluralism. Deliberative democrats take as their starting-point the lack of a prior consensus on policy issues. From this perspective, it seems important that potentially contested judgments are left as much as possible to the scrutiny of public deliberation. Accordingly, political equality is a means to ensure deliberation over potentially controversial issues, but should not, itself, rely on potentially contested value judgments. The second desideratum is thus to keep as minimal as possible the set of substantive value judgments that is imposed on the deliberative process. It suggests a weak criterion of political equality. I call a criterion of political equality weak if it is formulated with regard to a set of all-purpose means, for example in terms of Rawls's primary goods framework (5.2.a.).[2]

The dilemma that affects the specification of the content of political equality is the following. If, on the one hand, the substantive constraints on the deliberative process are kept to a minimum, only a weak criterion of political equality can be imposed on the deliberative process. This criterion may fail to ensure the effective equality of participants in the deliberative process, and this undermines the legitimacy of the outcomes of such a process. If, on the other hand, political equality is interpreted comprehensively, many substantive judgments will be packed into the conditions imposed on the deliberative process. They will be treated as exempt from deliberative evaluation. The stronger the criterion of political equality—the more emphasis is placed not just on general political resources, but on people's abilities to make effective use of these resources—the narrower the scope for democratic scrutiny. This, again, jeopardizes democratic legitimacy. Thus, a strong criterion of political equality will fail to ensure democratic legitimacy because it will exempt too many value judgments from delibera-tive democratic scrutiny. A weak criterion of political equality will fail to ensure democratic legitimacy because many will not have been able to par-ticipate in the deliberative process as effectively equals. In other words, the political egalitarian's dilemma reveals a clash between the attempt to ensure equal possibilities to participate in the democratic process and the require-ment of subjecting substantive judgments to deliberative evaluation.

The political egalitarian's dilemma shows that the tension between pro-cedure and substance resurfaces within deliberative democracy. The tension manifests itself in the following way. If, on the one hand, political equality is interpreted in the weak sense, claim (ii'), according to which deliberative democratic procedures are sufficient for legitimacy, will not have enough bite. For example, without a set of conditions that effectively eliminates limitations on people's opportunities to participate in the democratic pro-cess due to discrimination based on race or gender, it cannot be guaranteed that the outcomes will not be racist or sexist. The weaker the criterion of political equality, the more substantive judgments will unjustifiably pass as legitimate. To avoid the sanctioning of outcomes that violate fundamen-tal political values, legitimacy thus seems to require a strong criterion of political equality. But if political equality is interpreted in the strong sense, claim (i'), according to which democratic procedures are necessary for legit-imacy, will effectively be circumvented. A great range of potentially con-tested issues will be exempt from deliberation and will have been decided by other means than by democratic process. The stronger the criterion of political equality, the more the range of topics subjected to deliberation will be limited and the greater the reliance on substantive judgments that have not been democratically scrutinized. Thus, with a strong criterion of politi-cal equality, there will be insufficient reliance on democratic processes. The result is, again, that legitimacy is undermined.

Because of the ambivalence it exposes, the political egalitarian's dilemma forces us to conclude that, at least as defined by Cohen, deliberative demo-cratic decision-making procedures are not sufficient for legitimacy. Claim (ii') thus has to be replaced by:

(vii) Deliberative democratic procedures are not sufficient for legitimacy.

Quite obviously, this result clashes with the claim that Cohen tries to defend, i.e. that

(vi) Deliberative democratic procedures are necessary and sufficient for legitimacy.

The clash between these two claims has the exact same structure as Cohen's original procedure vs. substance dilemma, but this time the clash concerns deliberative democracy. Deliberative democracy, as I have characterized it here, is just as affected as aggregative democracy by this tension between the need to subject controversial substantive judgments to democratic decision-making and the expectation that the outcomes of such decision-making have a rational justification that is acceptable to all.

5.2. POLITICAL EQUALITY OF WHAT?

To render things less abstract, I now want to discuss how the political egalitarian's dilemma affects the attempt to specify the content of political equality. Amartya Sen has convincingly argued that defining the informational space to which principles of equality should apply is an essential feature of theorizing equality. As he puts it, all contemporary theories of justice, not just egalitarian ones, invoke "equality of *something*," but they differ greatly with regard to what it is that they recommend should be equalized (Sen 1992a: 12). The "equality of what?" debate in political philosophy, which Sen's contributions have triggered, addresses this issue within egalitarian theories of justice.[3] It has identified three main alternatives: welfare and opportunities for welfare, resources—including primary goods—and capabilities. My aim here is not to retrace the general debate, but to explore what political equality, or political fairness, in the context of a proceduralist conception of democratic legitimacy might require, and what informational framework might be most appropriate. The content of political equality is given by some account of the opportunities people have to participate in deliberative democratic processes. To specify this content, we need a framework that can capture relations of equality among political agents. The agency aspect thus plays a crucial role for political equality. This dimension is taken seriously in resourcist frameworks and in the capability approach. In both, the focus is on what persons need to pursue goals and values that matter to them. Because welfarist frameworks cannot accommodate the agency aspect (cf. section 2.2.c.), I shall thus refrain from discussing any further frameworks that focus on welfare or opportunities for welfare.

Many deliberative democrats have been drawn to the capability approach to interpret the requirements of political equality. As is well known, Sen developed the capability approach as an alternative to resourcist frameworks in general, but specifically to Rawls's primary goods framework. Sen influentially objected to the primary goods framework that it fails to be responsive to individual differences in the ability to make use of resources (Sen 1980). This objection has resonated with deliberative democrats who argue that political equality needs to focus on people's effective opportunities to participate in deliberative democratic processes (e.g. Bohman 1996, 1997; Knight and Johnson 1997).[4] In this section I want to address these issues. To simplify, I shall concentrate on the comparison between capabilities and primary goods, and not discuss resourcist frameworks in general. Let me start with an interpretation of political equality in terms of primary goods and then move on to those proposals that are based on the capability approach.[5]

5.2.a. Primary Goods

Primary goods are part of Rawls's theory of justice as fairness, but the framework can also be used to specify the more restricted requirements of political equality. This is so because, as discussed in the previous chapter, there is a common basis between justice and democratic legitimacy in Rawls's account, and political equality is part of both justice and legitimacy.

The primary goods framework is designed to capture certain general institutional features of the basic structure of society that affect the prospects of individuals, whatever their ideas of the good life are. Specifically, Rawls counts the following as primary goods (Rawls 1993: 181): "basic rights and liberties," "freedom of movement and free choice of occupation," "powers and prerogatives of offices and positions of responsibility," "income and wealth," and "the social bases of self-respect." The first primary good includes the following basic liberties and rights: political liberties (i.e. the right to vote and to be eligible for public office) and freedom of speech and assembly, liberty of conscience and freedom of thought, freedom of the person and the right to hold personal property, and the freedom from arbitrary arrest and seizure. The second and the third primary goods refer to access to the labor market and to powers and prerogatives of offices and to positions of responsibility in important political and economic institutions. The fourth primary good, income and wealth, is relatively straightforward. The case of the last primary good on the list, by contrast, is more complicated.[6] Note, first, that the emphasis lies on the social bases of self-respect and not on self-respect directly. It thus refers to the basic structure of society as well, and not, say, to an individual state of mind. In a society with feudal structures, for example, social groups that do not belong to the ruling classes are not granted the social bases for self-respect. This primary good is of a different kind than the others on the list. While the first four primary goods describe general means to develop and pursue a conception of the good, the social bases of self-respect ensure that the citizens have the possibility of experiencing it as worthwhile to do so. In this regard they are important for the development of a sense of justice, the second moral power attributed to citizens. It is for these reasons that Rawls regards the social bases of self-respect as the most important primary good on the list.

The value of primary goods is derived from fundamental political values of democratic societies, and not from individual conceptions of the good. As such, primary goods are different from the preference or utility frameworks used by economists. That is to say, they comprise what is necessary to assess whether the basic structure establishes fair cooperation and respects people as free and equals. Primary goods are not intended to be a surrogate of individual well-being. They are a measure of people's access to basic institutions—of the institutional conditions for the realization of the two fundamental moral powers that persons have.[7] I have argued in section 3.1.c. that these fundamental moral powers are compatible with and support a deliberative account of democracy, as they enable persons both to know what is to their advantage (the capacity for a sense of the good) and to take into account the need for establishing fair terms of cooperation (the capacity for a sense of justice). This suggests that the primary goods framework might be well-suited to specify the content of political equality in the context of deliberative democracy.

If primary goods are used in connection with the Rawlsian interpretation of the demands of legitimacy, the following results for political equality. I have argued that in the Rawlsian perspective, the ideas of legitimacy and justice are distinct but related (section 4.1.b.). Since legitimacy is weaker than justice, political equality demands less than full-blown justice. In the Rawlsian account, the requirements of democratic legitimacy are covered by the first principle of justice as fairness. This principle guarantees equality with respect to a list of basic liberties and rights, and includes the fair value of the political liberties. Ensuring that people can enjoy the fair value of the political liberties implies that the first principle does not just apply to the first primary good on the list. That would cover only formal equality. Instead, legitimacy makes demands on the distribution of the other primary goods as well. This Rawlsian view thus entails that the content of political equality is given by a social minimum of all primary goods.

5.2.b. The Capability Approach

A second interpretation of what the content of political equality might be is based on the capability approach. Sen developed the capability approach both as an alternative to Rawls's primary goods framework and to individual utility—the informational basis favored by economists (e.g. Sen 1985a, 1992a). In contrast to the former, the capability approach is sensitive to differences in individuals' ability to make effective use of their resources in the pursuit of their respective ends.

What characterizes the capability approach? A person's capability is determined by the functionings she can achieve. Functionings are a description of the various things an individual can do or be in a particular state, such as being well-nourished, being able to read, etc., and they are treated as objectively valuable. The identification of relevant functionings is the first step in any evaluatory exercise based on the capability approach. The second step consists in defining capability sets over the space of functionings. A person's capability set reflects "the alternative combinations of functionings the person can achieve, and from which he or she can choose one collection" (Sen 1993a: 31). The split between functionings and capabilities is the distinctive feature of the capability approach. It highlights the difference between "achievement" and "freedom" (Sen 1985b). The basic idea is that persons pursue their different aims and interests by realizing functionings they value. The capability approach can be used to analyze achievements—the range of functionings a person actually chooses to realize—but it is designed to be applicable to the broader exercise of capturing the positive freedom persons have. Insofar as the capability approach looks at which valuable functionings are effectively within a person's range of opportunities, it captures a positive notion of freedom.

Functionings may be well-being-oriented or agency-oriented—the capability approach, while applicable to the evaluation of well-being, is not welfarist (Sen 1985b). There is, however, an asymmetry in how the capability approach treats well-being and agency. If the capability approach is used to specify a person's well-being freedom, it refers to a specific objective—well-being. There will be a certain set of functionings that will be identified as necessarily part of individual well-being. And a person has well-being freedom to the extent to which his or her capability set includes these functionings. Agency-freedom, by contrast, is "freedom to achieve whatever the person, as a responsible agent, decides he or she should achieve" (Sen 1985b: 203–04). This implies that agency-freedom is necessarily conditional on the individual agent (Sen 1985b: 204)—which functionings ought to be in the capability set cannot be determined without taking into account the perspective of the agent in question.

It should also be noted that with regard to the agency aspect, there is an important difference between Martha Nussbaum's interpretation of the capability approach and Sen's interpretation. Nussbaum downplays the role of the agency dimension. According to her (2000: 14), the role of agency is already fully included into the distinction between capabilities and functionings. In this interpretation, agency is defined in relation to what an agent does to realize particular functionings and not others. Such an interpretation relies on an unduly narrow definition of agency, however, as agency is defined only relative to a given capability set and not relative to the identification and definition of relevant functionings and capability sets. In other words, it neglects the "open conditionality" (Sen 1985b: 204) that stems from the absence of any given objective and effectively reduces agency to the freedom to choose from a given set of alternatives. If that set of alternatives comprises well-being-related functionings, then it reduces agency-freedom to well-being freedom. But agency-freedom, in Sen's sense, is broader, and serves a different purpose than well-being freedom. It relates to the freedom persons have to set and pursue goals and values that they regard as worth pursuing.

Agency-freedom is of particular relevance for deliberative democracy as it captures, *inter alia*, people's opportunities to participate in processes of evaluation and decision-making that relate to collective action. The content of political equality, if interpreted on the basis of the capability approach, will be given by some subset of individual agency-freedoms. To specify the content of political equality, some list of functionings relevant to people's opportunities to participate in the deliberative decision-making process needs to be provided.[8] Deliberative democrats such as James Bohman, James Johnson and Jack Knight have used the capability approach to spell out the content of political equality.[9] Let me briefly discuss their proposals here.

Knight and Johnson's interpretation of political equality focuses on "equality of opportunity of political influence." They define it as follows (1997: 293):

> In one sense, equal opportunity of influence requires that asymmetries not give unfair advantage to participants. Equality entails that participation and decision making be voluntary and uncoerced. . . . In a second sense, equal opportunity of influence requires that asymmetries not place anyone in a position of unfair disadvantage. . . . This highlights the need for a distribution of power and resources in the society such that each individual citizen will have the personal resources to participate effectively in that process.

In an earlier proposal, Bohman interprets political equality as "effective social freedom." According to him (Bohman 1997: 393),

> [f]reedom is, on this account, the capability to live as one would choose. It includes the capability for effective social agency, the ability to participate in joint activities and achieve one's goals in them. For political liberties, the issue is effective use of public freedoms, which may not be possible even in the absence of direct coercion or prohibitions.

Both characterizations of political equality strongly echo the view Sen put forward in the "equality of what?" debate. In their defenses of the capability approach, both stress the importance of taking into account the effectiveness with which people translate resources into the possibility to participate in deliberative processes and criticize the primary goods framework for neglecting the possibility of differential effectiveness. For Bohman (1997: 322) it is a strength of the capability approach that "it not only elaborates a conception of equal standing in deliberation, it also makes central the fundamental diversity of human beings with regard to their public functioning." On this point, Knight and Johnson (1997: 298) agree with Bohman. Sen's argument that the primary goods framework—in contrast to the capability approach—neglects differences in people's worth of their freedom is, in their view, of particular importance in the domain of political equality. They also point out, however, that to make the capability approach workable in this context is not an easy task.

Identifying the capability set that is specific to political equality requires, on the one hand, an understanding of the functionings that are essential for people to be able to participate in deliberative decision-making. No one should be systematically excluded from democratic decision-making processes. On the other, due to the focus of the capability approach on effective freedoms, it also requires an understanding of the impediments that hinder people from being effective participants in democratic decision-making. No one should be assumed to consent to a particular decision—be "included"—if he or she has not had an effective opportunity to voice dissent.[10] The latter concern in particular brings to bear the emphasis of the capability approach on effective freedoms. It draws attention to a potentially wide range of impediments that hinder different people from voicing their dissent.

Knight and Johnson (1997: 298–99) have a proposal for a list of functionings that are relevant for political equality: the "capacity to formulate authentic preferences," "the effective use of cultural resources," and, most importantly in their view, "basic cognitive abilities and skills." Even this short list is sufficient to generate a fairly strong criterion of political equality because of the linkages between inequalities in the political sphere and inequalities in other spheres. Knight and Johnson argue that economic and social inequalities undermine, first, the capacity to formulate authentic preferences because of the problem of adaptive preferences—the tendency to adapt to adverse circumstances.[11] Second, they argue that social hierarchies put minority groups at a disadvantage in voicing their concerns effectively. Because cultural imperialism privileges some form of expression, access to education is thus necessary to give people from minority groups effective opportunities to articulate their concerns (Knight and Johnson 1997: 307). Finally, capabilities related to "basic cognitive abilities and skills," too, are linked to economic and social inequalities. One of Knight and Johnson's examples is a study that shows how childhood poverty may lead to diminished intellectual capacities in adults (Knight and Johnson 1997: 306). To ensure effective opportunities to participate in the deliberative process as an equal, they conclude, it is necessary to limit social and economics inequalities.

If the capability approach is used to specify the content of political equality, the emphasis is on how inequalities in the political sphere are linked to inequalities in a range of other spheres—socio-economic and cultural, health and education-related, etc. Descriptively speaking, it seems right and important to examine how social, cultural, and economic inequalities translate into political inequalities, and, conversely, to get an understanding of the multidimensionality of factors impacting on political equality. Normatively speaking, it also seems right that democratic legitimacy will be threatened if political equality is merely formal and if, as a result, people's effective abilities to participate in the deliberative process are undermined by unchecked inequalities in other spheres. But is this sufficient to argue that the content of political equality should be interpreted in terms of the capability approach, rather than in terms of a resourcist framework such as primary goods?

5.2.c. Political Equality and Proceduralist Legitimacy

I now want to argue that the choice between the two ways of interpreting the content of political equality that I have just discussed is affected by the political egalitarian's dilemma. Each informational framework accommodates one of the two desiderata for a theory of political equality in the context of deliberative democracy but not the other. The capability approach does better with accommodating the need to ensure that persons have effective opportunities to participate in deliberation as equals, whereas the primary goods framework does better with the need to avoid imposing controversial value judgments that are exempt from democratic scrutiny on the collective.

The advantage of the capability approach is that it highlights the multiple influences on people's opportunities to participate in the deliberative process. It draws attention to how democratic legitimacy will be threatened if people's effective abilities to participate in the deliberative process are undermined by unchecked social and economic inequalities. For these reasons, the capability approach is well-suited to push the case for a strong criterion of political equality and to highlight the potential brittleness of democratic legitimacy due to failures of securing effective political equality. Its initial appeal notwithstanding, a strong criterion of political equality based on the capability approach gives rise to a problem of its own, however. The problem is that it packs much of what would appear to be a subject for deliberation into the conditions that have to be met prior to deliberation. The role of political equality in proceduralist conceptions of democratic legitimacy is to specify the conditions that the decision-making process has to satisfy if its results are to be legitimate. As such, the content of political equality is not itself the subject of deliberation. Now, the more extensively the requirements of political equality are interpreted, the more substantive judgments are exempted from democratic deliberation. If, to take one of Knight and Johnson's examples, a certain educational program is seen as necessary for creating equal opportunities to participate in public deliberation, this makes it more likely that minority criticisms about cultural biases in education, and in the mainstream social and political discourse more generally, will be silenced. Since the conditions that frame the deliberative process are of decisive importance for democratic legitimacy, decision-making on these conditions will be separate from decision-making about issues in the regular course of the deliberative process. If the provision of a certain educational package is treated as a prerequisite for deliberation, it will not, at the same time, be a topic for deliberation. If it has been decided that the provision of education is the right strategy to counter the exclusionary effects of "cultural imperialism," the ways in which the educational system might support cultural biases in values and practices thus become harder to address. The same sort of problems affects the other suggestions that Knight and Johnson make. If certain measures against childhood poverty are imposed on the basis of beliefs about the link between poverty and cognitive abilities, a decision has been made about the needs of poor children that removes this—potentially contested—issue from deliberation.[12] And policies that aim at political empowerment and at breaking the link between adverse economic and social circumstances and adaptive preference formation may inadvertently limit the expression of "authentic" preferences as a result of taking a stance, in advance of the deliberative process, of what authentic and non-authentic preferences are.

A comprehensive understanding of politically relevant capabilities assumes that it is known what the appropriate distribution of economic and social resources is and what marginalized groups demand.[13] This interpretation of the requirements of political equality inadvertently carries the problem of political inclusion—that Bohman has correctly identified and that Knight and Johnson recognize too—into the definition of the conditions for democratic legitimacy. An interpretation of political equality based on the capability approach may have the unappealing consequence of including marginalized groups into processes of deliberative decision-making on the terms of the dominant groups. Specifying the content of political equality using the capability approach thus clashes with the desideratum of leaving substantive judgments to the deliberative process. Such judgments lack legitimacy because they have not been subjected to democratic scrutiny. This is, of course, just one of the horns of Cohen's procedure vs. substance dilemma.

Because of this problem with a strong criterion of political equality based on the capability approach, the primary goods framework suddenly looks more attractive again. As discussed earlier, in a Rawlsian interpretation, the content of political equality refers to primary goods that represent those aspects of the basic institutional structure of society that relate to the demands of legitimacy. Because it is concerned with features of basic social institutions, not of persons, the primary goods framework has an inbuilt "domain restriction."[14] The advantage of a weak criterion of political equality based on primary goods is that it avoids imposing constraints based on controversial substantive judgments on the deliberative process. Rawls's justification of his first principle of justice and of the primary goods framework is compatible with the general features of a political conception of justice. Such an interpretation of political equality is limited to the basic structure, respects the fact of reasonable pluralism, and, instead of drawing on comprehensive doctrines, only refers to the fundamental ideas implicit in the public political culture of a democratic society (Rawls 2001: 26–27). A strong criterion of political equality based on the capability approach, by contrast, does, by definition, not have such a domain restriction. Because it focuses on interpersonal differences in conversion, it stretches beyond the political sphere, and demands that the interlinkages between the political spheres and other spheres are taken into account. This implies that such a strong criterion cannot be specified by drawing only on fundamental political values, but will have to draw on comprehensive doctrines. As such, it cannot be uncontroversial. What is worse, contrary to its underlying aim, a strong criterion of political equality may end up building on the comprehensive doctrines of the privileged majority and silencing the perspectives of those who do not belong to this social group.

On the basis of this comparison between the two informational frameworks, the political egalitarian's dilemma can be rephrased as follows. If political equality is defined weakly in terms of primary goods, significant inequalities in people's abilities to effectively use their political liberties may be neglected. If this is the case, democratic legitimacy may be too readily assumed because some people are effectively excluded. If political equality is interpreted in terms of capabilities, the problem of effective inequalities can be avoided. The strong criterion of political equality based on the capability approach leads to legitimacy problems of its own, however. It will specify conditions that depend on an extensive set of evaluations of the value of certain functionings and about the determinants of people's capabilities. Many contested substantive judgments will be unduly bracketed from public deliberation, and this undermines the democratic legitimacy of the decisions taken. In sum, either way of specifying the content of political equality creates problems for democratic legitimacy.

The political egalitarian's dilemma reveals that even if it is granted that deliberative democracy imposes substantive constraints on the deliberative process, there is scope in the interpretation of these constraints, and the question remains what justifies the selection of a particular set of constraints. This leads to an ambiguity in the legitimacy requirement of deliberative democracy. The problem for how to interpret political equality arises in relation to claim (v). To repeat, it says that the substantive criteria—of which political equality forms an important part—are necessary to ensure that the outcomes of democratic procedures are acceptable to everyone. Perhaps paradoxically, the desideratum that all have effectively equal opportunities to participate in the deliberative process leads to a narrowing of the scope of deliberative evaluation, which then leads to a clash with the requirement that the outcomes of democratic procedures be acceptable to everyone. The very motivation for deliberative democracy lies in the acknowledgement that in pluralist societies, there is no prior consensus on substantive issues. Deliberation is seen as the necessary means for generating acceptance and legitimacy. Without deliberation, dissent over alternative outcomes fails to be registered, and this undermines the legitimacy of the decisions made.

One might object that I have given an overly static characterization of the problem of specifying the content of political equality. Does a dynamic interpretation of deliberative processes offer a way out of the difficulty posed by the political egalitarian's dilemma? Applied to the conditions framing deliberation, the dynamic interpretation addresses the issue of who is to determine these conditions. It insists on the importance of allowing deliberation over these conditions as well when they become problematic. Amy Gutmann and Dennis Thompson (2004), for example, argue that all principles governing deliberative processes—whether they are substantive or procedural—should be seen as contestable and as provisional. I agree that such an extended view of the scope of deliberation is indeed the only plausible one. In relation to the conditions of political equality, such deliberation may serve as a correcting force when the conditions are perceived as either too strong or too weak. It may, for example, lead to a demand for policies that increase effective participation for previously excluded groups, or to a demand for a change of policies that rest on controversial assumptions about the needs of the groups they target. But the dynamic interpretation does not solve the problem that the political egalitarian's dilemma encapsulates. Allowing for contestation, and for all principles to be provisional, may be the only way to proceed, but it does not eliminate the threat to democratic legitimacy posed by the political egalitarian's dilemma. The dynamic interpretation cannot escape the tension between attempting to ensure effectively equal opportunities for all to participate in the decision-making process and attempting to leave potentially controversial value judgments to the deliberative process. Contrary to Cohen's argument, the dilemma thus reveals how the tension between procedure and substance affects the specification of the content of the condition of political equality in deliberative democracy.

The thrust of Gutmann and Thompson's argument is to criticize Pure Proceduralist conceptions of legitimacy and to render unproblematic the inclusion of substantive principles in the ideal of deliberative democracy. The political egalitarian's dilemma casts doubt on this solution. Moreover, the political egalitarian's dilemma undermines those arguments for Rational Deliberative Proceduralism that rest on the ability of deliberative democracy to resolve the tension between procedural and substantive considerations. This raises the question of whether there are other, more effective, defenses of Rational Proceduralism, or whether conceptions of democratic legitimacy of this category ought to be abandoned in favor of some version of Pure Proceduralism. Of course, the political egalitarian's dilemma does not strengthen the case for Pure Proceduralism either—all proceduralist conceptions are affected by the dilemma. But the upshot of the dilemma is that, rather than hoping for some solution that would render the tension between procedural and substantive considerations unproblematic from the point of view of democratic legitimacy, a trade-off needs to be made between the two threats to democratic legitimacy.

In addition, the political egalitarian's dilemma also calls into question the readiness of many deliberative democrats to endorse a strong criterion of political equality. There is a tendency to demand that justice is fully realized prior to deliberation. But this amounts to putting the cart before the horse. If realizing justice is a plausible task for deliberative democracy, an account has to be given of how it can be expected that deliberative democracy will actually achieve this task; it will not do to simply pack justice into the conditions for legitimate deliberation. The political egalitarian's dilemma reveals that this strategy brings in problems of democratic legitimacy through the backdoor.

Insofar as the political egalitarian's dilemma reveals that making democratic legitimacy depend on substantive considerations is more problematic than it is often thought, a more deeply procedural interpretation of the requirements of democratic legitimacy in deliberative democracy gains some attractiveness. In the next two chapters, I will identify further problems with Rational Proceduralism and argue for a Pure Proceduralist conception of democratic legitimacy instead. I shall argue in Chapter 7 that the best response to the political egalitarian's dilemma is to take seriously democracy's constructive function (4.1.c.). This response relies on the possibility of endogenizing the process through which the members of the democratic constituency learn about the effects of different social states on different social groups. This can be achieved by including an idea of epistemic fairness in the idea of political fairness. Epistemic fairness relates to people's opportunities to contribute to the constructive function of deliberative democratic decision-making. This, I shall argue, counterbalances the exclusionary effects of a weak criterion of political equality and the inclusive effects of a strong criterion and thus renders the legitimacy of democratic decision-making more robust.

6 Public Reason

The main difference between Rational and Pure Proceduralist conceptions of democratic legitimacy lies in how the scope of political justification is defined. In Rational Proceduralist conceptions, legitimacy depends not just on an appropriately justified decision-making process, but also on some standards of justification that target the decisions themselves. In Pure Proceduralist conceptions, by contrast, the legitimacy of democratic decisions only hinges on them being the outcome of an appropriately justified decision-making process. Different accounts of democracy advocate different standards of justification, of course. In Kenneth Arrow's version of Rational Aggregative Proceduralism, for example, the standards for the justification of outcomes refer to the rationality of social preferences. In Philip Pettit's version of Rational Deliberative Proceduralism, these standards refer to a different interpretation of collective rationality. And as I shall explain it in Chapter 7, Rational Epistemic Proceduralism relies on procedure-independent standards of correctness.

I pursue several aims in this chapter. First, I want to clarify the distinction between Rational and Pure Proceduralism by discussing how the understanding of the relation between the justification of the decision-making process and the legitimacy of outcomes differs in these two categories of conceptions of legitimacy. I shall do so by focusing on deliberative democracy, and specifically on John Rawls's idea of public reason. I shall distinguish between two possible interpretations of his idea of public reason—a substantive interpretation and a procedural interpretation. According to the former, public reason applies to both the justification of what counts as a fair decision-making process and to the justification of the outcomes of that process. According to the latter, public reason applies only to the justification of what counts as a fair decision-making process. This second interpretation, which I shall argue is the more plausible one, thus supports a Pure Proceduralist conception, as it does not make the legitimacy of democratic decisions dependent on the availability of substantive reasons that would support a decision.

The idea of public reason is an essential element in Rawls's account of deliberative democracy.[1] Discussing this idea, together with the question of which conception of democratic legitimacy is most consistent with Rawls's writings on deliberative democracy, is my second aim in this chapter. It completes my characterization and defense of a broadly Rawlsian approach to democratic legitimacy. As I have argued in Chapter 5, however, Pure Deliberative Proceduralism is affected by the political egalitarian's dilemma. The Rawlsian conception of democratic legitimacy, as I shall reconstruct it, thus does not seem quite sufficient. In Chapter 7, I shall expand on it and argue that the fairness of the decision-making process should also be seen as depending on some account of epistemic fairness and hence on a more explicit acknowledgement of democracy's constructive function.

Before getting to epistemic democracy in the next chapter, I want to further strengthen the case for Pure Proceduralism by arguing against a view that is common in both aggregative and deliberative versions of Rational Proceduralism. This view holds that legitimate democratic decisions need to satisfy some requirements of collective rationality. My third aim in this chapter is thus to argue that it is not necessary for democratic legitimacy that the outcomes of the decision-making process are rational.

6.1. RAWLS'S IDEA OF PUBLIC REASON AND DEMOCRATIC LEGITIMACY

6.1.a. Rawls's Idea of Public Reason

Rawls's idea of public reason has attracted a host of criticisms. Some have objected that it is overly narrow and excludes contributions to the process of public deliberation that should not be excluded. Others have taken issue with the idea of public reason as freestanding—as making no reference to comprehensive (moral, religious, etc.) doctrines. Still others have argued that Rawls's idea of public reason is incomplete—that there are issues to be settled in political discussion that public reason cannot settle. Defenders of Rawls have attempted to respond to these objections and to argue that his idea of public reason can fulfill the tasks Rawls attributes to it.

In my view, these debates tend to fail to get to the core of the problem because they fail to address the relationship between Rawls's idea of public reason and his conception of democratic legitimacy. Rawls's own comments on the role of public reason in his conception of legitimacy are not always clear and he also seems to have changed his view on this issue over time. This has exacerbated confusion about his idea of public reason.

Rawls makes it clear that legitimacy demands public reason.[2] But is public reason meant to apply to the justification of the constraints the democratic decision process has to satisfy or to the justification of the democratic decisions themselves? Depending on how this question is answered, there are two interpretations of Rawls's idea of public reason. On one interpretation, call this the "substantive interpretation" of Rawls's idea of public reason, it applies not just to the framework in which democratic decision-making is embedded—the constitutional essentials—but has to extend to the substantive justification of the decisions made. In this view, the legitimacy of a particular decision will depend on its conformity with the content of public reason. This view is consistent with Rational Proceduralism. Rawls can sometimes be read to endorse this interpretation. I shall argue that this is not the interpretation we should favor and indeed the one that explains the many objections that have been leveled against Rawls's idea of public reason and against using a Rawlsian approach to democratic theory.

An alternative interpretation restricts public reason to the justification of the constraints that frame the decision-making process in a deliberative democracy. In this view, call it the "procedural interpretation" of Rawls's idea of public reason, democratic decisions are legitimate if they are the outcome of an appropriately constrained deliberative process. Public reason is invoked when it comes to the justification of the principles that should govern the process of democratic decision-making, but not—at least not directly—in relation to the content of public deliberation. Many passages in Rawls's writings suggest this procedural interpretation of public reason, which is consistent with a Pure Proceduralist conception of democratic legitimacy. I shall argue that this is the more plausible interpretation of Rawls's conception of democratic legitimacy. By interpreting Rawls's idea of public reason in this way, I shall, indirectly at least, also defend the idea against his critics.

But before it is possible to settle the question of how the idea of public reason should be interpreted, we first need a better understanding of the idea itself. According to Rawls, public reason has five aspects (Rawls 1999: 574–75):

> (1) the fundamental political questions to which it applies; (2) the persons to whom it applies (government officials and candidates for public office); (3) its content as given by a family of reasonable political conceptions of justice; (4) the application of these conceptions in discussions of coercive norms to be enacted in the form of legitimate law for a democratic people; and (5) citizens' checking that the principles derived from their conceptions of justice satisfy the criterion of reciprocity.[3]

Some of these aspects need more elucidation than others. The idea of public reason aims to tackle the problem of political legitimacy that I have characterized above: How is it possible, given the fact of reasonable pluralism, for citizens to justify the terms of the system of cooperation to each other? Rawls solves this problem by applying the method of "political"—as opposed to "metaphysical"—justification that he has developed in response to critics of his theory of justice as fairness (Rawls 1985). Public reason should thus be "freestanding" in the same way as his theory of justice is. That is, the goal is to characterize the idea of public reason with reference to fundamental political values alone and make it independent of comprehensive doctrines. This restricts the content of public reason (aspect 3) to what constitutes the family of political conceptions of justice. Because the content of public reason is thus restricted, its proper domain in the political sphere at large must be carefully specified. Rawls conceives of public reason as limited to matters of constitutional essentials and basic justice (aspect 1).[4] In addition, an account of the persons to whom public reason applies and how (aspects 2, 4, and 5) also needs to be given as it is obvious that, in many contexts, we will reason about political matters in terms of non-public reason.[5] The question is: in what context is it important that the restriction on reason is observed? Rawls answers that the proper domain of public reason is the "public political forum" (Rawls 1999: 575) and applies primarily—but not only—to judges, government officials, and candidates for public office. The public political forum is a separate domain contained within what Rawls calls the "public political culture." The latter is a normative category, encompassing all reasonable comprehensive doctrines. It is to be distinguished from "the background culture." This is a descriptive category. It captures actual public debates, which might be influenced by unreasonable doctrines.

With these conceptual and terminological distinctions in place, we can now address the following question: how should the relationship between Rawls's conception of democratic legitimacy and his idea of public reason be understood? Since public reason applies to the justification of these constitutional essentials and matters of basic justice, the question is how the justification of constitutional essentials and matters of basic justice relates to the legitimacy of specific policy proposals and new laws as they are made in the course of the democratic process. The answer will depend on how the relation between the public political forum—where only public reason applies—and the public political culture—the realm of a deliberative process in which the participants acknowledge each other as free and equals—is specified. Does Rawls's conception of democratic legitimacy demand that deliberation is reducible to public reason, or does it allow for the deliberative process in the public political culture to invoke a broader set of considerations?

6.1.b. A Procedural Interpretation of Rawls's Idea of Public Reason

If Rawls's conception of democratic legitimacy were a version of Rational Proceduralism, this would suggest a substantive interpretation of his idea of public reason. In this view, legitimacy demands that the substantive reasons given in the public political culture to support democratic decisions are identical—at least in principle—with the content of public reason. It would imply that in the deliberative process, people ought not make reference to their comprehensive doctrines, but instead attempt to justify their views to each other purely on the basis of—freestanding—public reason.

A democratic decision would only be legitimate if, beyond being the outcome of a fair process, it could be justified in terms of public reason.

If Rawls's conception of democratic legitimacy were of the Pure Proceduralist category, this would impose fewer restrictions on the deliberative process. This conception of democratic legitimacy fits with the procedural interpretation of Rawls's idea of public reason. In this interpretation, public reason only applies to the justification of the constitution that constrains the process of democratic decision-making, but is not required to extend to the substantive (as opposed to the procedural) reasons people might hold to justify a decision. That is to say, it is sufficient that the process in which decisions are taken and people exchange reasons for and against particular decisions is appropriately constrained. It is not necessary that people argue solely on the basis of public reason in the deliberative process. It is acceptable that they draw on their comprehensive doctrines. Note that if the deliberative process is appropriately constrained, the participants acknowledge each other as free and equals. That is to say, the scope of public deliberation is given by what Rawls calls the public political culture, which denotes the normatively limited domain of reasonable conceptions. As such, the deliberative process at all times respects the constraints imposed by the constitution, and public reason is available to remind people of these constraints. To make proper sense of the procedural interpretation of public reason, it is thus important to be aware of the difference between being reasonable—drawing on a comprehensive doctrine that is compatible with the political conception of justice—and employing public reason—arguing only from within a political conception of justice.

Unfortunately, Rawls is not always very clear about how we should interpret his idea of public reason, and hence about what conception of democratic legitimacy he advocates. Some parts of his writings suggest a substantive interpretation while others suggest a procedural interpretation of his idea of public reason. This, I contend, has created much confusion in the literature. Let me first give some examples for either interpretation before arguing that we should adopt the procedural interpretation of his idea of public reason.

A first piece of evidence for the substantive interpretation is when Rawls writes that public reason is the "form of reasoning appropriate to equal citizens who as a corporate body impose rules on one another backed by sanctions of state power" (Rawls 2001: 92). This reads just like a description of what a democratic society does when it decides on its laws or policies. It thus suggests that public reason ought to apply to the deliberative process at large. A further piece of evidence for the substantive interpretation may be found in some of what Rawls has to say on the relationship between public and non-public reason. Rawls states that the use of non-public reasons in the public political culture is admissible only if what he calls *the proviso* is satisfied: if, eventually, public reason can be invoked "to support whatever the comprehensive doctrines introduced are said to support" (Rawls

1999: 591). This, again, seems to suggest that the content of the reasons exchanged in the public political culture must ultimately be describable in terms of the content of public reason.

What about passages that suggest the procedural interpretation? Consider, first, what Rawls says on "political goodness." He writes: "citizens want to cooperate politically with one another in ways that satisfy the liberal principle of legitimacy: that is, on terms that can be publicly justified to all in the light of shared political values" (Rawls 2001: 202). What this characterization expresses is that political goodness—the realm of shared political values—can only be invoked to justify the constraints that shape the political process. According to the view Rawls expresses here, legitimacy requires that the process satisfy constraints everyone can accept. It does not entail that a particular outcome of the deliberative exchange of reasons ought to be justifiable in that way.

Other passages of *Justice as Fairness: A Restatement* similarly suggest that the shared political values that define the content of public reason ought to be invoked to justify the constitutional essentials, not to justify decisions made within a decision-making process that is thus constrained. Rawls emphasizes, for example, that he does not want to "say that a political conception formulates political values that can settle all legislative questions" (Rawls 2001: 41).[6] And he notes (Rawls 2001: 28):

> [I]f a political conception of justice covers the constitutional essentials, it is already of enormous importance even if it has little to say about many economic and social issues that legislative bodies must consider. To resolve these issues it is often necessary to go outside that conception and the political values its principles express, and to invoke values and considerations that it does not include. But as long as there is firm agreement on the constitutional essentials, the hope is that political and social cooperation between free and equal citizens can be maintained.

Since the political conception of justice defines the content of public reason, this passage constitutes clear evidence for the procedural interpretation, as it suggests that considerations other than those contained in public reason are necessary to make policy decisions.

A final piece of evidence is the way in which Rawls draws the distinction between justice and legitimacy in his "Reply to Habermas." There, Rawls argues that because "it is unreasonable to expect in general that human statutes and laws should strictly be just by our lights" (1995: 148, n. 30), a person may accept that a particular policy or law is legitimate, even if she does not regard it as just. Rawls thus insists that "citizens recognize the familiar distinction between accepting as (sufficiently) just and legitimate a constitution with its procedures for fair elections and legislative majorities, and accepting as legitimate (even when not just) a particular statute or a decision in a particular matter of policy" (1995: 148). This again clearly suggests the procedural interpretation of public reason, in which public reason applies to the justification of the constraints that shape the decision-making process, but not to the decisions themselves. This is consistent with the Pure Proceduralist idea that decisions are legitimate as long as they are the outcome of an appropriately constrained decision-making process.

Which interpretation of Rawls's idea of public reason should we adopt? Should we adopt the substantive interpretation, which fits Rational Proceduralism, or the procedural interpretation, which fits Pure Proceduralism? In my view, the confusion about Rawls's idea of public reason is a consequence of his failure to distinguish clearly between these two categories of conceptions of legitimacy and their implications for the role of public reason. It seems clear to me that even though the textual evidence I have cited supports both, Rawls's conception of legitimacy has to be Pure Proceduralist and cannot be a version of Rational Proceduralism. First, if he did indeed advocate Rational Proceduralism, his "Reply to Habermas" would not make sense. When Rawls insists on how the limited domain of his project distinguishes it from Juergen Habermas's project, he is not just insisting on a difference in degree, but on a difference in kind. For Habermas, the question is which course of action people can rationally justify to each other (under ideal circumstances). For Rawls, the question is how we can justify anything to each other, given reasonable pluralism. This is why he insists on the priority of the basic structure, and focuses, in his conception of legitimacy, on the justification of constitutional essentials and not on the justification of specific legislative decisions.

Second, and more importantly, the procedural interpretation is consistent with what Rawls has to say on public justification. Rawls introduces the idea of public justification for the case where legitimacy (or justice) is contested.[7] Public justification is another fundamental idea in Rawls's theory of justice as fairness. Rawls distinguishes three levels of publicity (1993: 66ff.). First, the principles of justice are publicly known and known to be effective. Everybody knows and accepts these principles and knows that everybody else does so too and that the basic structure is ruled and known to be ruled by these principles. Second, the general facts and beliefs from which the principles are derived are known and accepted. And, third, the full justification of the conception of justice is accessible. Political conceptions of justice are public in this full sense. This means that the coercive effects of the institutions of the basic structure can be publicly justified and are mutually acceptable to free and equal citizens.[8] The citizens recognize that they impose this power on themselves to regulate the fair terms of cooperation among them.

Rawls understands public justification as aiming at consensus: "Public justification is not . . . simply valid argument from given premises (though of course it is that). . . . [W]hen the premises and conclusions are not acceptable on due reflection to all parties in disagreement, valid argument falls short of public justification" (2001: 27). If there is disagreement in the course of the deliberative process about the legitimacy of a particular decision, appeal to shared fundamental values on which the political conception of justice rests helps to resolve conflicting questions. Note that by insisting on consensus and the collective endorsement of both the set of premises and their conclusions, this idea avoids the discursive dilemma (cf. 4.2.c. and 6.2.). It does so at the price of setting a very high standard for public justification, however. As a result, this makes the substantive interpretation of Rawls's idea of public reason very implausible. The substantive interpretation would entail the unrealistic hope that when there is disagreement, public reason can somehow miraculously produce an extended consensus that covers previously contested substantive ground. In the Rational Proceduralist view, controversies over the legitimacy of a decision have to be settled with regard to the content of public reason. In the Pure Proceduralist view and its procedural interpretation of public reason, public reason is invoked to appeal to the shared basis offered by the political values that constrain the democratic process. In this view, the question to be answered is not whether a particular decision can be supported by substantive reasons everyone can accept, but whether the decision came about through a process that everyone has reason to accept as legitimacy-generating. The procedural interpretation thus entails a more modest reading of Rawls's idea of public justification. In this view, public justification can only cover a limited domain. But it can help settle controversies about the legitimacy of particular decisions by referring the debate to the existing common ground on procedural considerations. Because Rawls defines the public political culture as the realm of reasonable conceptions of the good, there is, in this realm, always a possibility to appeal to a shared basis. While all sorts of reasons might be exchanged in the course of the deliberative process, when there is a conflict about whether a particular decision is legitimate, then public reason can be invoked and settle the question.

As I have explained it in Chapter 5, the shared basis in fundamental political values may be fairly thin, and not altogether immune to challenge. Over time, the deliberative process may produce questions about the best interpretation and implementation of the fundamental political values. This need not blur the distinction between Pure Proceduralist and Rational Proceduralist conception of legitimacy, however. Even if the justification of the constraints that should shape the decision-making process is occasionally itself called into question, the idea that there is a hierarchy, a lexicographic ordering, between the justification of these constraints, and the evaluation of alternative options in the course of a deliberative process that is shaped by certain constraints, is still plausible.

Reading Rawls as advocating a Pure Proceduralist conception of democratic legitimacy and the associated procedural interpretation of public reason not only presents a consistent account of the Rawlsian project, it also offers reply to those who have rejected the Rawlsian approach to deliberative democracy because it relies on the possibility of a consensus based on fundamental political values (cf. 4.1.b.). Insofar as these critics address their objection to the substantive interpretation of Rawls's idea of public reason, and to a Rational Proceduralist conception of legitimacy, I agree with them. But these critics have failed to consider the procedural interpretation of Rawls's idea of public reason and the possibility of a Pure Proceduralist conception of legitimacy. In addition, they tend to downplay the fact that any (non-instrumentalist) conception of democratic legitimacy makes reference to some ideals about the democratic decision-making process or about what it means be a participant in this process. In the terminology that I have used here, they make reference to some ideals of political equality, some idea of citizenship, and thus rely on the possibility of appealing to a shared basis. Chantal Mouffe (2000, 2006), for example, who in the recent debate has perhaps been one of the harshest critics of the Rawlsian approach and who has argued in favor of a more radically democratic approach instead, has to acknowledge that her "agonistic model of democracy" needs to put "some limits . . . to the kind of confrontation which is going to be seen as legitimate in the public sphere" (Mouffe 2000: 93). This is perfectly consistent with a Pure Proceduralist conception of democratic legitimacy as it does not deny that even if there is deep contestation on substantive matters, legitimacy demands that the decision-making process is appropriately constrained. Inevitably, there has to be some justification for these constraints, for otherwise the participants will not accept them as binding. Conversely, Pure Proceduralism does not demand that the justification of the constraints of the decision-making process extends to the justification of the decisions. To insist on the need for common ground when it comes to the justification of the constraints that ought to shape the decision-making process is thus perfectly compatible with a view of the process of public deliberation that is marked by disagreements, and in fact grows out of the recognition of the inevitable persistence of such disagreements.[9] These objections thus miss what I consider the most plausible reading of the Rawlsian project. Insofar as they have a target at all, it is probably the Rational Proceduralist conceptions of democratic legitimacy that dominate the current literature and perhaps some residues of Rational Proceduralism that linger in Rawls's own writings. It is to the Rational Proceduralist idea of political justification that I want to turn now.

6.2. DEMOCRATIC LEGITIMACY WITHOUT COLLECTIVE RATIONALITY

Rational Proceduralism is a prominent interpretation of the demands of democratic legitimacy. Much recent writing on the philosophy of democracy has either explicitly or implicitly assumed that the rationality of democratic decisions is an important feature of their legitimacy. Rationality can mean many things, of course, and different theories of democracy postulate different rationality requirements for legitimacy. Arrow, for example, claims that it is necessary for democratic legitimacy to demand that social preferences be rational in light of possible Condorcet cycles (2.1.a.). And Pettit argues in response to the discursive dilemma that the possibility of a conflict between the collective evaluation of an outcome and the collective evaluation of an independent set of premises that is logically connected to that outcome makes it necessary for legitimacy that democratic decisions satisfy rationality requirements that ensure consistency between the evaluation of the premises and the evaluation of the outcomes (4.2.c.). Against these authors, I shall argue here that the rationality requirements they want to impose are not necessary for democratic legitimacy.

What is at stake can be phrased in terms of the distinction between Rational and Pure Proceduralism (Chapter 4). I want to argue against the prominent versions of Aggregative and Deliberative Rational Proceduralism that have been put forward by Arrow and Pettit. My motivation for doing this is to add to the case for the Pure Proceduralist conception of democratic legitimacy that I want to defend in this book. By arguing against the versions of Rational Proceduralism propagated by Arrow and Pettit, I want to show that democratic legitimacy can be conceptualized without the rationality requirements that these authors think are necessary, and add plausibility to the view that inconsistencies of the decisions made need not undermine legitimacy.

6.2.a. Rational Proceduralism and Collective Rationality

The issue I want to raise here is analogous to the one raised in the recent debate on the normativity of rationality in moral philosophy. In this debate, a distinction is drawn between the normativity of reasons and the normativity of rationality (e.g. Broome 1999, 2005). According to a widely held view, what one ought to do or to believe depends on reasons. Beyond that, there is also the view that there is normativity in rationality—that one ought to do or believe what rationality requires one to do or to believe. This second view is currently under scrutiny. Are the requirements of rationality independently normative, or is there only the normativity of reasons?

Niko Kolodny, an important contributor to the debate, has argued that the normativity of rationality, which many just take for granted, is only apparent. He interprets the normativity of reasons as referring to a relationship between facts and attitudes. Rationality, by contrast, which he characterizes through a minimal coherence requirement, refers to "relations among a person's attitudes, viewed in abstraction from the reasons for them" (2005: 509). He grants that rationality captures intuitions about what one has reasons to do or to believe, but argues that these intuitions can be explained solely in terms of these reasons and without invoking a rationality requirement. If this is correct, it follows that requirements of rationality do not bind by themselves; only the underlying reasons bind.

Other contributors to this debate take a more moderate view, and explore the possibility that the normativity of rationality requirements is of a different kind than the normativity of reasons. According to John Broome (1999), requirements of rationality have normativity qua the logical relation they impose on reasoning, but this normativity is not one of reasons. In his interpretation, the normativity of rationality is expressed conditionally. In the case of instrumental rationality, Broome characterizes it as follows: "intending an end normatively requires you to intend what you believe to be a necessary means" (Broome 1999: 89). One can accept this normativity of rationality, but respond, not by intending the means, but by stopping to intend the end. The normativity of rationality thus "does not give you a reason to intend what you believe to be a necessary means" (ibid.).

Both Broome and Kolodny argue, in different ways, that it is not the case that requirements of rationality necessarily generate binding reasons. While I cannot retrace this debate here, I want to defend a similar point in relation to the bindingness of democratic legitimacy. Legitimacy is the concept that encapsulates the normativity of democratic decisions—it is the answer to the question of why, and under what conditions, democratic decisions ought to be respected. If a democratic decision is legitimate, one ought to accept the decision and act accordingly—when action is required. If a decision is illegitimate, it does not have this binding force. The normativity in question is clearly one of reasons: if a decision is legitimate, something must be the case that generates a reason to respect that decision. Many seem to assume that only democratic decisions that are, in some way, rational can be legitimate. The thought must be, roughly, that if a decision fails to satisfy requirements of rationality, the bindingness of legitimacy is jeopardized. On this view, only a rational decision can stand a chance of being a legitimate decision.

But is it really the case that, as a democratic collective, our decisions ought to satisfy some requirements of collective rationality? Does the binding force of legitimate decisions hinge on whether these decisions satisfy requirements of rationality? I want to argue here that this is not so. In light of the distinction between reasons and rationality, it is possible to see that this does not entail a denial that legitimate decisions generate reasons. It is only to deny that there is independent normative force in the fact that collective decisions satisfy some conditions of consistency.

A case for why satisfying requirements of collective rationality is necessary for democratic legitimacy depends, of course, on how one conceives of these rationality requirements. In this section I shall explore the arguments in favor of the consistency-based views that have been prominently put forward by Arrow and Pettit. Pettit's response to the discursive dilemma is similar to Arrow's response to the voting paradox in that both interpret the problems they discuss as showing that majoritarian endorsement cannot be sufficient for democratic legitimacy and argue that it is necessary that democratic decisions satisfy a collective rationality requirement. I shall argue that, contrary to what these authors claim, the rationality requirements that they impose are not necessary for democratic legitimacy, or at least that they have failed to show why they would be.[10]

Let me start with Arrow. In Arrow's framework, as discussed in Chapter 2, individual and social preference orderings have to satisfy the axioms of completeness and transitivity. In addition, there is also a condition stating that the alternative chosen is ranked as at least as good as any other alternative available—a maximizing condition (cf. 2.1.a.). The impossibility theorem shows that collective rationality is not easy to secure. The four normative conditions that Arrow also wants to impose on democratic decision-making clash with the requirement of collective rationality. Vice versa, rational social preferences can be obtained only if at least one of the four normative conditions on social welfare functions is dropped.

I do not want to argue that weakening the rationality conditions would offer a way out of the impossibility result. This strategy has been examined in great detail and already proved to be defective—one can obtain impossibility results even if the rationality conditions are maximally weakened (cf. Sen 1993b). My question is why the impossibility of achieving collective rationality is often seen as a problem in the first place. To put it in Arrow's own words, the question is why he thought it was a problem that his impossibility theorem demonstrates that "the doctrine of voters' sovereignty is incompatible with that of collective rationality" (1963: 60).

How does Arrow defend the requirement that the democratic evaluation of alternative policies needs to be based on a social preference ordering that satisfies the same axioms of rationality that economists typically impose on individual preferences? Arrow does not provide much argument for why the rationality of social preferences matters, which may be seen as an indication of how much he takes it for granted that rationality plays an important role in normative theories of democracy and in conceptions of democratic legitimacy. I want to argue here that imposing these conditions lacks warrant.

The most important reason that Arrow gives for imposing these requirements of collective rationality is in relation to what he calls the paradox of voting, which I discussed in Chapter 2. In the paradox of voting, the cyclic pattern in pairwise majority decisions implies that for each of the alternatives in question, there is a majority favoring it in pairwise comparisons. In the presence of cycles, there is a clash between different possible majority verdicts, which implies that any particular decision is arbitrary, as an alternative majority could be found. In addition, it implies that the decision is dependent on the order in which the alternatives were presented, and that democratic decision-making is thus vulnerable to manipulation: whoever has agenda-setting power can influence the outcome of the decision-making process.[11] Arrow sought to avoid these problems by making requirements of rationality a necessary element of democratic legitimacy. He asks (1963: 3): "Can we find . . . methods of aggregating individual tastes which imply rational behavior on the part of the community and which will be satisfactory in other ways?"

Towards the end of his short book, Arrow gives two further reasons why the rationality of social preferences matters. The first reason is that it eliminates path-dependency. Transitivity, he notes, ensures "independence of the final choice from the path to it. . .; from any environment, there will be a chosen alternative, and, in the absence of a deadlock, no place for the historically given alternative to be chosen by default" (Arrow 1963: 120). Path-dependency is thus judged negatively, as undermining legitimacy, and demanding that social preferences be transitive is a way to avoid it. The second reason is precisely to avoid deadlock, or "democratic paralysis," "a failure to act due not to a desire for inaction but an inability to agree on the proper action" (1963: 120). The combination of completeness and transitivity ensures that the collective decision-making mechanism will identify a best alternative in all situations, or at least a set of best alternatives, among which the collective is indifferent.[12]

I shall discuss these reasons for imposing requirements of collective rationality on social preferences in the next section. First I want to describe Pettit's argument for why the outcomes of democratic decision-making need to satisfy requirements of collective rationality. The argument is based on the discursive dilemma and refers to the context of deliberative democracy. This dilemma, which I have introduced in Chapter 4, captures a conflict between, on the one hand, the conclusion supported by the majoritarian evaluation of the premises and, on the other hand, the majoritarian evaluation of the conclusion. Depending on which decision-making procedure is chosen—the "premise-based" procedure or the "conclusion-based" procedure—the collective will come to a different view of what ought to be done.

In response to the discursive dilemma, Pettit (2003: 175ff.) argues the following. First, he notes that the history of past judgments will inevitably confront a collective with instances of the discursive dilemma and that this constrains democratic decision-making. It is to be expected that arguments for particular policy proposals will involve premises that have been the topic of past democratic evaluations. According to Pettit, this history constrains the judgments that the collective "ought to make in various new cases," as "only one particular judgment in this or that case will be consistent . . . with the past judgments" (Pettit 2003: 176). Secondly, Pettit takes it that a key feature of deliberative democracy is that it enables contestation and ensures that those acting on the collective's behalf are answerable to reason or, as he also calls it, "conversable" (Pettit 2001: 280ff.). In the ongoing deliberative process, decisions under consideration will be linked to commitments made earlier, and the tensions created by instances of the discursive dilemma raise questions for public deliberation. In his view, "every purposive group is bound to try to collectivize reason, achieving and acting on collective judgments that pass reason-related tests like consistency" (Pettit 2003: 177). As a result, a deliberative collective faces pressure to collectivize reason. Finally, Pettit argues, only the premise-based procedure will ensure that the collective is answerable to reason. Consistency can, of course, also be achieved with the conclusion-based procedure, by holding on to a particular decision and revising past judgments on some of the premises to which the decision is connected. But, Pettit argues, questioning past commitments each time when there is a clash would undermine the process of public deliberation. He thus thinks that the deliberative public "must avoid automatic recourse to the revision of past commitments; it must show that those commitments are sufficiently robust for us to be able to expect that the group will frequently be guided by them in its future judgments" (Pettit 2003: 177). Only the premise-based procedure can achieve that.

Pettit, like Arrow, interprets rationality as a form of consistency in the choices the democratic collective makes. The notion of collective rationality Pettit invokes combines a completeness requirement—there must be a judgment on all propositions—with two further requirements. The first, "consistency," demands that it is never the case that both a particular proposition and its negation are accepted. The second, "deductive closure," demands that the logical consequences of a proposition that is accepted are also accepted.[13]

6.2.b. Why be Rational?

What is the role Arrow and Pettit ascribe to such consistency-based collective rationality requirements? There are, in principle, two possibilities. According to the first, satisfying a rationality requirement is constitutive of the normative force of legitimate decisions. According to this view, because we ought to be rational, a legitimate decision—one we ought to respect—is one that is required by rationality; a decision that fails to satisfy a rationality requirement cannot be a decision that we ought to respect. Arguments for this view would have to build on the premise that rationality is normative—that we ought to do what rationality requires. Based on that, they would have to show that only rational collective decisions can bind and that they bind qua their rationality.

According to a second view, satisfying certain rationality requirements is instrumentally necessary for legitimacy: irrational decisions undermine other values seen as necessary for legitimacy and rational decisions safeguard the reasons for which we ought to respect a decision. According to this view, a legitimate decision—one we ought to respect—will be a rational decision. This second view is weaker than the first because it does not claim that legitimate decisions bind qua their rationality. It brackets the issue of what accounts for the binding force of legitimate decisions and merely claims that rationality is necessary for legitimate (and therefore binding) decisions.

The question to be discussed here is whether Arrow and Pettit succeed in justifying the rationality requirements they want to impose. My goal here is to argue that Arrow and Pettit do not succeed in defending either view and therefore fail to show that collective rationality is necessary for democratic legitimacy.

If I read him correctly, Pettit seems to be defending a variant of the first view—that a decision that fails to satisfy a rationality requirement cannot be a decision that we have reasons to respect. Pettit, as summarized above, offers a republican argument for the collective's need to form a consistent set of judgments. This links the legitimizing force of being answerable to reason to satisfying requirements of collective rationality. Pettit does not, however, have much to say on the link between rationality and normativity, it seems to me. None of the points he makes about the need for requirements of collective rationality addresses this issue. He seems to take it as given that the binding force of legitimate decisions is at least partly due to their satisfying some rationality requirements— that we ought to be rational—and does not provide an argument for why this is the case. As I mentioned it earlier, there is now a literature emerging that questions the independent normativity of requirements of individual rationality, interpreted as relations of consistency among the attitudes of an individual. Even if there is a successful argument to show that individual rationality requirements can independently generate an ought, it would take a further step to show that requirements of collective rationality, interpreted as relations of consistency among the decisions of a collective, can independently generate a binding reason. Pettit relies heavily on the possibility of showing this, as he prioritizes the normativity of collective rationality over the normativity of a majoritarian decision-making process. I am skeptical about the possibility for showing this, but developing an account of what explains the normativity of democratic legitimacy would be beyond the scope of this book and will have to be addressed elsewhere.

If we leave this fundamental point aside, there is the question whether Pettit's own actual argument is a plausible defense of the link between rationality and legitimacy. I do not think so. His argument rests on the legitimizing force of being answerable to reason. Christian List summarizes Pettit's view in the following way:

> [I]t is (often) necessary for democratic legitimacy to supplement collective decisions on actions or policies with supporting reasons. These reasons should themselves be collectively decided and publicly defensible. On this account, it is not enough for the legitimacy of an action or policy that the majority endorses this action or policy.

Such majority endorsement might stem from a spontaneous majority passion or lack any reasoned justification. (List 2006: 365)

It is correct, of course, that it must be possible to give reasons that one ought to respect a democratic decision for it to be legitimate. But it is not clear that the rationality requirements that Pettit wants to impose on the outcomes of collective decision-making are necessary to achieve that. Take the example of the communal center introduced earlier. In Pettit's view, the final decision, to be legitimate, has to be supported by the collective evaluation of the two criteria—that there is sufficient need in the community and that the site is appropriate. In this view, "answerability to reason" is thus interpreted substantively: it demands that the decision taken has to be supportable by the substantive considerations on which it depends. The rationality requirements, combined with the requirement to adopt the premise-based procedure, capture this interpretation of "answerability to reason." In this view, for a decision to build the center to be legitimate, it has to be the case that the collective has, as a collective, judged that there is sufficient need and that the site is appropriate. The legitimate collective decision is the one that is consistent with the collective evaluation of the premises.

But this is not the only way in which "answerability to reason" can be interpreted. An alternative interpretation is the one endorsed in Pure Proceduralist conceptions of democratic legitimacy. As defined above, Pure Proceduralist conceptions only impose some conditions of political fairness on the democratic process and refrain from imposing conditions that refer to the quality of outcomes. The reasons that determine the legitimacy of a decision are thus procedural ones—they cite features of the democratic decision-making process. As such, they will not invoke conditions that refer to consistency among the decisions themselves in the way in which the rationality requirements Pettit wants to impose would demand. In the example of the communal center, the reasons that would determine the legitimacy of a particular decision would be those that refer to the process. An illegitimate decision is one that has been reached in a decision-making process that does not satisfy the conditions that are seen as necessary for legitimacy.

This alternative Pure Proceduralist interpretation of the "answerability to reason" condition does not invoke features of the quality of the outcomes of the decision-making process, not even rationality requirements. In Pettit's argument, as well as in List's summary of it, there is an assumption that a decision that is legitimate in the sense that it is supported by reasons must be one that is supported by substantive reasons. But procedural reasons, surely, can be "publicly defensible" reasons. In fact, as I have argued in the case of Rawls's idea of public reason (6.1.b.), procedural reasons are much more likely to be publicly defensible than reasons that refer to the substantive content of a decision. It will be easier to agree on the principles that should regulate the "constitutional essentials," to use the Rawlsian term, which specify the decision-making process, than to agree on the goodness of alternative policies. Procedural reasons thus seem better candidates for determining the legitimacy of democratic decisions than reasons that refer to the substantive quality of outcomes.

In addition, because Pure Proceduralism is only backwards-looking—towards the process that generated a particular decision—it does not run into the kind of problem with honoring past commitments that affects Pettit's Rational Proceduralist conception. Pettit's argument for why it is important to satisfy collective rationality requirements thus proposes a solution for a problem that only arises if one has already accepted the normativity of collective rationality. Because his argument is circular, Pettit has failed to show that collective rationality is necessary for legitimacy.

Arrow's arguments for the need to satisfy requirements of collective rationality tend to be of the instrumental variant. Arrow, as we saw, invokes rationality to avoid manipulable cycles in the pattern of majority voting, as well as arbitrary path-dependencies and indecision. From the perspective of a Pure Proceduralist interpretation of deliberative democracy and its associated conception of justification, Arrow's concerns can be met without invoking his rationality requirements.

Let me start with the argument from manipulation. I certainly agree that it is plausible to demand that absence of manipulation is necessary for democratic legitimacy. The thought must be that the possibility to rig the outcome of democratic decision-making undermines the legitimacy. That seems correct. But if a decision has come about as a result of a manipulation, does that not by itself constitute a reason for doubting the legitimacy of the decision? What would demanding consistency of the social preference ordering add? It can be answered that demanding consistency may help eliminate the possibility of manipulation. While this is true, this does not make satisfying the rationality requirement, by itself, a criterion for legitimacy. If absence of manipulation is a necessary condition, then a decision made in a decision-making process that satisfies this condition is legitimate (provided all other necessary conditions are satisfied), even if it is irrational in the sense that it violates some condition of consistency.

What about the charge that in the presence of cycles, decisions may be arbitrary? This worry is also linked to Arrow's second argument for imposing requirements of collective rationality, which is that they ensure that the reasons for choosing an alternative are not path-dependent, but reside in how the alternative chosen compares to all other alternatives. Presumably, the worry is that with path-dependency, the choice is made on the basis of reasons that should not influence the decision. Arrow's own example is a status-quo bias. Again, the question is whether this is a sufficient argument for imposing requirements of collective rationality. I do not think it is. First, there is the question whether path-dependencies are such a terrible thing. Let me grant that it makes sense to demand that legitimate decisions do not suffer from arbitrary biases, such as a status-quo bias. But while it is true that complete, transitive social preferences rule out path-dependencies, this only proves that collective rationality is sufficient, not that collective rationality is necessary. Like in the case of manipulation, if what is at stake can be covered by procedural criteria, then it is not necessary that the outcomes satisfy requirements of collective rationality. An arbitrary status quo bias occurs, I contend, if the democratic process is such that the preferences of those who prefer the status quo to an alternative arrangement receive undue weight—for example, because they succeed in politically marginalizing those who would prefer, with good reasons, an alternative arrangement. The procedural solution to this problem is to demand that the democratic process allows for a fair hearing of all concerns and that there is fair uptake of criticisms of existing arrangements and objections to arguments that support them (cf. Chapter 7). The irrationality of particular decisions may, again, be taken as an indicator that there are issues that need further deliberation, or of problems with the fairness of the decision-making process, but it need not, by itself, undermine legitimacy.

Arrow's last argument—from the need to avoid indecision—targets not the full set of rationality requirements, but only the completeness condition. This condition demands that the social preference ordering is defined for any pair of alternatives. Its rationale is that the collective ought to be able to make a choice in any given situation. It is not clear to me that this is indeed a requirement of democratic legitimacy. If there is indecision, extending deliberation may be the better response if the concern is with the legitimacy of the final decision. But even if it were a condition of legitimacy, it could very easily be interpreted procedurally, to require that the democratic decision-making process have mechanisms that bring the process to a close—at least to a temporary one. There is no need to cast this criterion with reference to a rational social preference ordering. In this procedural view, it is sufficient that the process generates a decision—any decision.

In sum, none of the arguments that Pettit and Arrow provide show that legitimate democratic decisions need to satisfy consistency-based requirements of collective rationality. There is at least the possibility of a Pure Proceduralist response to each of the issues they raise and to each of the concerns they address in the attempt to defend their respective version of Rational Proceduralism.

7   Epistemic Democracy

Let me briefly take stock of what has, hopefully, been achieved so far. In Chapters 2 and 3, I have rejected the aggregative account of democracy and defended the deliberative account. In Chapters 4–6, I have addressed the question of how democratic legitimacy should be interpreted, focusing on the distinction between Rational and Pure Proceduralist conceptions of democratic legitimacy. I have argued against Rational Deliberative Proceduralism, but I have not done so by embracing Pure Deliberative Proceduralism. The reason for that is that I believe that it does not have a satisfactory solution to the problem that the political egalitarian's dilemma, described in Chapter 5, poses. In this final chapter, I shall develop and defend an alternative Pure Proceduralist conception of democratic legitimacy. I shall first introduce an additional account of democracy—epistemic democracy. Put very generally, in the epistemic interpretation, democratic decision-making processes are valued at least in part for their knowledge-producing potential and defended in relation to this. There are different versions of the epistemic account of democracy. Some rest on aggregative democracy while others rest on deliberative democracy. In addition, they draw on different epistemologies. Arguments in support of an epistemic account of democracy depend, of course, on how epistemic democracy is characterized and what the underlying epistemology is. Many assume that the epistemic dimension refers to a procedure-independent standard for the correctness of the outcomes of the democratic decision-making process. The commonly held view is that it furthers legitimacy if there is some way in which democratic decision-making can track outcomes that are "truly" in the best interest or "truly" just. This leads to conceptions of legitimacy of the category of Rational Epistemic Proceduralism. I shall argue against this view. I shall develop a Pure Proceduralist conception of democratic legitimacy that works for epistemic democracy and defend it against Rational Epistemic Proceduralism.

7.1. THE EPISTEMOLOGY OF DEMOCRACY

7.1.a. The Standard Account of Epistemic Democracy

One interpretation of epistemic democracy has been particularly influential; I shall call this the "standard account of epistemic democracy." Christian

List and Robert Goodin (2001: 277) give the following brief but representative characterization:

> For epistemic democrats, the aim of democracy is to 'track the truth.' For them, democracy is more desirable than alternative forms of decision-making because, and insofar as, it does that. One democratic decision rule is more desirable than another according to that same standard, so far as epistemic democrats are concerned.

By the standard account I shall denote any characterization of epistemic democracy that centers on the truth-tracking potential of democratic decision-making processes, and in which truth refers to a procedure-independent standard of correctness. According to such accounts, there exists, independently of the actual decision-making process, a correct decision and the legitimacy of democratic decisions depends, at least in part, on the ability of the decision-making process to generate the correct outcome.

The particular epistemology that the standard account invokes is a social epistemology of the variant that Alvin Goldman has called a veritistic consequentialist epistemology. A veritistic epistemology "is concerned with the production of knowledge, where knowledge is . . . understood in the 'weak' sense of *true belief*" (1999: 5). As a consequentialist social epistemology, it is concerned with the effect of social practices and institutions on epistemic (veritistic) value, i.e. with how they promote or impede the acquisition of knowledge (Goldman 1999: 87).[1]

Let me go into some more detail. Joshua Cohen influentially characterized the standard account of epistemic democracy as a combination of the following three properties (1986: 34): (i) "an independent standard of correct decisions"; (ii) "a cognitive account of voting"; and (iii) "an account of decision-making as a process of the adjustment of beliefs." The first property is the assumption that there is a sense in which a particular decision is correct—truly just or representing the common good. It is characteristic of the standard account of epistemic democracy that what it treats as a correct outcome is logically independent of the decision-making process; it exists prior to and outside of the actual democratic process. The second property couples this account of what determines the quality of the outcomes with an account of voting behavior, or, more generally, of the input to the democratic process. According to the cognitive account, Cohen writes (1986: 34) "voting expresses beliefs about what the correct policies are . . ., not personal preferences for policies." The standard account of epistemic democracy replaces individual preferences about alternative policy proposals, and reasons supportive of particular ends and means, with individual beliefs about correct outcomes and reasons that support these beliefs. Democratic decision-making is thus not about the values people hold, but about their beliefs. The third property, finally, applies to the process of democratic decision-making. It demands that individuals adjust their beliefs about correct outcomes in light of the available evidence. As Cohen puts it, "the epistemic conception treats processes of decision making as, potentially, rational processes of the formation of common judgments" (1986: 34). In this perspective, insofar as the rationality of collective decision-making is invoked, it no longer refers to the rational pursuit of certain values, but to people's beliefs about the correctness of outcomes.

As I have characterized it, the standard account of epistemic democracy is compatible with both aggregative and deliberative democracy. The move from non-epistemic to epistemic aggregative democracy consists in a move from aggregating individual preferences about alternative social states to aggregating individual beliefs about them. The move from the standard interpretation of deliberative democracy to its epistemic variant, similarly, entails a shift in the account of what deliberation is conceived to be about. According to the standard account of epistemic deliberative democracy, people deliberate about which outcome is likely to be truly in the common interest, or truly just. This contrasts with the non-epistemic account of deliberative democracy, according to which people exchange reasons about the value of alternative outcomes.

A variant of epistemic democracy of the kind that fits Cohen's definition can be attributed to Jean-Jacques Rousseau (1763), and his concern with the distinction between private wills and the general will. In his account, the correct outcome of democratic decision-making is the one that represents the general will. The decision-making process is cast as one in which the participants express their beliefs about what the general will is. In the recent literature, the dominant interpretations of such an account of epistemic democracy invoke the Condorcet jury theorem (Black 1958; Grofman and Feld 1988; List and Goodin 2001). In its original formulation, the Condorcet jury theorem says that if there are two alternatives, and one of them is the correct outcome, and if each voter is more likely than not to be correct, then a majority is more likely to be correct than a single individual, and the probability that a majority will vote for the correct outcome increases with the size of the body of voters. If the size of the constituency approaches infinity, the probability that the majority will be correct reaches 1. This follows from the law of large numbers on which the Condorcet jury theorem rests. In its original formulation, the theorem works for two alternatives. But List and Goodin (2001) have recently extended the result to plurality voting among many options, thus showing that those objections to the relevance of the Condorcet jury theorem for epistemic democracy that rest on it only being applicable to the case of two options fail.[2]

In this first interpretation of epistemic democracy, the Condorcet jury theorem is at the core of a defense of democracy. The argument shows that, under certain conditions, the democratic aggregation of people's beliefs about the correct policy is likely to identify the correct outcome. As such, this constitutes a defense of aggregative epistemic democracy; it does not invoke deliberation. But a case for deliberative epistemic democracy can easily be constructed on the basis of the Condorcet jury theorem. It can be argued that public deliberation improves the formation of individual preferences by facilitating the exchange of reasons and information about the correct outcome. If this holds, it then follows in the context of the Condorcet jury theorem that, compared to majority voting without deliberation, deliberative decision-making has a higher probability that the correct outcome will be chosen (Estlund 1989; Waldron 1989).

The main problem with this defense of democracy is that there is no feedback loop (e.g. Estlund 1997, 2008; Goodin 2003; Anderson 2006). It does not explain why people who held a different view than the one adopted by the majority should change their minds once the outcome is known. The Bayesian interpretation of the standard account of epistemic democracy is sometimes seen as improving the interpretation based on the Condorcet jury theorem precisely because it addresses individual belief formation.[3] The Bayesian formula specifies a rationality requirement for individual belief formation. It tells individuals how to update their beliefs about the probability of a proposition being true when additional information is available. Applied to democratic decision-making, the Bayesian perspective tells individuals how they ought to make use of the information contained in how a majority votes, or in the reasons that find most support in public deliberation. As such, it attributes a different role to probabilistic calculations than is the case in the Condorcet jury theorem. As Goodin (2003: 111) puts it, "Condorcet tells us 'what is the probability that the majority will choose outcome K, given the fact that outcome K is the right outcome'," whereas "Bayes tells us 'what is the probability that outcome K is right, given the fact that the majority has chosen K'." By staying firmly in the realm of subjective beliefs, the Bayesian interpretation of epistemic democracy can supply the participants in democratic decision-making with reasons to defer to a majority verdict they initially disagreed with.

Many, including myself would argue, however, that the Bayesian perspective exaggerates the reasons the participants have to defer to a majority view.[4] The problem is that in this perspective, participants are too readily asked to accept a particular decision as correct. The account thus fails to make sense of the phenomenon of persisting opposition that tends to accompany majority decisions. The opposition that remains after a democratic decision has been made is often deep in the sense that it cannot simply be explained as an expression of error. Instead, the possibility needs to be acknowledged that it reflects differences in judgment that have their roots in a reasonable pluralism of values and an ingrained diversity of epistemic positions. It seems more plausible to characterize the deliberative process as having to come to terms with the implications of accepting what John Rawls calls the "burdens of judgment" (1993: 54ff.), as opposed to assuming that it strives towards an outcome that all are rationally required to endorse.

The problem that arises with the Bayesian perspective is a variant of a more general problem that those who attach value to truth-tracking need to grapple with. If respecting this pluralism and diversity is seen as essential to the ideal of democracy, it becomes important to avoid the potentially anti-democratic implications of emphasizing correctness. A simple, but probably not very compelling, epistemic account of social evaluation and policy choice would take correct outcomes as the goal, but not place any value on how these outcomes are chosen. Such an account would have no problems with an "epistocracy" (Estlund 1993, 1997, 2008)—the idea that there is a small group of experts that could determine the correct outcome. Epistemic democrats face the challenge of safeguarding themselves from such an account, and need to make room for the possibility of reasonable, persisting opposition. In Chapter 4, I presented two arguments against democratic instrumentalism. The first argument rejects democratic instrumentalism on the grounds that it fails to take individual agency seriously enough by assuming that there is an ideal outcome that can be identified without the participation of the individuals concerned. In an epistemic account of democracy, this issue gains new importance, especially in the standard account of epistemic democracy with its assumption of a correct outcome.

David Estlund is very aware that importing correctness into the philosophy of democracy is a difficult endeavor. He cautions: "The moral challenge for any epistemic conception of political authority . . . is to let truth be the guide without illegitimately privileging the opinions of any putative experts" (2008: 102).[5] His version of the standard account of epistemic democracy, which I regard as the most sophisticated one, assigns an important role to veritistic consequentialist epistemology in political justification, but seeks to minimize the anti-democratic implications of doing so. His proposal is best understood against the background of a distinction that is often made between an epistemic account of the value of democracy and a procedural account.[6] As explained before according to proceduralism, the legitimacy of a democratic decision depends, at least in part, on it being the outcome of an appropriately constrained decision-making process. Estlund (2008) objects, rightly, that such a dichotomy is misleading. One can be an epistemic democrat, in the sense of the standard account, and a proceduralist at the same time. What Estlund proposes is a more explicitly proceduralist interpretation of the standard account. He aims at "making truth safe for democracy" (Estlund 1993, 2008), by safeguarding the participants in democratic decision-making from having to surrender their judgment to some epistemic authority. The main argument he offers against epistocracy, the attempt to assign political authority to those with superior wisdom and expertise about what correct outcomes would be, starts from the claim that it would have to be possible to justify such authority at least to reasonable people. Since even reasonable people will disagree on who is and who is not an expert, however, such "invidious comparisons" (Estlund 2008: 36) will never be acceptable to all of them.[7] Epistocracy thus lacks legitimacy.

Estlund's proposal also rejects the instrumentalism of defenses of epistemic democracy that rest on the Condorcet jury theorem. Compared to the version of the standard account based on the Condorcet jury theorem, Estlund puts relatively more value on democratic procedures, and less on correctness. His interpretation of epistemic democracy highlights how alternative institutionalizations of the democratic process will differ in their truth-tracking potential, and he argues that the justification of a particular decision-making process should take this into account. In this interpretation, epistemic considerations thus figure as a selection device among alternative institutional arrangements of the democratic decision-making process. What distinguishes his account of epistemic democracy from its Condercetian and Bayesian counterparts is that he makes the democratic process the main object of the justificatory exercise, not the decisions made. His main question is not whether a decisions is correct, but which democratic decision-making processes are most likely to generate correct outcomes. If there is a choice among alternative democratic decision-making procedures with different truth-tracking potential, he argues that the one that best tracks correct outcomes should be implemented. He calls the conception of legitimacy that shapes this account "epistemic proceduralism"—in a deliberate attempt to bridge the alleged gap between epistemic and proceduralist accounts of the value of democracy.

Note that although Estlund seeks to de-emphasize correctness and to foreground the legitimizing force of procedures, his account does not abandon the idea that democratic procedures ought to track correct outcomes as they exist procedure-independently. According to him, the value of the democratic decision-making process depends, at least in part, on its ability to track the correct outcome. This is compatible with all three properties of the standard account of epistemic democracy, as identified by Cohen (1986). It assumes an independent standard of correct decisions (i), adopts a cognitive account of democratic decision-making (ii), and views deliberation as a process of adjusting beliefs (iii). To be sure, Estlund is at pains to emphasize the importance of procedural fairness and to minimize reliance on procedure-independent standards, but, true to Cohen's first property, his proposal nevertheless takes correctness to be a procedure-independent criterion for the quality of the outcomes of collective decision-making. As such, it is still a version of the standard account of epistemic democracy as I have defined it above.

What speaks for Estlund's account is that it is better able to respect individual agency than rival versions of the standard account of epistemic democracy (cf. my first argument against democratic instrumentalism). First, it attributes independent value to individual participation under conditions of fairness and thus places greater emphasis on fair procedures than the other versions. In addition, it respects individual agency by explicitly not requiring individuals to defer to a majority view when they believe that they have good reasons to hold a different view. While holding on to the assumption of the standard account of epistemic democracy that there is a correct outcome and that democratic decision-making processes differ in their truth-tracking potential, it honors the possibility of error in any judgment—even the judgment of a vast, well-informed majority—and refuses to ask individuals to surrender their own judgment to the outcome of a probabilistic calculation.

I agree with Estlund that it is important to insist on the independent importance of procedures even in an account of epistemic democracy. But while, for this reason, I regard his interpretation of the standard account of epistemic democracy as superior to the more instrumentalist ones, there is still a problem with his account. The problem is that while it treats democratic processes as having knowledge-producing potential, it does not have a convincing account for what the epistemic value is of sustained controversial democratic deliberation. In other words, Estlund's proposal, while relying on the constructive function of deliberative decision-making (cf. 4.1.c.), does not have a good account of this function. As such, it neglects what I have identified as the second tenet of the case for democratic proceduralism.

The problem I have in mind is that the legacy of the opposition between epistemic and procedural democracy that I have mentioned above still shows in his account. In his recent book, Estlund sets up a contrast between his epistemic proceduralism and "deep proceduralism" (2008: 29). Deep proceduralism, he writes, "never appeals to the existence of any procedure-independent standard for better or worse political decisions" (2008: 30). This, he argues, distinguishes it from his epistemic proceduralism, which relies on such standards. The distinction between epistemic and deep proceduralism relies on a sharp contrast between the value of procedural fairness and epistemic value. As he puts it in an early article, "procedural fairness . . . is not a cognitive process" (1997: 196). What this opposition between epistemic proceduralism and deep proceduralism fails to acknowledge is how the epistemic dimension may be rooted in a fair decision-making process. My goal is precisely to argue for a view of this sort. But several intermediate steps will be needed before I can get to that. First I want to show that the opposition between procedural values and epistemic values may not be as clear-cut as Estlund suggests.

All accounts of deliberative epistemic democracy take seriously the constructive function, and an argument for why epistemic democracy is preferable to non-epistemic accounts of deliberative democracy can be built on this: non-epistemic accounts of democracy have no real argument for why the exchange of reasons matters. But different accounts interpret it differently and Estlund's epistemic proceduralism tends to portray this constructive function too minimally. This shows in how he argues against Deliberative Proceduralist conceptions of democratic legitimacy. According to Estlund, defending deliberative democracy on grounds of the fairness of the procedures fails to render it plausible why delibera-tion is important in the first place: choosing an outcome randomly, e.g. by flipping a coin, could be just as fair (Estlund 1997: 178; 2008: 82ff.). If the objection is adapted to target Pure Aggregative Proceduralism, it is valid. But as an objection against Deliberative Proceduralist conceptions it is not, at least not in this strong form. The aim of deliberation does not reduce to selecting a particular outcome. It has importance also because of its contribution to how participants form their preferences, and to how the political agenda is determined. Many deliberative democrats tend to emphasize these features as part of the argument for why the specific fair-ness conditions that deliberative democracy imposes make it preferable to aggregative democracy.[8] But note that these features are part of the learning process that deliberative decision-making enables, that is, of the constructive function of democracy. Tossing a coin neglects this construc-tive function of deliberative democratic decision-making, and the strong version of Estlund's objection thus misfires.

This said, there is a weaker form of Estlund's objection that I think is valid. In its weaker form, the objection states that Deliberative Proce-duralism cannot account for the constructive function of deliberative deci-sion-making. In particular, such non-epistemic conceptions of democratic legitimacy do not have an account for how deliberative democracy contrib-utes to the discovery of flaws in existing policy proposals or of new policy proposals. But note that a variant of this weaker objection also applies to Estlund's version of epistemic proceduralism. Because he uses the epistemic argument only as a selection device, not as part of a defense of deliberative democratic decision-making, he dissociates the value of democratic pro-cedures from the value of this learning process. As such, it, too, neglects important aspects of the constructive function of democracy, and is thus vulnerable to a similar objection.

7.1.b. Deweyan Epistemic Democracy

Some have argued that John Dewey's account of epistemic democracy is preferable to the standard account for precisely the reason that it is better able to explain the learning process inherent in deliberative decision-mak-ing and the epistemic value of persisting disagreement. Elizabeth Ander-son, for example, has recently argued that the main advantage of Deweyan epistemic democracy compared to the standard account is "that it allows us to represent dissent, even after a decision has been made, as epistemically productive, not merely as a matter of error" (2006: 9). Such dissent alerts to deficiencies in a chosen policy, and can prompt a new search for better policies. The claim she defends in her article is that "John Dewey's experi-mentalist account of democracy offers a better model of the epistemology of democracy than alternatives"—and better than the standard account with its foundation in veritistic social epistemology in particular.[9]

I agree that insofar as a Deweyan account of epistemic democracy has a better explanation of the constructive function of deliberative decision-making than the standard account, this provides an argument for it. I want to explore here how pragmatist social epistemology deals with the constructive function of deliberative democracy. As we shall see, while I am sympathetic to defenses of Deweyan epistemic democracy based on how he accounts for the epistemic value of democratic deliberation, I think that a Deweyan account runs into a problem of its own. The problem is one that does not arise in Estlund's epistemic proceduralism, and this suggests that there is need for a third alternative. But let me first explore in some more detail what exactly the Deweyan epistemological defense of democracy entails and then discuss its merits and flaws.

In contrast to the standard account of epistemic democracy, Dewey's epistemology is not veritistic. In his view, epistemic value cannot be reduced to knowing things as they are, and as they exist independently of our inquiry into them. Dewey dismisses what he called the "spectator theory of knowledge," which conceives of knowledge as being about fixed objects that exist independently of the subject and that the subject observes, as if seeing them in a mirror. He thus rejects the veritistic epistemology on which the standard account of epistemic democracy is based. Instead, he conceives of knowledge, and of the process of inquiry, as oriented towards solving problems that affect people's lives.

Central to his epistemology is the process of inquiry, as modeled on the methods of experimental science. In *The Public and its Problems* (1927: 163) Dewey writes:

> The layman takes certain conclusions which get into circulation to be science. But the scientific inquirer knows that they constitute science only in connection with the methods by which they are reached. Even when true, they are not science by virtue of their correctness, but by reason of the apparatus which is employed in reaching them.

He trusts the process of scientific inquiry to contribute to "increasing knowledge of things as they are" (1939: 3). But, in contrast to veritistic epistemology, he does not place value on achieving correctness as such. In his view, in line with the pragmatist tradition, the isolated pursuit of inquiry into things as they are may have negative consequences. Instead, it is the sustained attempt to improve people's living conditions through experimental interaction with the—natural and social—environment that he sees as the aim of the process of inquiry. According to Dewey, "[s]cience is converted into knowledge in its honorable and emphatic sense *only* in application" (1927: 174, his emphasis), and by application he means "recognized bearing upon human experience and well-being" (ibid.).

Dewey explicitly applied his epistemology to the theory of democracy, rejecting any principled distinction between scientific inquiry and inquiry in other spheres. According to him (1939: 4):

> Democracy as compared with other ways of life is the sole way of living which believes wholeheartedly in the process of experience as end and as means; as that which is capable of generating the science which is the sole dependable authority for the direction of further experience . . . For every way of life that fails in its democracy limits the contacts, the exchanges, the communications, the interactions by which experience is steadied while it is also enlarged and enriched.

In this account, free, open, and sustained social inquiry is part and parcel of effective problem solving. Knowledge, in Dewey's sense, does not exist in single individuals' minds, nor in small groups. Only when inquiry is conducted in such a way that all can take part and contribute to the attempt to solve common problems and test proposed solutions is knowledge its product.[10] (Deliberative) democracy is the form of life that enables this inquiry, and thus that enables effective problem solving. In contrast to forms of association that try to constrain social inquiry and the collective engagement with its results, democracy enables the formation of judgments about what ought to be done.[11] This, roughly, is Dewey's epistemic defense of democracy.

What I regard as the most attractive part of Dewey's account is how it attributes epistemic value to democratic participation. Note that—as a result of this insistence on the need for democratic participation—Dewey firmly rejects the naïve instrumentalist view that I have discussed earlier (4.1.c.). He has the following to say about those who attempt to further the common good without participation of those who are supposed to benefit:

> There is a moral tragedy inherent in efforts to further the common good which prevent the result from being either good or common—not good, because it is at the expense of the active growth of those to be helped, and not common because these have no share in bringing the result about. The social welfare can be advanced only by means which enlist the positive interest and active energy of those to be benefitted or 'improved'. . . . [W]ithout active cooperation both in forming aims and in carrying them out there is no possibility of a common good.[12]

Dewey, like other epistemic democrats, rejects the idea of an "epistocracy"—he refuses to trust a small group of experts with bringing about a good outcome and insists on the importance of democratic participation. But he attributes a different value to participation than versions of the standard account of epistemic democracy. For Dewey, democratic participation has epistemic value, but not simply in relation to its contribution to the discovery of an independently existing correct outcome. For Dewey, as we just saw, people's participation in the evaluation and testing of the results of social inquiry is necessary for the results to count as knowledge. Participation is an essential requirement in the effective solution of social problems; without participation there is no collective experimentation and hence no knowledge. Dewey's epistemic defense of democracy thus supports the ideal of democratic inclusion on epistemic grounds. For social inquiry to yield good results, it has to be open to the diversity of people's perspectives and experiences.

Dewey's insight into the epistemic value of democratic participation sheds light on what is missing in Estlund's account of epistemic democracy. Of course, Estlund's account supports including a diversity of perspectives and experiences insofar as this increases veritistic value. As he stresses, "thinking together" is likely to improve the outcome of collective decision-making, as "[m]ore minds will tend to bring more relevant reasons into play, and this (other things equal) has epistemic value" (Estlund 2008: 181). Such benefits of deliberation are one consideration that will influence which democratic process counts as the best truth-tracker. Unlike Dewey, however, he does not have an argument for why including a diversity of perspectives and experiences is part of what confers epistemic value on the outcome. The same applies to the interpretation of the standard account based on the Condorcet jury theorem. All that this account requires is that there are sufficient numbers of participants that are all more likely than not to identify a correct outcome. On both versions of the standard account, the value of including a diversity of perspectives and experiences is not an end, as in Dewey's account, but only a means towards veritistic value. Dewey's experimentalism has a more explicitly procedural account, in which sustained and controversial deliberation is constitutive of the epistemic value of the outcomes; it being the result of such a process is part of what it means for the outcome to be correct. Because the standard account fails to incorporate this value of epistemic diversity, it can only offer a relatively thin description of the constructive function of deliberative democratic decision-making.

How the Deweyan epistemic defense of democracy can make sense of the constructive function of deliberative democratic decision-making constitutes its main advantage over the standard account. Anderson (2006) is right to stress how Dewey's insistence on sustained, free, and open inquiry enables his account not just to accommodate persisting disagreement, but to attribute positive epistemic value to it. But should we thus abandon the standard account and replace it by a Deweyan account of epistemic democracy? I do not think so. The reason is that Dewey's epistemology is affected by a problem of its own—one that Estlund's account of epistemic democracy has a better handle on. Dewey's epistemology presupposes a doubtful harmony about the ends of inquiry and this clashes with the first argument for proceduralism that I have discussed—respect of (reasonable) pluralism.[13]

Dewey's moral philosophy is consequentialist.[14] He thus has to assume that there are some shared goals that can give direction to the aim of problem-solving and inform the assessment of the consequences of different proposals—even if he grants that democratic procedures are necessary to help determine what these shared goals are. We saw that Dewey has no difficulty with recognizing epistemic diversity. This sets his account apart from the standard account of epistemic democracy. But if individual agency expresses itself not only in diverse epistemic perspectives, but also in an irreducible pluralism of values, the possibility must be acknowledged that there are no shared goals, and hence no shared view of how social problems might best be solved. Persisting (reasonable) pluralism undermines the consequentialist ideal. As a result, the normative anchor for Dewey's epistemic defense of democracy loses its grip.

The focus on problem-solving makes Dewey's epistemology consequentialist even if not veritistic.[15] There is a parallel between Dewey's and Estlund's accounts of epistemic democracy that stems from the consequentialist structure of their epistemologies—in spite of the differences in their views about veritistic value. Both argue for the importance of the deliberative process (what Dewey calls the process of inquiry)—Estlund on grounds of respect of individual agency and Dewey on grounds of its knowledge-producing potential—and then advise us to select that institutional arrangement that is best able to bring about the desired outcome. In Estlund's account, the idea is to select that institutional organization of deliberative decision-making that has the greatest truth-tracking potential. In Dewey's account, the idea is to ensure that the deliberative process effectively contributes to solving social problems.

Estlund's version of the standard account of epistemic democracy and Dewey's pragmatist account each have something to offer that the other lacks. Their consequentialist epistemologies stand in the way of acknowledging both tenets of proceduralist conceptions of legitimacy that I have identified earlier: (i) respect of reasonable value pluralism and the constitutive role of democratic participation and (ii) the constructive function of inclusive democratic deliberation. Dewey's account of epistemic democracy is more helpful than Estlund's account for making sense of the constructive function of deliberative democratic decision-making. Estlund's epistemic proceduralist conception of democratic legitimacy, by contrast, avoids letting epistemic considerations trump respect of reasonable value pluralism and recognizes the link between respect of individual agency and the constitutive role of inclusive democratic procedures in a conception of legitimacy. Dewey's epistemic defense of democracy can account for the productive value of epistemic diversity, but has difficulties with the argument that links democratic procedures to respect of value pluralism and individual agency. Unlike Estlund's version of epistemic proceduralism, it thus fails to support what I had identified as the first tenet of the argument for proceduralism.

7.1.c. A Proceduralist Epistemology for Democracy

Given these weaknesses of consequentialist epistemologies, I now want to propose a third epistemology of democracy. This epistemology is proceduralist. According to Goldman, proceduralist epistemology focuses exclusively on "the intrinsic merits of intellectual practices to judge their epistemic worth or propriety" (1999: 75). In contrast to veritistic epistemology, it dispenses with the idea that a procedure-independent standard is necessary to assess the quality of the knowledge-producing practices.

Epistemologies that fit this definition have been developed by many social epistemologists, but most notably by feminist epistemologists and philosophers of science (e.g. Longino 1987, 2002a; Harding 1991, 1998). I shall base my account here on the proposal Helen Longino puts forward in her book *The Fate of Knowledge* (2002a). Longino addresses the so-called "science wars" and seeks to identify a viable middle-ground between those who defend traditional epistemology and philosophy of science and those who argue that the knowledge-producing practices of science are social through and through. Her strategy is to argue that cognition is as an inherently social process—rooted in a set of knowledge-producing social practices to which certain normative criteria apply.

Her argument rests on a distinction between three senses of knowledge: (i) knowledge-producing practices; (ii) knowing; and (iii) the content of knowledge (Longino 2002a: 77–78). Different epistemologies and philosophies of science have different interpretations of these three senses of knowledge and how they are related. In traditional epistemology—and for those in the "rational" camp in the science wars—knowing describes a state where an epistemic subject accepts a certain proposition, the proposition is true, and the epistemic subject is justified in believing that the proposition is true. The content of knowledge is what is thus known to epistemic subjects. Knowledge-producing practices, finally, are those processes of belief acquisition that justify belief. In those strands in (empirical) science studies that represent the "social" side of the dichotomy, by contrast, all three senses of knowledge are interpreted in social terms. Knowledge-producing practices are a set of social practices that shape the evaluation of propositions in the relevant community. Knowing refers to a state in which an epistemic subject accepts a proposition, and both the proposition itself and the fact that the epistemic subject accepts the proposition are acceptable in the relevant community. The content of knowledge again refers to what is thus known by epistemic subjects. Such empirical approaches are descriptive, not normative, about knowledge.

In Longino's hybrid view, the process of knowledge production is social because it is embedded in practices that are shaped by the interactions among epistemic subjects and the background assumptions that facilitate these interactions. She rejects the idea that this process can be reduced to the rational justification of belief. In this regard, she takes on board insights from social studies of science. At the same time, she also rejects the idea that this would force her to take a purely descriptive approach. Instead, she argues that it is possible to locate normativity in these social practices themselves. Her alternative account, she writes (Longino 2002a: 205), locates justification, or the production of knowledge, not just in the testing of hypotheses against data, but also in subjecting hypotheses, data, reasoning, and background assumptions to criticisms from a variety of perspectives. . . . Because the assumptions that constitute the intellectual context of observation and reasoning are, by their nature, usually not explicit but tacit patterns of thought, the function of critical interaction is to make them visible as well as to examine metaphysical, empirical, and normative implications. These discursive practices are both constructive and justificatory. . . . Sociality does not come into play at the limit of or instead of the cognitive. Instead, these social practices *are* cognitive.

The key difference between Longino's view of the knowledge-producing process and the more widely held veritistic view is that it supports the idea that epistemic value resides in the process itself, not in its outcome. Her hybrid view is in continuation with traditional epistemology in the sense that she holds on to the idea that there are normative criteria that apply to knowledge-producing practices. But she breaks with the traditional approach by dissociating normativity from a procedure-independent standard for what counts as a good outcome. In consequence, she defines knowing and the content of knowledge entirely in relation to the process of knowledge production—and not in relation to a procedure-independent idea of truth. Her epistemology is proceduralist because it dispenses with procedure-independent criteria for what counts as knowing or for what defines the content of knowledge. It is normative, and not just empirical, because it has a set of criteria that distinguishes among knowledge-producing practices and knowing and its content depend on the appropriateness of the procedure of which they are the outcomes.

With regard to the conditions that the knowledge-producing process ought to satisfy, Longino (2002a: 128ff.) proposes a list of four. The first condition, "publicly recognized forums for the criticism of evidence, methods, and of assumptions and reasoning," demands that criticism of original research is not marginalized. This condition is concerned with creating space for critical discourse—within the venues of original research. The second, "uptake of criticism," addresses the transforming potential of critical discourse. Uptake is understood as cutting both ways: i.e. both defenders of a certain knowledge claim and its critics should be responsive to each other. The third criterion demands "publicly recognized standards by reference to which theories, hypotheses, and observational practices are evaluated and by appeal to which criticism is made relevant to the goals of the inquiring community." Public, not just implicit, standards help both defenders of a certain claim and their critics to identify their points of agreement and disagreement and structure the process in which arising problems are handled. This criterion ensures that critical discourse is orderly and constructive, rather than chaotic and destructive. Longino adds that these standards need not be static, but can themselves come under scrutiny. Finally, she lists "tempered equality . . . of intellectual authority," a criterion that warns of illegitimate associations between social, political, and/or economic privilege and power with epistemic privilege and power.

These four conditions give answers to the "where," "why," "how" and "who" questions about processes of knowledge–production. None of these criteria refers to a procedure-independent ideal of a good outcome. This is more straightforward with the conditions that refer to the "where" and the "who"—publicly recognized forums and equality of intellectual authority. But even the "why" and the "how"—uptake of criticism and publicly recognized standards—do not imply an ideal of a correct outcome that would exist procedure-independently and that the procedure would be supposed to track. Epistemic values, in this account, are best interpreted as irreducibly procedural—there is nothing beyond critically engaging with each other in transparent and non-authoritarian ways. What Longino puts at the center of her epistemology is the demand that knowledge claims be scrutinized from a variety of perspectives, and in particular that it is possible to subject the background assumptions embedded in the scientific practices that support these claims to critical examination of their "metaphysical, empirical, and normative implications."[16]

Acknowledging the influence of background assumptions embedded in scientific practices forms an important part of her claim that cognition is an irreducibly social process. In fact, it probably constitutes the main difference between her social epistemology and the theory Philip Kitcher presents in *Science, Truth, and Democracy* (2001). Since both emphasize the productive role of democratic values in social epistemology, it will be helpful to briefly discuss this difference. Compared to his earlier book, *The Advancement of Science* (Kitcher 1993), Kitcher's more recent interpretation of social epistemology recognizes blurred boundaries between the epistemic and the social. He introduces the idea of significance graphs to capture the role of social influences on what counts as scientifically significant. A significance graph is a map that informs us how certain topics have become relevant. It is made of directed arrows between such items as "questions, answers, hypotheses, apparatus, methods, and so forth" that contribute to the construction of epistemic significance (Kitcher 2001: 78). Since maps are always drawn to answer particular questions—about the topography, about streets and highways, about landmarks, etc.—no map is neutral. Significance graphs, similarly, do not just depend on epistemic goals and conditions, but on social factors too. A significance graph represents how what is known—what the map depicts—is at least partly socially constructed.

Kitcher (2001) thus recognizes that research agendas pursued within science may have a social component and that scientific inquiry, left to itself, may not be able to best manage these social influences and protect itself from arbitrariness. Borrowing from Rawlsian terminology, Kitcher (2001:

117–135) proposes the ideal of a well-ordered science in response. A well-ordered science is accountable to society at large through democratic control over the aims of inquiry. According to Kitcher, democratic evaluation should ensure that the research agendas pursued within science are not the product of social biases, but are indeed conducive to produce significant truth. It is thus an instrument for the maintenance of the rationality of scientific inquiry.

The interesting contrast with Longino's proposal is the following. For Kitcher, democracy plays a role only at the level of science policy—it is necessary for the shaping the aims of inquiry. For Longino, however, democratic values also play a role at the level of scientific inquiry itself—as conditions that shape scientific practices.[17] This contrast has its origin in how cognitive agency is modeled. According to Kitcher, social factors have some influence on the aims that scientists pursue—in addition to purely epistemic aims. And scientific practices are simply the result of the interactions among interest-maximizing individuals.[18] Kitcher seems to think that drawing a significance graph is a straightforward task. In his model, its nodes and paths are the result of the maximizing behavior of the epistemic agents and can be reconstructed and explicated as such. On the basis of such a graph, in well-ordered science, a democratically organized public should decide which of the currently possible research agendas most further the common good—as opposed to what best satisfies the aims of the scientists.

Longino's social epistemology rests on a more subtle notion of the social influences on scientific practices than Kitcher's theory. In Longino's theory, there are important social factors in the background assumptions that shape scientific practices—they frame the options that scientists perceive. On this view, social factors embedded in scientific practices help mold scientific significance without conscious activities by particular agents. But this makes it more difficult to examine their diverse influences than Kitcher assumes and also more important from a normative point of view. Joseph Rouse (1996: 142–43) puts the problem in the following way:

> precisely because what is at issue in a practice and what is at stake in conflicts over those issues are assumed to be what 'everybody knows', these issues and stakes often remain only partially articulated and therefore less susceptible to normative constraint.

Longino's proceduralist epistemology targets precisely this influence and the need for normative conditions that apply within scientific inquiry—to scientific practices themselves. Her proposal thus argues for the importance of democratic values not just at the level of science policy, but at the level of scientific inquiry as well. Kitcher's ideal of a well-ordered science neglects this problem because he treats the influence of background assumptions on how scientific inquiry is conducted as unproblematic. It allows for the possibility that democratic evaluation of the ends of scientific research may be productive, but it does not consider how democratic values may be fruitfully brought to bear on the process of inquiry itself by creating room for the scrutiny of the influence of tacit background assumptions.

While Longino developed her social epistemology in the context of philosophy of science, it is, just like veritistic social epistemology or pragmatist epistemology, applicable to the context of democratic theory. In Chapter 3, I had characterized deliberative democracy on the basis of two main features: public reasoning and political equality. The epistemic account of deliberative democracy based on a proceduralist epistemology changes the interpretation of these two features in the following way. First, it incorporates the epistemic dimension into a concern with fair procedures by stressing the epistemic value of fair deliberative processes. As such, it interprets political equality more extensively, as including criteria that specify epistemic fairness. That is to say, it demands that there are criteria that regulate public deliberation at the fact-gathering and analysis stages of processes of policy formulation in addition to the more commonly recognized criteria that refer to equal possibilities to participate in the deliberation over given policy proposals. The idea is that exclusion from those stages of the policy-evaluation and selection process that are crucial for the shaping of the evidence-basis on which particular policies rest is just as problematic as exclusion from other stages of this process. One way to make sense of this could be by extending the interpretation of political equality based on primary goods by adding goods that are defined in relation to access to the consultational stages of the policy-making process. For example, beyond rights and liberties, freedom of movement and choice of occupation, powers and prerogatives of offices and positions of responsibility, income and wealth, and the social bases of self-respect, the list could include goods that lobbying groups need to have influence on the deliberative process, such as access to information, to funding of research projects, and to official and unofficial hearings. This reinterpretation of what a fair process includes has consequences for how the exchange of reasons is interpreted as well. An account of deliberative democracy based on proceduralist epistemology portrays public deliberation as an ongoing process of critical engagement and learning with conflicting representations of what the problems are, what it takes to solve them, and the reasons people have for valuing alternative options thus construed. It can thus take seriously the constructive function of democratic decision-making processes without abandoning respect of value pluralism.

It seems to me that a proceduralist interpretation of epistemic democracy provides the appropriate framework for Iris Marion Young's interpretation of deliberative democracy (Young 1997, 2000). Young addresses the question of how it can be expected that deliberative democracy is a good means to reach justice. Her answer explicitly invokes the epistemic dimension: the "structure and norms of ideal deliberative democracy . . . *provide the epistemic conditions* for the collective knowledge of which proposals are most likely . . . to promote results that are wise and just" (Young 2000: 30; my emphasis). According to Young, social differences matter epistemically. As explained previously (3.1.a.), she rejects a description of deliberative democracy that centers on an orientation towards the common good. Acknowledging the epistemic dimension of deliberative decision-making on the basis of a proceduralist epistemology explains her worry about appeals to the common good. Appeals to the common good are problematic when they are based on tacit assumptions about common knowledge that are not themselves subject to democratic scrutiny. If experiences and analyses of the consequences of injustice will vary for social groups, deliberation needs to take this situatedness of knowledge into account. Public deliberation, then, is not just about the common good, but extends to the epistemic bases on which people reason about the common good. Invoking a proceduralist epistemology thus supports Young's claim that "difference" should be seen as a resource for deliberative democracy if it is to fulfill its goal of inclusive public reasoning (Young 1997, 2000).[19]

Let me end this section by discussing some differences between such an account of epistemic democracy and the other two accounts discussed earlier—the standard account, particularly in Estlund's interpretation, and the Deweyan account. It differs from Estlund's epistemic proceduralism by offering a way of capturing the knowledge-producing potential of democratic process without including any conditions that target the veritistic quality of outcomes. The account proposed here includes epistemic concerns without referring to the idea that there exists, procedure-independently, a correct outcome of democratic decision-making.[20] Because it gives an account of the cognitive dimension of deliberative decision-making, the version of epistemic proceduralism advocated here is better able than Estlund's to capture the constructive function of democratic deliberation. It values epistemic diversity and explains why the expression of dissent, and collective action organized around dissent, can be the engines for the evaluation and transformation of unjust or otherwise problematic arrangements through democratic processes. What it shares with Estlund's proposal is a commitment to the first proceduralist tenet that individual agency and reasonable value pluralism ought to be respected. But since it can better accommodate the second tenet—the constructive function of deliberative democratic decision-making—it is preferable to Estlund's account.

How does the account of epistemic democracy that I am advocating here differ from a Deweyan account and why would it be preferable? Longino's proceduralist epistemology shares with Deweyan epistemology an emphasis on sustained critical interaction. In fact, at times,

Dewey himself sounds like a proceduralist. Consider the following passage, for example:

> The true purity of knowledge exists not when it is uncontaminated by contact with use and service. It is wholly a moral matter, an affair of honesty, impartiality and generous breadth of intent in search and communication. The adulteration of knowledge is due not to its use, but to vested bias and prejudice, to one-sidedness of outlook, to vanity, to conceit of possession and authority, to contempt or disregard of human concern in its use. (1927: 175–76)

This passage, with its insistence on "honesty, impartiality and generous breadth of intent in search and communication," certainly makes clear that for Dewey, too, there are important procedural epistemic values. And Dewey, like Longino, insists on epistemic inclusiveness—to uncover "vested bias and prejudice." Both, finally, have a positive account for why epistemic diversity is productive.

The proceduralist account of epistemic democracy thus shares with Deweyan epistemic democracy a rich account of the constructive function. But it avoids the consequentialist orientation that is tied to pragmatist epistemology. As we saw, the pragmatist case for respecting epistemic diversity and for inclusive epistemic practices is based on a consequentialist focus on effective problem-solving. In an account of epistemic democracy based on proceduralist social epistemology, by contrast, the case rests on making the process of deliberative inquiry—not its outcome—the source of epistemic value. It defends a set of practices in which epistemic agents critically engage with each other under conditions of transparency and reciprocity as the bedrock of an account of the knowledge-producing potential of deliberation. And it accommodates the possibility of an irreducible plurality in the aims of inquiry instead of stipulating a particular goal for epistemic practices. There is no reference to procedure-independent standards of correctness, or to the ability of democratic procedures to contribute to the common good by solving social problems. As a result, a proceduralist account of epistemic democracy has the advantage over one based on Dewey's consequentialist epistemology in that it does not run into the problem that the latter has with the fact of reasonable value pluralism and with attributing more than instrumental value to individual agency.

Because it can thus accommodate both proceduralist tenets it is preferable not just to Estlund's version of the standard account of epistemic democracy, but to Deweyan epistemic democracy as well. The account of epistemic democracy I have sketched here offers a way of incorporating the epistemic dimension into a concern with fair procedures by stressing the epistemic value of fair deliberative processes. In the next section I want to give further plausibility to an interpretation of epistemic deliberative democracy that relies on such a proceduralist epistemology, by defending its corresponding conception of democratic legitimacy against the Rational Proceduralist conceptions linked to accounts of epistemic democracy based on consequentialist epistemologies.

7.2. EPISTEMIC PROCEDURALISM

The taxonomy I developed in Chapter 4 drew on Rawls's distinctions among forms of procedural justice and used these distinctions to identify two main categories of conceptions of democratic legitimacy: Pure and Rational Proceduralism, where the latter combines Rawls's categories of perfect and imperfect proceduralism. I now want to extend this taxonomy to the case of epistemic democracy. Most epistemic democrats seem to be of the view that Rational Proceduralism is the default conception of democratic legitimacy. By building on a proceduralist epistemology, I shall argue that there is a plausible, and preferable, Pure Proceduralist alternative conception of democratic legitimacy that works for epistemic democracy.

7.2.a. Rational Epistemic Proceduralism

Extending the taxonomy to include the epistemic account of democracy adds two more fields to the existing matrix: Rational Epistemic Proceduralism (and its perfect and imperfect subcategories) and Pure Epistemic Proceduralism.[21] The matrix thus looks as represented in Table 7.1.

The conception of legitimacy that underlies Deweyan epistemic democracy, as I have characterized it in the last section, is a version of Rational Epistemic Perfect Proceduralism. It combines both features of perfect proceduralism: there is a procedure-independent way of characterizing the ideal outcome—i.e. a social state that maximizes the common good—and there is a procedure that, ideally, leads to this outcome—the deliberative process. Dewey characterizes the conception of legitimacy in the following way (1978: 431):

Table 7.1 Categories of Conceptions of Democratic Legitimacy II

	Aggregative Democracy	Deliberative Democracy	Epistemic Democracy
Pure Proceduralism: Political Fairness	Pure Aggregative Proceduralism	Pure Deliberative Proceduralism	Pure Epistemic Proceduralism
Rational Proceduralism: Political Fairness and Political Quality	Rational Aggregative Proceduralism	Rational Deliberative Proceduralism –Perfect –Imperfect	Rational Epistemic Proceduralism –Perfect –Imperfect

> The moral criterion by which to try social institution and political
> measures may be summed up as follows: The test is whether a given
> custom or law sets free individual capacities in such a way as to make
> them available for the development of the general happiness or the
> common good.

Since I have already argued in the previous section that its dependence
on the common good constitutes a weakness of Deweyan epistemic
democracy, I shall not pursue his conception of democratic legitimacy
any further.

The conception of legitimacy that is implicit in interpretations of the
standard account of epistemic democracy that draw on the Condorcet
jury theorem also falls into the category of Rational Epistemic Perfect
Proceduralism. According to this interpretation of democratic legitimacy,
a collective decision is legitimate if it is correct. But a democratic decision-making procedure is seen as necessary to achieve correctness in this
account. For as long as the competence of the members of the democratic
constituency is limited yet above a certain threshold, a large number of
people are more likely to chose the correct outcome than a single person,
or a small group of people. To ensure correctness, and hence legitimacy,
the decision-making power should not rest in the hands of a few, but be
divided equally among all members of the democratic constituency.

Estlund's interpretation of the standard account is pitched against this
version of Rational Epistemic Perfect Proceduralism, which he calls the
"correctness theory of democratic legitimacy" (Estlund 2008: 99). His
main objection, as I have discussed it earlier, is that it fails to give a sufficient explanation for why those who disagree with the outcome of the
democratic decision-making process ought to treat them as binding and
hence demands too much deference from the participants of democratic
decision-making. To correct for that, Estlund's alternative conception of
democratic legitimacy puts more emphasis on procedures. The conception
of legitimacy that he advocates "requires that the procedure can be held,
in terms acceptable to all qualified points of view, to be epistemically the
best (or close to it) among those that are better than random" (Estlund
2008: 98).

Estlund calls his conception "epistemic proceduralism" and he sometimes
refers to it as "purely" procedural (e.g. Estlund 2008: 108, 116). As I use
the Rawlsian terminology here, however, a Pure Proceduralist conception
of legitimacy refrains from including any reference to procedure-independent standards. In Estlund's epistemic proceduralism, procedure-independent standards of correctness influence the selection of the procedure that
has the capacity to be legitimacy-generating. As such, his conception of
legitimacy is not purely procedural. Instead, it is better described as having
the structure of imperfect proceduralism. It assumes a procedure-independent standard for correct outcomes and defends a particular democratic

procedure in terms of its ability to approximate these outcomes, factoring in implications of the impossibility of guaranteeing that the procedure always gets it right. It is a feature of an imperfect proceduralist conception of democratic legitimacy that a particular decision may fail to reach the ideal outcome—i.e. the correct outcome in the case of epistemic democracy based on veritistic epistemology—yet still be legitimate. This feature plays an important role in Estlund's epistemic proceduralism, but it is accounted for in imperfect proceduralism and does not render his conception of legitimacy purely procedural. To put my point differently, whereas Pure Proceduralism is monistic about legitimacy, Estlund's imperfect proceduralist conception is non-monistic, as it both insists that (deliberative) democratic procedures of decision-making are essential for political legitimacy and requires that these procedures approximate, as much as possible, an ideal outcome. As such, it falls in my category of "Rational Epistemic Imperfect Proceduralism."

Both the conception of democratic legitimacy that Estlund advocates and the one underlying the use of the Condorcet jury theorem are thus versions of Rational Epistemic Proceduralism. In both versions, democratic legitimacy depends on the truth-tracking potential of the democratic process. For both it holds that the greater the truth-tracking potential, the more legitimate are its outcomes. The only difference between them is that Estlund's conception of democratic legitimacy demands less deference from individual participants to majority judgments than versions of Rational Epistemic Perfect Proceduralism do, because it loosens the link between legitimacy and correct outcomes.

What speaks for Estlund's account is that it is better able to explain why democratic procedures are constitutive for legitimacy than rival versions of the standard account of epistemic democracy—for example, those based on the Condorcet jury theorem. First, Estlund does not attribute merely instrumental value to democratic procedures. Instead, he uses the truth-tracking criterion as a selection device among procedures that satisfy criteria that render them "recognizably democratic." In Estlund's Rational Epistemic Proceduralism, democratic procedures thus play an irreducible role for legitimacy. Second, it respects individual agency by explicitly not requiring individuals to defer to a majority view when they believe that they have good reasons to hold a different view. While holding on to the assumption that there is a correct outcome and that democratic decision-making processes differ in their truth-tracking potential, it acknowledges the implications of the "burdens of judgment." It admits the possibility of error in any judgment—even the judgment of a vast, well-informed majority—and refuses to ask individuals to surrender their own judgment to the outcome of a probabilistic calculation.

Still, as I have argued above, I do not think that Estlund's characterization is the best way for thinking about the epistemic dimension of deliberative democracy. The main problem with Estlund's argument for Rational

Epistemic Proceduralism is that it underestimates the epistemic value of democratic procedures themselves. In the next section, I want to show that the conception of democratic legitimacy that is associated with a proceduralist account of epistemic democracy is preferable to his version of Rational Epistemic Proceduralism.

7.2.b. Pure Epistemic Proceduralism Defended

Pure Epistemic Proceduralism requires public deliberation among members of the democratic constituency under conditions of political equality and epistemic fairness. This conception of democratic legitimacy lies in between Rational Epistemic Proceduralism and Pure Deliberative Proceduralism. While Pure Deliberative Proceduralism and Pure Epistemic Proceduralism are alike in that they both define legitimacy purely on the basis of procedural fairness, they differ in that the latter includes criteria that specify epistemic fairness. Pure Epistemic Proceduralism is thus distinct from variants of Deliberative Proceduralism in that it explicitly refers to the epistemic dimension. But because it does so in a proceduralist way, it also differs from Rational Epistemic Proceduralism.

The Pure Epistemic Proceduralist conception of democratic legitimacy is preferable to the Pure Deliberative Proceduralist conception because it is less static. The proceduralist epistemology on which it relies can account for the social learning process that deliberative decision-making enables. As such Pure Epistemic Proceduralism it is better equipped to deal with the challenges of the political egalitarian's dilemma than Pure Deliberative Proceduralism (cf. Chapter 5). If political fairness is interpreted so as to include epistemic fairness, this gives participants in the deliberative process additional resources to counteract the effects of overly weak or overly strong criteria of political equality. I have argued that if political equality is too weak, some will be effectively excluded from the deliberative process. If epistemic fairness prevails, however, this will allow those affected to draw attention to this situation. Conversely, if political equality is too strong, some will find that the deliberative process rests on substantive judgments that they do not endorse. Again, if epistemic fairness prevails, this allows them to challenge these presumptions. Pure Epistemic Proceduralism is not immune to the threats to legitimacy that the political egalitarian's dilemma poses, of course. But by allowing for collective learning about the effects of different constraints on the deliberative process, it gives support to a dynamic interpretation of how these constraints get established. Including conditions of epistemic fairness in the political fairness constraints provides some (procedural) safeguards against the adverse effects of overly weak and overly strong criteria of political equality.

Pure Epistemic Proceduralism is preferable to Estlund's interpretation of Rational Epistemic Proceduralism because the latter commits us to unnecessary problematic claims about the epistemic dimension of democratic legitimacy. Specifically, I want to raise three objections against Estlund's version of Rational Epistemic Proceduralism: (i) that it is not a practicable conception of legitimacy, (ii) that it makes unnecessary demands, and (iii) that it is normatively misleading.

A first problem with Rational Epistemic Proceduralism, as Estlund is well aware, is that correctness is difficult, if not impossible, to determine. Judgments about correctness tend to be fallible and historically and socially situated. Correctness thus seems primarily something to aspire to, but not something that is ever at hand. There are, in other words, only claims about correctness; correctness itself, interpreted as a procedure-independent notion, is elusive. If a procedure-independent standard is elusive, however, it is difficult to see how democratic legitimacy can hinge on its normative cutting power.

In reply, Estlund might say that we know enough about correct outcomes to design the democratic process in such a way as to increase its ability to track them. The process should be fine-tuned, as far as it is possible, to maximize their truth-tracking potential. For example, if it is known that certain biases—e.g. sexism or racism—tend to detract from correctness, then legitimacy requires that the democratic processes be designed in such a way as to curtail their effects on the outcomes.

It seems obviously right to demand that harmful biases need to be contained for legitimacy. But the crucial question is whether the way in which Rational Epistemic Proceduralism recommends that we do this is right. I do not think it is and this leads me to my second objection to Estlund's version of Epistemic Proceduralism. To fix ideas, I want to discuss a distinction that Rational Epistemic Proceduralism makes between two possible outcomes of a decision-making process that meets the political fairness constraint that is inherent to deliberative democracy. It distinguishes between, on the one hand, the case where such a fair process leads to a correct outcome and, on the other, the case where such a process leads to a biased outcome. The first is qualified as legitimate, whereas the second fails to ensure legitimacy. An unfair process, i.e. a decision-making process that violates constraints that would render it "recognizably democratic," cannot, of course, establish legitimacy—independently of the outcomes it generates. On this, Rational Epistemic Proceduralism and Pure Epistemic Proceduralism concur—in contrast to democratic instrumentalism.

I do not find the differential treatment of the outcomes of fair processes plausible. How should one make sense of the idea of a fair deliberative process that leads to a biased outcome? Consider the following example. Suppose the outcome of collective decision-making is sexist. It endorses a policy proposal that claims to increase the common good or social justice but rests on sexist premises about family life. Now, a fair procedure should ensure that everybody is able to participate in the process as an equal. It should enable all those affected by and opposed to sexism to effectively challenge these premises—Longino's criterion of uptake of criticism that I discussed above underlines this demand. If the procedure is genuinely fair, one would thus not expect a sexist proposal to go through. Conversely, if a sexist proposal goes through, is this not likely to be the result of unfair procedures, in which women may have been nominally treated as equals, but not effectively so? I find it difficult to see how a deliberative process can be called fair if deliberation over policy alternatives leaves unchallenged background assumptions that undermine the equal standing of all participants. A proceduralist epistemology explains what is at stake here. But if the procedure is unfair, then we do not need Rational Epistemic Proceduralism to explain the lack of legitimacy of the outcome. It will be sufficient to argue that the procedures did not meet the standards of procedural fairness. In this Pure Proceduralist view, bias is treated not as an additional concern, but as a part of the very concern with procedural fairness. My second objection to Estlund's proposal is thus that the assumption of a procedure-independent standard of correctness is unnecessary to address his concerns. The illegitimacy of a biased outcome can be attributed to unfair procedures. This renders Pure Epistemic Proceduralism more parsimonious than Rational Epistemic Proceduralism.

Third, there is the related question of how to avoid the problem of "privileging the opinions of any putative experts" of which Estlund rightly warns us (7.1.a.). The truth-tracking view commits us to a strategy of bias-avoidance. The very idea of there being a correct outcome demands that this outcome be neutral. At first sight, Rational Epistemic Proceduralism may thus seem to avoid this problem, as it would call illegitimate any outcome that is not correct, but chosen under the influence of biased "experts." The alternative view is the one that is also stressed by Young (1997, 2000; cf. 3.1.a. and 7.1.c.): to treat difference not as something to be eliminated from, but as a resource for knowledge production. According to this view, social influences of all sorts are always present in epistemic practices—be it in science or in other contexts—and not all such influences need to be valued negatively. Which biases are and which are not harmful has to be determined in an inclusive process. In the example above, it trusts that sexist premises will be more effectively challenged from the vantage point of a—biased—feminist perspective than from the alleged vantage point of—bias-neutral—truth.

The advocate of the truth-tracking view can reply to this that if it is known that the inclusion of feminist values and beliefs improves the truth-tracking potential of the knowledge-producing process, then it would also recommend including them. But that is not a satisfactory solution. It leaves out the issue of how we learn about biases in the first place. The problem is that even if we know what potential sources of bias are—e.g. values and beliefs related to gender—we will not know in every instance how these biases influence deliberation. This is so because bias-inducing values and beliefs typically operate at the level of background assumptions—i.e. as part of the frame of inquiry, but not as its objects. The truth-tracking view can only contain those biases about which a sufficient amount is already known, so that the process of inquiry can be fine-tuned accordingly. The truth-tracking account only becomes effective, so to speak, "after the fact"—once it is considered established how a bias operates. This overlooks how the discovery of biased background assumptions and their effects is typically a contested process—it overlooks, in other words, the constructive function of democracy. The biases-as-resource view, by contrast, is concerned precisely with this process. It emphasizes that the problematic biases are not those we already know about, but those that remain hidden. As such, it manifests more caution about possible biases than the bias-avoidance view with its dependence on the neutrality of a correct outcome and warns against smothering the process of discovery through claims to correctness. The bias-avoidance strategy, to put the point bluntly, bets on the wrong horse.

This third objection is the most serious. It challenges Estlund's version of Rational Epistemic Proceduralism for being normatively misleading. The difference between the two views is that the bias-avoidance view is part of a consequentialist epistemology, whereas the biases-as-resources view is part of a proceduralist epistemology. As part of a consequentialist epistemology, the bias-avoidance view values biases instrumentally in relation to their truth-tracking potential. It can deal with biases only insofar as their effects on the correct outcome are already known. The bias-as-resources view demands that knowledge-producing practices be as inclusive and as public as possible, to facilitate contestation from a multitude of perspectives. It values procedural fairness from the epistemic point of view as well; political and epistemic fairness are just two sides of the same coin.

Pure Epistemic Proceduralism acknowledges that there are epistemic and non-epistemic reasons to value deliberative democracy. The received view of deliberative democracy focuses on non-epistemic reasons—such as reciprocal justification, for example—and brackets the issue of epistemic values. Estlund has criticized this interpretation and argued that we should value deliberative democracy for epistemic reasons as well and conceive of the requirements of democratic legitimacy accordingly. In his account, the epistemic reason for valuing deliberative democracy lies in its truth-tracking potential. I agree with Estlund that deliberative democracy is valuable for both epistemic and non-epistemic reasons. But I have argued that the two need not be seen as conceptually independent. I have used my taxonomy of alternative conceptions of democratic legitimacy to show how Rational Epistemic Proceduralism is not the only possible conception of legitimacy in epistemic democracy. Pure Epistemic Proceduralism is a coherent and preferable alternative conception. My goal has been to show how Pure Epistemic Proceduralism, because it does not presuppose the existence of a correct outcome for democratic decisions, alleviates some of the problems that Rational Epistemic Proceduralism creates, while accommodating the concerns Rational Epistemic Proceduralism aims to address with fewer epistemological commitments. My argument shows that making democratic legitimacy depend on correctness is not necessary and possibly misleading because it is content with the elimination of biases we already know and may smother the process of discovery of biases not yet recognized. The account I presented rests on a link between procedural fairness and epistemic value. More so than alternative interpretations of epistemic democracy, it gives a grip on the idea that inclusive public deliberation is valuable not just for the ideal of political equality that it embodies, but also for its epistemic contribution.

Notes

NOTES TO CHAPTER 1

1. Riley (1982) has an excellent discussion of different contractarian positions on political legitimacy.
2. By interpreting democratic legitimacy in this way, I am focusing on internal legitimacy. I shall bracket issues of external legitimacy, i.e. the reasons, say, the international community has to respect the decisions of a particular democratic state. For a treatment of external legitimacy, see Buchanan (2004a).

NOTES TO CHAPTER 2

1. There is an additional condition, reflexivity, which demands that individuals rank each alternative as at least as good as itself. This is a technical condition, and I shall not discuss it any further.
2. For a critique of this model, see Sen (1977a). In the last decade, criticism of the standard model of rational choice has intensified and alternatives have been explored; see e.g. Gintis *et al.* (2005) and evaluations in Peter and Schmid (2007).
3. Furthermore, the decision-making mechanisms are not part of the social states. Individual preferences over alternative mechanisms are therefore not considered. On this see Sen (1986b).
4. Arrow (1963: 106): "This position [of locating social values in the actions taken by society through its rules for making social decisions] is a natural extension of the ordinalist view of values; just as it identifies values and choices for the individual, so I regard social values as meaning nothing else than social choices."
5. Note that the weak Pareto condition is not identical with full unanimity, understood as unanimity about what to do, as it only refers to how individuals rank pairs of alternatives. On this issue, see Sen (1976).
6. For example, assume that the preference ordering of three individuals is *xyz*, the preference ordering of two individuals is *yzx*, and the ordering of another two individuals is *zyx*. This yields x as a winner. If the last two individuals mentioned were to change their preferences over the pair *y*, *z*, there would be four individuals with *yzx*, and two with *xyz*, yielding y as the winner. The Independence axiom identifies this as inadmissible.
7. "[The fundamental problem of social choice is] the construction of constitutions. In general, of course, there is no difficulty in constructing a rule if one is content with arbitrary ones. The problem becomes meaningful if reason-

able conditions are suggested, which every constitution should obey. [. . .] I suggest here four conditions which seem very reasonable to impose on any constitution" (Arrow 1967: 225).

8. This holds provided the number of alternatives is at least three and the number of individuals at least two.

9. Sen (1986a, 1995) has a nice version of the proof.

10. For a critical evaluation of Riker's claims, see e.g. Coleman and Ferejohn (1986) and Cohen (1986).

11. The literature on social choice theory is very vast, and I cannot do justice to it here. I shall only discuss those results that are of particular relevance to my project here. Good surveys are Plott (1976), Sen (1977c, 1986a, 1995), and Blackorby, Donaldson and Weymark (1984), among others.

12. "[T]he difficulties in forming a social welfare function arise from the differing social attitudes which follow from the individualistic hypothesis [which assumes that individual preferences depend on the goods the individual consumes], especially in the case of similar tastes for individual consumption. It follows that the possibility of social welfare judgments rests upon a similarity of attitudes toward social alternatives" (Arrow 1963: 69).

13. See Arrow (1963: 75). Single-peaked preferences were already discussed by Black (1948).

14. See e.g. Saari (2001).

15. Sen (1986a) explores alternatives to completeness.

16. An individual has a veto if for every pair of alternatives society must regard x as at least as good as y whenever he or she strictly prefers x to y. In Sen's (1970a: 75) terminology, if an individual has a veto, he or she is "semidecisive" over every pair of alternatives.

17. Even weaker than quasi-transitivity is acyclicity. It merely requires that a preference ranking contains no circles. An example of a preference ranking that satisfies acyclicity would be the ranking (xPy, yPz and xIz). Acyclicity is sufficient to derive a social choice from a social preference ranking. But it can again be shown that in any acyclic collective decision function that satisfies a set of rather weak conditions someone has a veto (Mas-Colell and Sonnenschein 1972). Further results of this sort are discussed in Sen (1977c, 1986a) or Suzumura (1983), for example.

18. Sugden also argued that these rationality conditions may be unduly blurring the difference between individual choice and democratic choice. As he puts it, "a voting system has the property of collective rationality if all the decisions that it produces are consistent with one ordering of end states. Thus a voting system that has this property yields decisions that are so consistent with one another that they might have been made by a single public official, acting on the basis of a social welfare ordering" (1981: 152).

19. See also Saari (1995).

20. See Bentham (1823), Mill (1859, 1861), Sidgwick (1893). The term classical utilitarianism is used to distinguish the original form from the various reformulations that have since been put forward, even if there are significant variations within classical utilitarianism too. Riley (1988) has a discussion of Mill's utilitarianism in relation to social choice theory.

21. According to Mill, the Greatest Happiness principle is "a mere form of words without rational signification, unless one person's happiness . . . is counted for exactly as much as another's" (1861: 198).

22. See for example Arrow (1973). For a critical examination of the concept see Gibbard (1987).

23. To be precise, they imply "strict-ranking welfarism": nothing but individual preferences should count for social choice as long as these preferences are

strict, i.e. of the "better-than" form, and not merely of the "at-least-as-good" form (see Sen 1979: 540–41).

24. For axiomatizations of different such social welfare functions, see Hammond (1976); see also Strasnick (1976). For reviews of the literature on this issue, see Blackorby, Donaldson and Weymark (1984), Sen (1986a), and Roemer (1996).

25. Fleurbaey (2007) argues for the possibility of social choice even without interpersonal comparisons.

26. Arrow wrote (1963: 9): "The viewpoint will be taken here that interpersonal comparisons of utilities have no meaning."

27. Putnam (2002) has a good discussion of the impossibility of separating facts and value judgments in this context.

28. I shall discuss the capability approach in Chapter 5.

29. This is not to say that Sen should be accused of this one-sidedness. In Chapters 3 and 4, I shall discuss how Sen attributes a role to democratic participation both in the evaluation of alternative social states, and in the identification of the relevant informational framework.

30. Williams (1973: 137). See also Sen and Williams (1982: 1–22).

31. For extended discussions of this point, see Parfit (1984: 493ff.) and Griffin (1986).

32. The term "adaptive preferences" is from Elster (1983).

33. Voorhoeve (2006) revisits this problem.

34. See for example Rawls (1982: 168). See also Dworkin (1981), G. Cohen (1989), Arneson (1990), Daniels (1990), Roemer (1996).

35. On the tension between the principle of consumer's sovereignty and the correction of preferences, see Scanlon (1991: 28ff.).

36. Some aspects of the problems that arise from the exclusion of non-utility information in welfare economics and Arrow's framework are well-known from the extensive philosophical debate on utilitarianism and rights. The literature on the difficulties of utilitarianism with incorporating right is very extensive. The issue experienced a revival after the publication of Rawls's *A Theory of Justice* (1971), but it already figured prominently in Mill's thinking, see Mill (1859, 1861). As I cannot pursue this issue here, see for example Dworkin (1977), Griffin (1986), Sen and Williams (1982, 1–22), Brandt (1992), or the collective volumes edited by Frey (1984) and Waldron (1984).

37. The large literature in moral philosophy on "agent-relativity" discusses the importance of taking agency seriously. For a powerful argument in support of the claim that taking agency seriously makes a fundamental difference in moral evaluation and is incompatible with consequentialist ethics, see Korsgaard (1996).

38. Sen (1970b). The liberal paradox has triggered extensive debates. See, among others, Gibbard (1974), Nozick (1974), Riley (1988), Gaertner, Pattanaik and Suzumura (1992), Pettit (1997), List (2004). For some of Sen's replies, see Sen (1976, 1992b). In what follows, I shall draw on Peter (2003).

39. Sen (1986c) defends the assumption of interdependence along these lines.

40. Though some have argued against such an interpretation of liberalism—e.g. Barry (1986).

NOTES TO CHAPTER 3

1. See, for example, Cohen (1997a, b), Manin (1987), Gutmann and Thompson (1996, 2004), Bohman (1996), Young (2000), Dryzek (2000), Estlund (2008), among others. For a good overview, see Freeman (2000).

2. Cohen explicates this dimension in the following way: "Deliberation is *reasoned* in that the parties to it are required to state their reasons for advancing proposals, supporting or criticizing them. They give reasons with the expectation that those reasons (and not, for example, power) will settle the fate of their proposal" (1997a: 74, his emphasis).

3. The other main feature that characterizes deliberative democracy—deliberation among free and equal participants—complements the account.

4. Deliberative democrats are not the first to stress these effects. Mill (1859) has a detailed discussion of them.

5. Basically all deliberative democrats stress this transformative effect of public deliberation on individual preferences; but particularly influential discussions of this issue can be found in Elster (1986), Cohen (1997b), Fearon (1998), and Young (2000), among others. For some recent attempts to explore the transformative effects of public deliberations with the tools of game theory or even social choice theory, see Austen-Smith and Federsen (2006) and List (2008).

6. Elster (1986: 112–13) expresses the same thought: "In a political debate it is paradigmatically impossible to argue that a given solution should be chosen just because it is good for oneself. By the very act of engaging in a public debate—by arguing rather than bargaining—one has ruled out the possibility of invoking such reasons." Mill (1859) also stressed this point.

7. Knight and Johnson (1994: 286) have a view of this kind: "[I]f the point of deliberation is to reach decisions, it is important not to attribute too much to such outcomes. This is a pragmatic position. The outcome of democratic procedures represents *a*—not *the*—common good. A "common good" is fashioned, not discovered" (emphasis in the original).

8. According to Cohen, "ideal deliberation aims to arrive at a rationally motivated *consensus*" (1997a: 75; his emphasis).

9. See also Phillips (1999).

10. Cohen's description of one of the main tenets of deliberative democracy emphasizes this pluralism: "A deliberative democracy is a pluralistic association. The members have diverse preferences, convictions and ideals concerning the conduct of their own lives. While sharing a commitment to the deliberative resolution of problems of collective choice . . ., they also have divergent aims, and do not think that some particular set of preferences, convictions, or ideals is mandatory" (Cohen 1997a: 72).

11. By insisting on the importance of deliberation, understood as a public exchange of reasons, this interpretation also avoids the common charges raised against what is dismissively called "identity politics." On this issue, see also Benhabib (2002).

12. For a discussion of this distinction, see Wall (2007).

13. The distinction between the horizontal and the vertical distinction of political power is from Dworkin (2000: 190–91).

14. Young characterizes this function (2000: 83): "A democratic process is inclusive not simply by formally including all potentially affected individuals in the same way, but by attending to social relations that differently position people and condition their experiences, opportunities, and knowledge of society. . . . Not only does the explicit inclusion of different social groups in democratic discussion and decision-making increase the likelihood of promoting justice because the interests of all are taken into account. It also increases that likelihood by increasing the stock of knowledge available to participants."

15. For a recent account of these ideas, see Rawls (2001). My presentation draws on Peter (2009).

16. "Cooperation is distinct from merely socially coordinated activity, for example, from activity coordinated by orders issued by some central authority.

Cooperation is guided by publicly recognized rules and procedures that those cooperating accept and regard as properly regulating their conduct" (Rawls 1993: 16). And: "Cooperation involves the idea of fair terms of cooperation [. . .]. Fair terms of cooperation specify an idea of reciprocity: all who are engaged in cooperation and who do their part as the rules and procedures require, are to benefit in an appropriate way as assessed by a suitable benchmark of comparisons" (ibid.).

17. Rawls (1993: 58) writes: "[M]any of our most important judgments are made under conditions where it is not to be expected that conscientious persons with full powers of reason, even after free discussion, will all arrive at the same conclusion. [. . .] These burdens of judgment are of first significance for a democratic idea of toleration."

18. The fair value contrasts with the formal equality that the first principle of justice as fairness demands for other basic rights and liberties. The same distinction appears in the second principle of justice as fairness, in the distinction between fair and formal equality of opportunity. On this, see Rawls (2001: 148ff.); see also Brighouse (1997).

19. Rawls discusses the idea of the basic structure as the first subject of justice extensively in Rawls (1971: 7–11; 1993: 257–88; 2001: 135–179).

20. What I write here rests on certain claims about Rawls's idea of public reason. There is quite a lot of confusion about the role of Rawls's idea of public reason in deliberative democracy in the literature. I cannot go into this issue at this stage. In section VI.1. I will argue that Rawls's idea of public reason is a procedural idea and should not be interpreted as justifying particular decisions on substantive grounds.

21. This is, unfortunately, all very rough; I shall develop these points in Chapters 4 and 6.

22. Goodin (2003) has an account of deliberative democracy that puts great emphasis on this individual component of deliberation.

23. It is perhaps interesting to note that very early on, Buchanan has objected to social choice theory that it neglects the process of preference formation (Buchanan 1954: 120): "[T]he extension of [the assumption of given preferences] to apply to individual values in the voting process disregards one of the most important functions of voting itself. The definition of democracy as 'government by discussion' implies that individual values can and do change in the process of decision-making." This quote is interesting because the view expressed is in some conflict with Buchanan's other writings on collective decision-making. As a matter of fact, Buchanan has not, to my knowledge, pursued this issue any further.

24. See also Elster (1986).

25. For an objection against Sunstein along these lines, see Ferejohn (1993). As a way out of this problem, Thaler and Sunstein (2008) propose an approach that maintains the welfare-enhancing goal, but involves means that do not seek to tamper with individual preferences, only "nudge" individuals to choose options that are better for them.

26. As Goodin nicely puts the point, "[m]erely 'registering preferences'," as advocated in aggregative democracy, "stops well short of genuinely 'respecting preferences'. That has us respecting the mark on the ballot, rather than the person or the reasoning for which it stands" (Goodin 2003: 48). And he urges us "to take people's preferences more seriously than that. Doing so requires us to make a genuine attempt at understanding what the other is trying to say to us: what the other is asserting and why. . . . [T]he object of our respect is people's reasons rather than brute expression of their preferences" (ibid.). Young (2000: 19–20) expresses the same point when she objects to aggregative democracy

that it "lacks any distinct idea of a public formed from the interactions of democratic citizens and their motivation to reach some decision" . . . and it relies only on a "thin and instrumentalistic form of rationality."

27. For a recent defense of this "all-things considered" approach to rational choice, see Hausman (2007).

28. Sen (1977a) raised this objection against rational choice theory. For discussions of the link between Sen's critique and a Kantian theory of practical reason, see Anderson (2001) and Pauer-Studer (2007). For an evaluation of Sen's critique in light of recent developments in rational choice theory, see Peter and Schmid (2007).

29. Beitz (1989) has a helpful discussion of this distinction.

30. The problem here is related to the difficulty that aggregative democracy has with dealing with different modes of evaluation; cf. my discussion of Sen's liberal paradox and related problems.

31. See, among others, Benhabib (1994), Knight and Johnson (1994), Cohen (1997a, b), King (2003) and Chambers (2004).

32. I shall properly introduce the distinction between a normative and a positive interpretation of legitimacy in the next chapter.

33. The authors also mention the possibility of making voting itself public. This option is discussed by Brennan and Pettit (1990).

34. This possibility has also been discussed by Pildes and Anderson (1990).

35. Cf. Dryzek and List (2003: 9): "deliberation can focus not only on first-order decisions concerning specific outcomes, but also on second-order decisions concerning institutional arrangements, for instance concerning taxation or welfare provision. Deliberation could reach agreement on the choice of some interpersonally significant standard for assessing people's interests or welfare (such as Rawlsian primary goods)."

36. Knight and Johnson (1994) also have an early defense of deliberative democracy that focuses on the area of intersection between social choice theory and deliberative democracy. They suggest turning to social choice theory to analyze the endogenous difficulties of aggregative democracy and blame deliberative democrats for failing to take social choice theory seriously. According to them, deliberation can answer both concerns that Riker raises. Like Dryzek and List (2003), they argue that deliberation may help to establish the dimensions of the conflict, thus enabling single-peaked preferences and hence reducing instability and manipulability. They also argue, however, that because deliberative democracy rests on a different conception of democratic legitimacy than aggregative democracy, the possible ambiguity that bothers social choice theorists need not bother deliberative democrats. These arguments rely on a confusion about which of the two strategies to adopt. On the one hand, they reject the conception of legitimacy that underlines aggregative democracy. On the other, however, they seem to take it for granted that avoiding cycles is essential for democratic legitimacy.

37. I shall focus on Cohen, but many deliberative democrats have written on how deliberative democracy combines considerations of procedure and substance, and indeed on how this is a key feature of deliberative democracy. See my discussion of Habermas in 2.1.c.; see also Gutmann and Thompson (1996, 2004), for example. For an excellent overview of the recent literature on deliberative democracy, see Freeman (2000).

NOTES TO CHAPTER 4

1. On political obligations, see also Gilbert (2006).

2. Buchanan (2002) also has a legitimacy-based view.
3. Here I shall focus on Rawls's approach to the concept of legitimacy, i.e. on the role he attributes to legitimacy in normative theory. In section 6.1., when I discuss Rawls's idea of public reason, I shall address the question what the Rawlsian conception of democratic legitimacy is—i.e. what legitimacy, in the Rawlsian view, demands of the democratic decision-making process.
4. See also Rawls (1995: 170ff.).
5. It is essential that the first principle is interpreted with regard to such a list of liberties and not, as A Theory of Justice has suggested, as a principle of "basic liberty." Justice as fairness does not assign special value to freedom as such, only to a specific list of rights and liberties.
6. Rawls states (1993: 228–29): "A principle specifying the basic rights and liberties covers the second kind of constitutional essentials. But while some principle of opportunity is surely such an essential, for example, a principle requiring at least freedom of movement and free choice of occupation, fair equality of opportunity (as I have specified it) goes beyond that and is not such an essential. Similarly, though a social minimum providing for the basic needs of all citizens is also an essential, what I have called the 'difference principle' is more demanding and is not."
7. Rawls (1995: 175) writes: "legitimacy is a weaker idea than justice and imposes weaker constraints on what can be done. . . . [D]emocratic decisions and laws are legitimate, not because they are just but because they are legitimately enacted in accordance with an accepted legitimate procedure. It is of great importance that the constitution specifying the procedure be sufficiently just, even though not perfectly just . . . But it may not be just and still be legitimate, provided it is just enough in view of the circumstances and social conditions."
8. As Rawls (1993: 330) explains: "the guarantee of fair value for the political liberties is included in the first principle of justice because it is essential to establish just legislation and to make sure that the fair political process specified by the constitution is open to everyone on a basis of rough equality."
9. I shall address the question of what political equality might entail in Chapter 5.
10. The idea is well expressed by Korsgaard (1997: 309): "it is the procedures themselves that confer normativity on those results. . . . And the normativity of the procedures themselves springs not from the quality of their outcomes, but rather from the fact that we must have such procedures if we are going to form a general will. In order to act together—to make laws and policies, apply them, enforce them, in a way that represents, not some of us imposing our private wills on others, but all of us acting together from a collective general will—we must have certain procedures that make collective decision and action possible, and normatively speaking, we must stand by their actual results."
11. In Chapter 7 I shall add: (5) Rational Epistemic Proceduralism, and (6) Pure Epistemic Proceduralism. The terminology is inspired by Estlund (1997), but there are some important differences between his and my interpretation of some of these labels. Moreover, the way in which I use the terms also differs from how List and Goodin (2001) use similar terms.
12. See Dahl (1956). Dahl (1989), however, defends a view that is closer to Rational Aggregative Proceduralism.
13. The four axioms are: Decisiveness, Anonymity, Neutrality, and Positive Responsiveness. These labels are used in the contemporary literature and differ somewhat from May's original characterization. For a statement of May's theorem as it is used today, see Mueller (1989: 96ff.).
14. Goodin and List (2006) generalize May's theorem for the case of more than two alternatives.

15. Rawls defines perfect proceduralism through the requirement that there is an "independent" criterion for what constitutes a desirable outcome (Rawls 1971: 85). Since Habermas's interpretation of rational justification is intrinsically linked to the deliberative process, it may seem incompatible with perfect proceduralism. To this it can be replied that there is a sense in which Habermas's interpretation of rational justification stands for a desirable state independently of the process through which it was reached—it is a social state that all have reasons to endorse. On this view, (ideal) deliberation then becomes the procedure that can guarantee that this ideal state is reached. This is the structure of perfect proceduralism. Bellamy defends a similar view. He argues that Habermas's interpretation of deliberative democracy on the basis of discourse ethics "sounds like a pure proceduralist argument, but turns out to be a form of perfect proceduralism" (Bellamy 2005: 35).
16. Benhabib (1994) also endorses Rational Deliberative Perfect Proceduralism; some passages of Cohen (1997a) also suggest this conception.
17. Gaus (1997) has a forceful argument against this view.
18. See e.g. Pettit (2001a, b, 2003), List and Pettit (2002, 2004), List (2006).
19. The labels for the two decision-making procedures are from Bovens and Rabinowicz (2003).
20. But see Goodin (2003) for an account that puts great emphasis on the individual component of deliberation in deliberative democracy.
21. My defense of Pure Epistemic Proceduralism in Chapter 7 will also invoke this constructive function, and attribute value to public deliberation without committing to a Rational Proceduralist conception of legitimacy.

NOTES TO CHAPTER 5

1. I believe that although my argument is different, the bottom-line is the same as in Estlund's rejection of Cohen's claim (cf. Estlund 2008: 85ff.). As I will explain in Chapter 7, however, I will draw different conclusions from this than Estlund.
2. The distinction between a weak and a strong criterion of political equality echoes Sen's distinction between "means" and "freedoms" (Sen 1990).
3. This debate originated in the early 1980s with an article by Sen with that title (Sen 1980) and continues until today (e.g. Fleurbaey 2002; Pogge 2002; Vallentyne 2005). For an early assessment of the debate, see Daniels (1990).
4. Christiano (1996), by contrast, advocates a resourcist framework.
5. I shall focus on the differences between interpretations of political equality based on the primary goods framework and on the capability approach, but I do not mean to exaggerate this point. I do not mean to suggest that it is impossible to capture the aims of primary-goods-based social evaluation in the capability approach. Note that Rawls (1993: 178ff.) has acknowledged the possibility of incorporating basic capabilities into his framework in response to Sen's critique. But I want to bracket this issue here. My goal is to address the interpretations put forward by those deliberative democrats who have strongly argued in favor of the capability approach.
6. On the social bases of self-respect, see especially Rawls (1971: 440–46; 544–48).
7. According to Rawls (1982: 163), "primary goods are certain features of institutions or of the situation of citizens in relation to them. . . . We are not required to examine citizens' psychological attitudes or their comparative levels of well-being; and the relevant features of institutions . . . are open to public view."
8. In the attempt to use the capability approach to specify political equality, the ideal of equal participation takes the place of the ideal of human flourishing

that underlies Nussbaum's interpretation of the capability approach (Nussbaum 2000, 2003).

9. Sen has not, to my knowledge, applied the capability approach to the specification of political equality, but he has argued in several places for the importance of "political freedoms"—the opportunity to exercise political rights (e.g. Sen 1999a: 146ff.). This relates to Sen's argument for the constructive function of democracy that I have introduced in Chapter 4 and to which I will return in Chapter 7. On the suitability of the capability approach to specify "democratic equality," see also Anderson (1999, 2003) and Daniels (2003).

10. I borrow the distinction between being "excluded" and being "included" from Bohman (1996, 1997).

11. I have discussed this problem in II.2.b.

12. As an unintended consequence, such policies might even produce exclusionary effects of their own. A policy based on the assumption that people who have been poor in their childhood have, on average, fewer cognitive skills than those who have not been poor, may feed into existing discriminatory biases and practices against people from a background of poverty.

13. I shall address epistemic considerations in Chapter 7.

14. As Pogge (2002: 1–2) puts it, the main difference between a resourcist approach such as the primary goods framework and the capability approach is the following: "Capability theorists assert, while resourcists deny, that a public criterion of social justice should take account of the individual rates at which persons . . . can convert resources into valuable functionings."

NOTES TO CHAPTER 6

1. "There are three essential elements of deliberative democracy. One is an idea of public reason. . . .. A second is a framework of constitutional democratic institutions that specifies the setting for deliberative legislative bodies. The third is the knowledge and desire on the part of the citizens generally to follow public reason. . ." (Rawls 1999: 580).

2. "A liberal conception of political legitimacy aims for a public basis of justification and appeals to free public reason" (Rawls 2001: 186).

3. Rawls adds: "Moreover, such reason is public in three ways: as the reason of free and equal citizens, it is the reason of the public; its subject is the public good concerning questions of fundamental political justice, which questions are of two kinds, constitutional essentials and matters of basic justice; and its nature and content are public, being expressed in public reasoning by a family of reasonable conceptions of political justice reasonably thought to satisfy the criterion of reciprocity" (1999: 575).

4. "In matters of constitutional essentials, as well as on questions of basic justice, we try to appeal only to principles and values each citizen can endorse" (Rawls 2001: 41).

5. Non-public reason is "the reason appropriate to individuals and associations within society" (Rawls 2001: 92).

6. He also notes the following, however: "It is a further desideratum that all legislative questions that concern or border on these [constitutional] essentials or are highly divisive, should also be settled, as far as possible, by guidelines and values that can be similarly understood" (Rawls 2001: 41).

7. "So understood, justification is addressed to others who disagree with us. . . . To justify our political judgments to others is to convince them by public reason, that is, by ways of reasoning appropriate to fundamental political questions, and by appealing to beliefs, grounds, and political values

it is reasonable for others also to acknowledge. Public justification proceeds from some consensus: from premises all parties in disagreement, assumed to be free and equal and fully capable of reason, may reasonably be expected to share and freely endorse" (Rawls 2001: 27).

8. "When a political conception of justice satisfies [the publicity condition], and basic social arrangements and individual actions are fully justifiable, citizens can give reasons for their beliefs and conduct before one another confident that this avowed reckoning itself will strengthen and not weaken public understanding. The political order does not, it seems, depend on historically accidental or established delusions, or other mistaken beliefs resting on the deceptive appearance of institutions that mislead us as to how they work" (Rawls 1993: 68).

9. See also Cohen (1993).

10. In the next chapter, I shall also address epistemic rationality.

11. The influential interpretation of the impossibility result as revealing that democratic decisions are arbitrary and manipulable is from Riker (1982).

12. The latter creates a problem, of course, as some additional criterion will have to be used to select one alternative from the set. The story of Buridan's ass, who starved to death between two identical haystacks, is often used to illustrate this problem that indifference creates.

13. See List and Pettit (2002: 97) and List and Pettit (2004: 213–14). Pettit, like Arrow, invokes the same rationality requirements for individuals as for the democratic collective.

NOTES TO CHAPTER 7

1. Buchanan (2004b) links this epistemology to a defense of political liberalism.

2. For an extensive discussion of the Condorcet jury theorem, see Goodin (2003: 91–108).

3. For a detailed discussion, see Goodin (2003: 109–121).

4. Goodin (2003) has a very good discussion of this problem.

5. On this, see also Christiano (2001).

6. List and Goodin (2001), for example, follow this strategy.

7. As he puts it in an earlier article (Estlund 1997: 183): "reasonable citizens should . . . refuse to surrender their moral judgment on important matters to anyone. Then, unless all reasonable citizens actually agreed with the decisions of some agreed moral/political guru, no one could legitimately rule on the basis of wisdom. So there might be political truth, and even knowers of various degrees, without any moral basis for epistocracy."

8. See my section III.2.; see also Christiano (1996) and Cohen (1997a, b), for example.

9. Anderson (2006: 9). Dewey's theory can be found in The Public and its Problems (1927), and in a short article entitled "Creative Democracy" (1939). For a helpful reconstruction of Deweyan epistemic democracy, see Putnam (1990).

10. "Knowledge cooped up in a private consciousness is a myth, and knowledge of social phenomena is particularly dependent upon dissemination, for only by distribution can such knowledge be either obtained or tested" (Dewey 1927: 176–77).

11. "Communication of the results of social inquiry is the same thing as the formation of public opinion. . . . For public opinion is judgment which is formed and entertained by those who constitute the public and is about public affairs" (Dewey 1927: 177).

12. Dewey quoted in Putnam (1990: 1676). As I shall argue below, Dewey's rejection of the naïve instrumentalist view does not imply Deweyan epistemic democracy is not instrumentalist in some other way.
13. On this, see also Talisse and Aikin (2005).
14. For a discussion of this, see Putnam (1990: 1676).
15. Goldman calls pragmatist social epistemology "utility consequentialism" (1999: 72). He characterizes it as "the view that social belief-causing practices should be evaluated by the amount of utility . . . that they would produce" (ibid.).
16. Her interpretation of the influence of tacit patterns of thought on scientific inquiry also leads her to endorse "nonmonism." Nonmonism is a claim about the content of knowledge and denies "that there is exactly one (correct, complete, consistent) account" (Longino 2002a: 91). She thus rejects Kitcher's realism.
17. Longino (2002b) comments on this.
18. In reaction to Kitcher (1993), Longino (2002a: 75) writes: "The distinction between the pure and the sullied suggests that either inquirers have no preconceptions or they are deliberately trying to insinuate their social views where they do not belong (or to advance their careers). This reinscription of cognitive Manichaeanism presupposes a simplistic account of cognitive agency and misunderstands what social and cultural analysts, including feminist scholars, of the sciences have been claiming: that values and social preconceptions are embedded in scientific concepts and practices and are carried, for the most part, unconsciously by scientific practitioners."
19. According to her (Young 2000: 83): "A strong communicative democracy . . . needs to draw on social group differentiation, especially the experience derived from structural differentiation, as a resource. A democratic process is inclusive not simply by formally including all potentially affected individuals in the same way, but by attending to social relations that differently position people and condition their experiences, opportunities, and knowledge of society. . . . Not only does the explicit inclusion of different social groups in democratic discussion and decision-making increase the likelihood of promoting justice because the interests of all are taken into account. It also increases that likelihood by increasing the stock of knowledge available to participants."
20. In section 7.2., I shall argue that the standard account's focus on correctness is normatively misleading.
21. For simplicity's sake, I shall refrain from further differentiating between aggregative and deliberative versions of epistemic democracy and base my arguments mostly on the deliberative version.

Bibliography

Anderson, Elizabeth. 1999. "What is the Point of Equality?" *Ethics* 109:287–337.

Anderson, Elizabeth. 2001. "Unstrapping the Straightjacket of 'Preference': On Amartya Sen's Contributions to Philosophy and Economies." *Economies and Philosophy* 17:21–38.

Anderson, Elizabeth. 2003. "Sen, Ethics, and Democracy." *Feminist Economics* 9(2–3):239–261.

Anderson, Elizabeth. 2006. "The Epistemology of Democracy." *Episteme* 3 (1–2):9–23.

Arneson, Richard. 1990. "Liberalism, Distributive Subjectivism, and Equal Opportunity for Welfare." *Philosophy and Public Affairs* 19:158–194.

Arneson, Richard. 2003. "Debate: Defending the Purely Instrumental Account of Democratic Legitimacy." *The Journal of Political Philosophy* 11(1):122–132.

Arrow, Kenneth. 1963. *Social Choice and Individual Values*. New Haven: Yale University Press.

Arrow, Kenneth. 1967. "Values and Collective Decision-Making." In P. Laslett and W. G. Runciman (eds.) *Philosophy, Politics, and Society*. Oxford: Basil Blackwell, 215–232.

Arrow, Kenneth. 1973. "Some Ordinalist-Utilitarian Notes on Rawls's Theory of Justice." *Journal of Philosophy* 70. Reprinted in K. Arrow *Social Choice and Justice*. Oxford: Basil Blackwell, 1984, 96–114.

Arrow, Kenneth. 1984. *Social Choice and Justice*. Oxford: Basil Blackwell.

Austen-Smith, David and Timothy Feddersen. 2006. "Deliberation, Preference Uncertainty and Voting Rules." *American Political Science Review* 100:209–218.

Barry, Brian. 1986. "Lady Chatterley's Lover and Doctor Fisher's Bomb Party." In Jon Elster and Aanund Hylland (eds.) *Foundations of Social Choice Theory*. Cambridge: Cambridge University Press, 11–43.

Beitz, Charles R. 1989. *Political Equality*. Princeton: Princeton University Press.

Bellamy, Richard. 2005. "Constitutionalism and Democracy." http://www.ucl.ac.uk/spp/download/seminars/0405/Richard-Bellamy-Const-and-Democ.doc.

Benhabib, Seyla. 1994. "Deliberative Rationality and Models of Democratic Legitimacy." *Constellations* 1(1):25–53.

Benhabib, Seyla. 2002. *The Claims of Culture*. Princeton: Princeton University Press.

Bentham, Jeremy. 1823 (1907). *An Introduction to the Principles of Morals and Legislation*. Reprinted. Oxford: Clarendon Press.

Berlin, Isaiah. 1969. *Four Essays on Liberty*. Oxford University Press.

Black, Duncan. 1948. "On the Rationale of Group Decision-making." *Journal of Political Economy* 56:23–34.

Black, Duncan. 1958. *The Theory of Committees and Elections*. Cambridge: Cambridge University Press.

Blackorby, Charles, David Donaldson and John A Weymark. 1984. "Social Choice with Interpersonal Comparisons: A Diagrammatic Introduction." *International Economic Review* 25:327–356.

Blau, Julian H. 1975. "Liberal Values and Independence." *The Review of Economic Studies* 42(3):395–401.

Bohman, James. 1996. *Public Deliberation*. Cambridge, MA: MIT Press.

Bohman, James. 1997. "Deliberative Democracy and Effective Social Freedom: Capabilities, Resources, and Opportunities." In James Bohman and William Rehg (eds.) *Deliberative Democracy: Essays on Reason and Politics*. Cambridge, MA: MIT Press, 321–348.

Bohman, James. 1998. "The Coming of Age of Deliberative Democracy." *Journal of Political Philosophy* 6:399–423.

Bohnet, Iris and Bruno Frey. 1994. "Direct-Democratic Rules: The Role of Discussion." *Kyklos* 47:341–354.

Borda, Jean-Charles de. 1784. "Mémoire sur les élections au scrutin." Mémoires de l'Académie Royale des Sciences année 1781. In I. McLean and A.B. Urken (eds. and transl.) 1995. *Classics of Social Choice*. Ann Arbor: University of Michigan Press, 83–89.

Bovens, Luc and Wlodek Rabinowicz. 2003. "Democracy and Argument—Tracking Truth in Complex Social Decisions." In Anne van Aaken, Christian List, and Christoph Lütge (eds.) *Deliberation and Decision*. Aldershot: Ashgate Publishing, 143–157.

Brandt, Richard. 1992. *Morality, Utilitarianism, and Rights*. Cambridge: Cambridge University Press.

Brennan, Geoffrey and Philip Pettit. 1990. "Unveiling the Vote." *British Journal of Political Science* 20(3):311–333.

Brighouse, Harry. 1997. "Political Equality in Justice as Fairness." *Philosophical Studies* 86:155–184.

Broome, John. 1999. "Normative Requirements." *Ratio* 12:398–419.

Broome, John. 2005. "Does Rationality Give Us Reasons?" *Philosophical Issues* 15:321–337.

Buchanan, Allen. 2002. "Political Legitimacy and Democracy." *Ethics* 112(4):689–719.

Buchanan, Allen. 2004a. *Justice, Legitimacy, and Self-Determination*. Oxford: Oxford University Press.

Buchanan, Allen. 2004b. "Political Liberalism and Social Epistemology." *Philosophy and Public Affairs* 32(2):95–130.

Buchanan, James. 1954. "Social Choice, Democracy, and Free Markets." *Journal of Political Economy* 62:114–123.

Chambers, Simone. 2004. "Democracy, Popular Sovereignty, and Constitutional Legitimacy." *Constellations* 11(2):153–173.

Christiano, Thomas. 1996. *The Rule of the Many*. Boulder, CO: Westview Press.

Christiano. Thomas. 2001. "Knowledge and Power in the Justification of Democracy." *Australasian Journal of Philosophy* 79(2):197–215.

Christiano, Thomas. 2004. "The Authority of Democracy." *The Journal of Political Philosophy* 12(3):266–290.

Cohen, Gerald A. 1989. "On the Currency of Egalitarian Justice." *Ethics* 99:906–944.

Cohen, Joshua. 1986. "An Epistemic Conception of Democracy." *Ethics* 97(1):26–38.

Cohen, Joshua. 1993. "Moral Pluralism and Political Consensus." In David Copp, Jean Hampton and John Roemer (eds.) *The Idea of Democracy*. Cambridge: Cambridge University Press, 270–291.

Cohen, Joshua. 1997a. "Deliberation and Democratic Legitimacy." In James Bohman and William Rehg (eds.) *Deliberative Democracy*. Cambridge, MA: MIT Press, 67–91.

Cohen, Joshua. 1997b. "Procedure and Substance in Deliberative Democracy." In James Bohman and William Rehg (eds.) *Deliberative Democracy*. Cambridge, MA: MIT Press, 407–437. Reprinted from Benhabib, Seyla (ed.) 1996. *Democracy and Difference*. Princeton: Princeton University Press, 95–119.

Coleman, Jules and John Ferejohn. 1986. "Democracy and Social Choice." *Ethics* 97(1):6–25.

Condorcet, Marie Jean Antoine Nicolas de Caritat, Marquis de. 1785. Essai sur l'application de l'analyse à la probabilité des décisions rendues à la pluralité des voix. Paris: l'Imprimerie Royale. In I. McLean and A.B. Urken (eds. and transl.) 1995. *Classics of Social Choice*. Ann Arbor: University of Michigan Press, 91–113.

Connolly, William (ed.) 1984. *Legitimacy and the State*. Oxford: Basil Blackwell.

Dahl, Robert. A. 1956. *A Preface to Democratic Theory*. Chicago: Chicago University Press.

Dahl, Robert A. 1989. *Democracy and Its Critics*. New Haven and London: Yale University Press.

Daniels, Norman. 1990. "Equality of What: Welfare, Resources, or Capabilities?" *Philosophy and Phenomenological Research* Suppl. Vol. 50:273–296.

Daniels, Norman. 2003. "Democratic Equality: Rawls's Complex Egalitarianism." In Samuel Freeman (ed.) *The Cambridge Companion to Rawls*. Cambridge: Cambridge University Press, 241–276.

Dasgupta, Partha and Eric Maskin. 2004. "The Fairest Vote of All." *Scientific American* 290(3):92–97.

Dewey, John. 1927. *The Public and its Problems*. Athens: Swallow Press.

Dewey, John. 1939. "Creative Democracy." http://www.beloit.edu/~pbk/dewey.html.

Dewey, John. 1978. *Ethics 1908. The Middle Works, 1899–1924, Volume 5*. Jo Ann Boydston (ed.). Carbondale and Edwardsville: Southern Illinois University Press.

Dryzek, John S. 2000. *Deliberative Democracy and Beyond*. Oxford: Oxford University Press.

Dryzek, John S. and Christian List. 2003. "Social Choice Theory and Deliberative Democracy: A Reconciliation." *British Journal of Political Science* 33(1):1–28.

Dworkin, Ronald. 1977. *Taking Rights Seriously*. London: Duckworth.

Dworkin, Ronald. 1981. "What is Equality? Part I: Equality of Welfare." *Philosophy and Public Affairs* 10(3):185–246.

Dworkin, Ronald. 1986. *Law's Empire*. Cambridge: Harvard University Press.

Dworkin, Ronald. 2000. *Sovereign Virtue*. Cambridge: Harvard University Press.

Elster, Jon. 1983. *Sour Grapes: Studies in the Subversion of Rationality*. Cambridge: Cambridge University Press.

Elster, Jon. 1986. "The Market and the Forum." In Jon Elster and Aanund Hylland (eds.) *Foundations of Social Choice Theory*. Cambridge: Cambridge University Press, 103–132.

Estlund, David. 1989. "Democratic Theory and the Public Interest: Rousseau and Condorcet Revisited." *American Political Science Review* 83:1317–1322.

Estlund, David. 1993. "Making Truth Safe for Democracy." In David Copp, Jean Hampton, and John E. Roemer (eds.) *The Idea of Democracy*. Cambridge: Cambridge University Press, 71–100.

Estlund, David. 1997. "Beyond Fairness and Deliberation: The Epistemic Dimension of Democratic Authority." In James Bohman and William Rehg (eds.) *Deliberative Democracy: Essays on Reason and Politics*. Cambridge, MA: MIT Press, 173–204.

Estlund, David. 2000. "Political Quality." In Ellen Frankel Paul, Fred D. Miller, and Jeffrey Paul (eds.) *Democracy.* Cambridge: Cambridge University Press, 127–160.

Estlund, David. 2008. *Democratic Authority.* Princeton: Princeton University Press.

Fearon, James D. 1998. "Deliberation as Discussion." In Jon Elster (ed.) *Deliberative Democracy.* Cambridge: Cambridge University Press, 44–68.

Ferejohn, John. 1993. "Must Preferences be Respected in a Democracy?" In David Copp, Jean Hampton, and John Roemer (eds.) *The Idea of Democracy.* Cambridge: Cambridge University Press, 231–241.

Fishburn, Peter C. 1973. *The Theory of Social Choice.* Princeton: Princeton University Press.

Fleurbaey, Marc. 2002. "Equality of Resources Revisited." *Ethics* 113:82–105.

Fleurbaey, Marc. 2007. "Social Choice and Just Institutions: New Perspectives." *Economics and Philosophy* 23:15–43.

Freeman, Samuel. 2000. "Deliberative Democracy: A Sympathetic Comment." *Philosophy and Public Affairs* 29(4):371–418.

Frey, Raymond G. (ed.). 1984. *Utility and Rights.* Oxford: Basil Blackwell.

Gaertner, Wulf, Prasanta K. Pattanaik, and Kotaro Suzumura. 1992. "Individual Rights Revisited." *Economica* 59:161–177.

Gaus, Gerald F. 1997. "Reason, Justification, and Consensus: Why Democracy Can't Have It All." In James Bohman and William Rehg (eds.) *Deliberative Democracy: Essays on Reason and Politics.* Cambridge, MA: MIT Press, 205–242.

Gibbard, Allan. 1974. "A Pareto-Consistent Libertarian Claim." *Journal of Economic Theory* 7:388–410.

Gibbard, Allan. 1987. "Ordinal Utilitarianism." In G. R. Feiwel (ed.) *Arrow and the Foundations of the Theory of Economic Policy.* New York: New York University Press, 135–153.

Gilbert, Margaret. 2006. *Political Obligations.* Oxford: Oxford University Press.

Gintis, Herbert, Samuel Bowles, Robert T. Boyd, and Ernst Fehr (eds.). 2005. *Moral Sentiments and Material Interests: The Foundations of Cooperation in Economic Life.* Cambridge, MA: MIT Press.

Goldman, Alvin. 1999. *Knowledge in a Social World.* Oxford: Oxford University Press.

Goodin, Robert. 2003. *Reflective Democracy.* Oxford: Oxford University Press.

Goodin, Robert and Christian List. 2006. "A Conditional Defense of Plurality Rule: Generalizing May's Theorem in a Restricted Informational Environment." *American Journal of Political Science* 50(4):940–949.

Griffin, James. 1986. *Well-Being: Its Meaning, Measurement and Moral Importance.* Oxford: Clarendon Press.

Grofman, Bernard and Scott L. Feld. 1988. "Rousseau's General Will: A Condorcetian Perspective." *The American Political Science Review* 82(2):567–576.

Gutmann, Amy and Dennis Thompson. 1996. *Democracy and Disagreement.* Cambridge, MA: Harvard University Press.

Gutmann, Amy and Dennis Thompson. 2004. *Why Deliberative Democracy?* Princeton: Princeton University Press.

Habermas, Juergen. 1990. *Moral Consciousness and Communicative Action.* Transl. by Christian Lenhardt and Shierry Weber Nicholsen. Cambridge, MA: MIT Press.

Habermas, Juergen. 1996. *Between Facts and Norms.* Transl. by William Rehg. Cambridge, MA: MIT Press.

Habermas, Juergen. 1998. *The Inclusion of the Other.* Cambridge, MA: MIT Press.

Hammond, Peter J. 1976. "Equity, Arrow's Conditions, and Rawls' Difference Principle." *Econometrica* 44:793–804.

Harding, Sandra. 1991. *Whose Science? Whose Knowledge? Thinking from Women's Lives*. Ithaca: Cornell University Press.

Harding, Sandra. 1998. *Is Science Multicultural?* Bloomington and Indianapolis: Indiana University Press.

Harsanyi, John. 1955. "Cardinal Welfare, Individualistic Ethics, and Interpersonal Comparisons of Utility." *Journal of Political Economy* 62:309–321.

Hausman, Daniel. 2007. "Sympathy, Commitment, and Preference." In Fabienne Peter and Hans Bernhard Schmid (eds.) *Rationality and Commitment*. Oxford: Oxford University Press, 49–69.

Hirschman, Albert. 1989. "Having Opinions: One of the Elements of Well-Being?" *American Economic Review* 79:75–79.

King, Loren A. 2003. "Deliberation, Legitimacy, and Multilateral Democracy." *Governance* 16 (1):23–50.

Kitcher, Philip. 1993. *The Advancement of Science*. New York: Oxford University Press.

Kitcher, Philip. 2001. *Science, Truth, and Democracy*. Oxford and New York: Oxford University Press.

Knight, Jack and James Johnson. 1994. "Aggregation and Deliberation: On the Possibility of Democratic Legitimacy." *Political Theory* 22(2):277–296.

Knight, Jack and James Johnson. 1997. "What Sort of Equality Does Deliberative Democracy Require?" In James Bohman and William Rehg (eds.) *Deliberative Democracy*. Cambridge, MA: MIT Press, 279–319.

Kolodny, Niko. 2005. "Why Be Rational?" *Mind* 114:509–563.

Korsgaard, Christine. 1996. "The Reasons We Can Share." In Korsgaard *Creating the Kingdom of Ends*. Cambridge: Cambridge University Press, 275–310.

Korsgaard, Christine. 1997. "Taking the Law into Our Own Hands: Kant on the Right to Revolution." In A. Reath, B. Herman, and C. Korsgaard (eds.), *Reclaiming the History of Ethics: Essays for John Rawls*. Cambridge: Cambridge University Press, 297–328.

List, Christian. 2004. "The Impossibility of a Paretian Republican: Some Comments on Pettit and Sen." *Economics and Philosophy* 20(1):1–23.

List, Christian. 2006. "The Discursive Dilemma and Public Reason." *Ethics* 116(2):362–402.

List, Christian. 2008. "Group Deliberation and the Revision of Judgments: An Impossibility Result." London School of Economics, http://personal.lse.ac.uk/list/PDF-files/JudgmentRevision.pdf.

List, Christian and Robert Goodin. 2001. "Epistemic Democracy: Generalizing the Condorcet Jury Theorem." *Journal of Political Philosophy* 9(3):277–306.

List, Christian and Philip Pettit. 2002. "Aggregating Sets of Judgments: An Impossibility Result." *Economics and Philosophy* 18:89–110.

List, Christian and Philip Pettit. 2004. "Aggregating Sets of Judgments: Two Impossibility Theorems Compared." *Synthese* 140(1–2):207–235.

Longino, Helen. 1987. *Science as Social Knowledge*. Princeton: Princeton University Press.

Longino, Helen. 2002a. *The Fate of Knowledge*. Princeton: Princeton University Press.

Longino, Helen. 2002b. "Reply to Philip Kitcher." *Philosophy of Science* 69:573–577.

Manin, Bernard. 1987. "On Legitimacy and Political Deliberation." *Political Theory* 15:338–368.

Mas-Colell, Andrew and Hugo Sonnenschein. 1972. "General Possibility Theorems for Group Decisions." *Review of Economic Studies* 39:185–192.

May, Kenneth O. 1952. "A Set of Independent, Necessary, and Sufficient Conditions for Simple Majority Decision." *Econometrica* 20(4):680–684.

McLean, Iain. 1995. "The First Golden Age of Social Choice, 1784–1803." In William A. Barnett, Hervé Moulin, Maurice Salles, and Norman J Schofield (eds.) *Social Choice, Welfare, and Ethics. Proceedings of the Eighth International Symposium in Economic Theory and Econometrics.* Cambridge: Cambridge University Press, 13–33.

Mill, John Stuart. 1859 (1998). "On Liberty." In John Gray (ed.) *On Liberty and other Essays.* Oxford: Oxford University Press, 1–128.

Mill, John Stuart. 1861 (1998). "Utilitarianism." In John Gray (ed.) *On Liberty and other Essays.* Oxford: Oxford University Press, 129–201.

Mouffe, Chantal. 2000. *The Democratic Paradox.* New York and London: Verso.

Mouffe, Chantal. 2006. "Rawls: Political Philosophy without Politics." In Mouffe (ed.) *The Return of the Political.* New York and London: Verso, 41–59.

Mueller, Dennis. 1989. *Public Choice II.* Cambridge: Cambridge University Press.

Nozick, Robert. 1974. *Anarchy, State and Utopia.* Oxford: Basil Blackwell.

Nussbaum, Martha. 2000. *Women and Human Development.* Cambridge: Cambridge University Press.

Nussbaum, Martha. 2003. "Beyond the Social Contract: Toward Global Justice." *The Tanner Lectures in Human Value.* http://www.tannerlectures.utah.edu/lectures/volume24/nussbaum_2003.pdf.

Parfit, Derek. 1984. *Reasons and Persons.* Oxford: Oxford University Press.

Pauer-Studer, Herlinde. 2007. "Instrumental Rationality versus Practical Reason: Desires, Ends, and Commitment." In Fabienne Peter and Hans Bernhard Schmid (eds.) *Rationality and Commitment.* Oxford: Oxford University Press, 73–104.

Peter, Fabienne. 2003. "Gender and the Foundations of Social Change: The Role of Situated Agency." *Feminist Economies* 9(2):13–32.

Peter, Fabienne. 2004. "Choice, Consent, and the Legitimacy of Market Transactions." *Economics and Philosophy* 20(1):1–18.

Peter, Fabienne. 2009. "Rawlsian Justice." In Paul Anand, Prasanta Pattanaik, and Clemens Puppe (eds.) *Handbook of Rational and Social Choice.* Oxford: Oxford University Press, pp. 433–456 (forthcoming).

Peter, Fabienne and Hans Bernard Schmid (eds.). 2007. *Rationality and Commitment.* Oxford: Oxford University Press.

Pettit, Philip. 1997. *Republicanism: A Theory of Freedom and Government.* Oxford: Oxford University Press.

Pettit, Philip. 2001a. *A Theory of Freedom.* Oxford: Oxford University Press.

Pettit, Philip. 2001b. "Deliberative Democracy and the Discursive Dilemma." *Philosophical Issues* 11:268–299.

Pettit, Philip. 2003. "Groups with Minds of Their Own." In F. F. Schmitt (ed.) *Socializing Metaphysics.* New York: Rowman & Littlefield, 167–193.

Phillips, Anne. 1999. *Which Equalities Matter?* Cambridge: Polity Press.

Pigou, Arthur C. 1929. *The Economics of Welfare.* 3rd Edition. London: Macmillan.

Pildes, Richard and Elizabeth Anderson. 1990. "Slinging Arrows at Democracy: Social Choice Theory, Value Pluralism, and Democratic Politics." *Columbia Law Review* 90:2121–2214.

Plott, Charles. 1976. "Axiomatic Social Choice Theory: An Overview and Interpretation." *American Journal of Political Science* 20:511–596.

Pogge, Thomas. 2002. "Can the Capability Approach be Justified?" *Philosophical Topics* 30(2):167–228. Online at http://mora.rente.nhh.no/projects/EqualityExchange/Portals/0/articles/pogge1.pdf.

Postema, Gerald. 1995. "Public Practical Reason: An Archeology." *Social Philosophy and Policy* 12:43–86.

Putnam, Hilary. 1990. "A Reconsideration of Deweyan Democracy." *Southern California Law Review* 63:1671–1697.

Putnam, Hilary. 2002. *The Collapse of the Fact/Value Dichotomy and Other Essays*. Cambridge, MA: Harvard University Press.

Rawls, John. 1971. *A Theory of Justice*. Cambridge, MA: Harvard University Press.

Rawls, John. 1982. "Social Unity and Primary Goods." In Amartya Sen and Bernard Williams (eds.) *Utilitarianism and Beyond*. Cambridge, MA: Cambridge University Press,159–185.

Rawls, John. 1985. "Justice: Political not Metaphysical." *Philosophy and Public Affairs* 14:223–252.

Rawls, John. 1993. *Political Liberalism*. New York: Columbia University Press.

Rawls, John. 1995. "Reply to Habermas." *The Journal of Philosophy* 92(3):132–180.

Rawls, John. 1999. *Collected Papers*. Samuel Freeman (ed.). Cambridge, MA: Harvard University Press.

Rawls. John. 2001. *Justice as Fairness: A Restatement*. Cambridge, MA: Harvard University Press.

Riker, William H. 1982. *Liberalism Against Populism*. San Francisco: W. H. Freeman.

Riley, Jonathan. 1988. *Liberal Utilitarianism: Social Choice Theory and J.S. Mill's Philosophy*. Cambridge: Cambridge University Press.

Riley, Patrick. 1982. *Will and Political Legitimacy*. Cambridge, MA: Harvard University Press.

Robbins, Lionel. 1938. "Interpersonal Comparisons of Utility: A Comment." *Economic Journal* 48:635–641.

Roemer, John. 1996. *Theories of Distributive Justice*. Cambridge, MA: Harvard University Press.

Rouse, Joseph. 1996. *Engaging Science: How to Understand its Practices Philosophically*. Ithaca: Cornell University Press.

Rousseau, Jean-Jacques. 1763 (1987). "On the Social Contract." In J.J. Rousseau *Basic Political Writings*. Indianapolis: Hackett, 141–227.

Saari, Donald G. 1995. "Inner Consistency or not Inner Consistency: A Reformulation is the Answer." In William A. Barnett, Hervé Moulin, Maurice Salles, and Norman J. Schofield (eds.) *Social Choice, Welfare, and Ethics. Proceedings of the Eighth International Symposium in Economic Theory and Econometrics*. Cambridge: Cambridge University Press, 187–212.

Saari, Donald G. 2001. *Decisions and Elections: Explaining the Unexpected*. Cambridge: Cambridge University Press.

Samuelson, Paul A. 1938. "A Note on the Pure Theory of Consumers' Behavior." *Economica* 5:61–71.

Sanders, Lynn. 1997. "Against Deliberation." *Political Theory* 25(3):347–376.

Scanlon, Thomas. 1991. "The Moral Basis of Interpersonal Comparisons." In Jon Elster and John Roemer (eds.) *Interpersonal Comparisons of Well-Being*. Cambridge: Cambridge University Press, 17–44.

Scanlon, Thomas. 1998. *What We Owe To Each Other*. Cambridge, MA: Harvard University Press.

Sen, Amartya. 1969. "Quasi-transitivity, Rational Choice and Collective Decisions." *Review of Economic Studies* 36:381–393.

Sen, Amartya. 1970a. *Collective Choice and Social Welfare*. San Francisco: Holden-Day.

Sen, Amartya. 1970b. "The Impossibility of a Paretian Liberal." *Journal of Political Economy* 78:152–157.

Sen, Amartya. 1976. "Liberty, Unanimity and Rights." *Economica* 43:217–245.

Sen, Amartya. 1977a. "Rational Fools." *Philosophy and Public Affairs* 6:317–344.

Sen, Amartya. 1977b. "On Weights and Measures: Informational Constraints in Social Welfare Analysis." *Econometrica* 45:1539–1572.

Sen, Amartya. 1977c. "Social Choice Theory: A Re-Examination." *Econometrica* 45:53–89.

Sen, Amartya. 1979. "Personal Utilities and Public Judgments; or: What's Wrong with Welfare Economics?" *The Economic Journal* 89:537–558.

Sen, Amartya. 1980. "Equality of What?" In S. M. McMurrin (ed.) *The Tanner Lectures on Human Values* Vol.1. Salt Lake City: University of Utah Press, 195–220.

Sen, Amartya. 1985a. *Commodities and Capabilities*. Amsterdam: North-Holland.

Sen, Amartya. 1985b. "Well-Being, Agency and Freedom." *Journal of Philosophy* 82:169–221.

Sen, Amartya. 1986a. "Social Choice Theory." In K. Arrow and M. D. Intriligator (eds.) *Handbook of Mathematical Economics*. Amsterdam: North-Holland, 1073–1181.

Sen, Amartya. 1986b. "Information and Invariance in Normative Choice." In W. P. Heller, R. M. Starr, and D. A. Starrett (eds.) *Social Choice and Public Decision Making: Essays in Honor of Kenneth J. Arrow*. Cambridge: Cambridge University Press, 29–55.

Sen, Amartya. 1986c. "Foundations of Social Choice Theory." In Jon Elster and Aanund Hylland (eds.) *Foundations of Social Choice Theory*. Cambridge: Cambridge University Press, 213–248

Sen, Amartya. 1990. "Justice: Means versus Freedoms." *Philosophy and Public Affairs* 19:111–121.

Sen, Amartya. 1992a. *Inequality Re-examined*. Oxford: Clarendon.

Sen, Amartya. 1992b. "Minimal Liberty." *Economica* 59:139–59.

Sen, Amartya. 1993a. "Capabilities and Well-being." In Martha Nussbaum and Amartya Sen (eds.) *Quality of Life*. Oxford: Clarendon, 30–53.

Sen, Amartya. 1993b. "Internal Consistency of Choice." *Econometrica* 61(3):495–521.

Sen, Amartya. 1995. "Rationality and Social Choice." *American Economic Review* 85:1–24.

Sen, Amartya. 1999a. *Development as Freedom*. New York: Knopf.

Sen, Amartya. 1999b. "Democracy and Social Justice." Paper presented at the Seoul Conference on Democracy, Market Economy and Development, February 26–27, 1999.

Sen, Amartya. 2002. *Rationality and Freedom*. Cambridge, MA: Harvard University Press.

Sen, Amartya and Bernard Williams (eds.). 1982. *Utilitarianism and Beyond*. Cambridge: Cambridge University Press.

Sidgwick, Henry. 1893 (1981). *The Methods of Ethics*. 7th Edition. Indianapolis: Hackett.

Simmons, A. John. 2001. *Justification and Legitimacy*. Cambridge: Cambridge University Press.

Strasnick, Steven. 1976. "The Problem of Social Choice: Arrow to Rawls." *Philosophy and Public Affairs* 5:241–273.

Sugden, Robert. 1981. *The Political Economy of Public Choice*. Oxford: Martin Robertson.

Sunstein, Cass. 1991. "Preferences and Politics." *Philosophy and Public Affairs* 20:3–34.

Suzumura, Kotaro. 1983. *Rational Choice, Collective Decisions and Social Welfare*. Cambridge: Cambridge University Press.

Talisse, Robert and Scott Aikin. 2005. "Why Pragmatists Cannot be Pluralists." *Transactions of the Charles S. Peirce Society* XLI:101–118.

Thaler, Richard and Cass Sunstein. 2008. *Nudge*. New Haven: Yale University Press.

Valadez, Jorge M. 2001. *Deliberative Democracy, Political Legitimacy, and Self-Determination in Multicultural Societies*. Boulder, CO: Westview Press.

Vallentyne, Peter. 2005. "Capabilities vs. Opportunities for Well-being." *Journal of Political Philosophy* 13(3):359–371.

Voorhoeve, Alex. 2006. "Preference Change and Interpersonal Comparisons of Welfare." *Royal Institute of Philosophy Supplement* 59:265–279.

Waldron, Jeremy (ed.). 1984. *Theories of Rights*. Oxford: Oxford University Press.

Waldron, Jeremy. 1989. "Democratic Theory and the Public Interest: Rousseau and Condorcet Revisited." *American Political Science Review* 83:1322–1328.

Waldron, Jeremy. 1999. *Law and Disagreement*. Oxford: Oxford University Press.

Wall, Steven. 2007. "Democracy and Equality." *Political Quarterly* 57:416–438.

Weber, Max. 1964. *The Theory of Social and Economic Organization*. Basingstoke: Macmillan.

Williams, Bernard. 1973. "A Critique of Utilitarianism." In J. J. C. Smart and Bernard Williams (eds.) *Utilitarianism: For and Against*. Cambridge: Cambridge University Press, 75–150.

Wolin, Sheldon. 1996. "The Liberal/Democratic Divide. On Rawls's Political Liberalism." *Political Theory* 24(1):97–119.

Young, Iris Marion. 1996. "Communication and the Other: Beyond Deliberative Democracy." In Seyla Benhabib (ed.) *Democracy and Difference*. Princeton: Princeton University Press, 120–135.

Young, Iris Marion. 1997. "Difference as a Resource for Democratic Communication." In James Bohman and William Rehg (eds.) *Deliberative Democracy: Essays on Reason and Politics*. Cambridge, MA: MIT Press, 383–406.

Young, Iris Marion. 2000. *Inclusion and Democracy*. Oxford: Oxford University Press.

Index